Leonard Bloomfield

SPOKEN
DUTCH

Spoken Language Services, Inc.

© 1944 Linguistic Society of America

© 1978, 1991 Spoken Language Services, Inc.

Library of Congress Number 75-15107
ISBN 0-87950-054-9

Published by
Spoken Language Services, Inc.
P.O. Box 783
Ithaca, New York 14851

INTRODUCTION

1. This course in spoken Dutch contains all the vocabulary and all the grammar necessary for you to converse on ordinary topics, fluently and with a good pronunciation. It is designed to give you that ability as quickly as possible. It is based on the principle that if you are to understand a language when it is spoken, you have got to practice listening to it, and that if you are to make yourself understood in a language, you must practice speaking it.

Dutch is the language of about ten million people in the Netherlands, the Netherlands East Indies, and the other Dutch colonies. *Flemish*, spoken by a little over five million people in Belgium, and *Afrikaans*, spoken by a few more than three million people in south Africa, are close enough to Dutch that people who speak the three languages can understand each other with little difficulty. Dutch is more similar to English than is any other of the world's important languages, but you must be careful not to be overimpressed by the similarity, or you will relax your efforts and not learn as well as you should.

The speakers of Dutch do not all speak in just the same way, any more than do all the speakers of English.

There are variations from one place to another and from one social group to another. The variety taught in this manual will be understood and accepted everywhere and by people in all walks of life. But if you find yourself with Dutch people who speak somewhat differently from what you have learned, try to talk as they do. They will not resent your imitating them, but will be pleased that you are learning their language.

2. To take this course you need two things:

1. This manual.

2. A native speaker of Dutch, called the *Guide*; or, if none is available, the set of cassette recordings made to accompany the manual.[1]

In addition, if you are studying in a group, one of the group should be selected to act as *Leader*. The manual itself is the teacher, telling you what you need to know

---

[1] Even if you have a Guide you can still use the records to good advantage: for extra drill; for another kind of Dutch pronunciation; and when the Guide is temporarily unavailable. The records cannot answer questions, but they can give you the same word or sentence over and over again in exactly the same way.

at each stage *about* the language. The Guide, or the records, will give you not facts *about* the language, but *the language itself*. The Leader's job is to see that the group follows instructions, doing the right thing at the right time with maximum efficiency. Note especially that neither Leader nor Guide is supposed to do what a teacher ordinarily does in a language course, selecting and arranging material, and presenting and explaining it. The manual does the selection, arrangement, and explaining.

3. The course is divided into five major *Parts*. Each Part consists of six *Units*, the last of which is a review Unit. Each Unit except those devoted to review is divided into the following *Sections*:

A. Basic Sentences (and Hints on Pronunciation in the first few Units)
B. Word Study.
C. What Would You Say?
D. Listening In.
E. Conversation.
 Finder List.

Each Unit should take five or six hours to master. This, however, is merely an estimate, and more time should be spent whenever it seems advisable.

The **Basic Sentences** are arranged to give you a number of new words, first in short phrases, and then in complete sentences. On the printed page they are presented in parallel columns, the English to the left, the Dutch to the right, and a special simplified spelling of the Dutch in the middle. But *do not attempt to read the Dutch to yourself*. The printed page is only a secondary help. The primary business is listening to the Guide or the records as they give the material of the Basic Sentences orally, using what your eyes see on the page only to supplement what you are getting through your ears.

The **Hints on Pronunciation** will explain some of the more difficult points about pronouncing Dutch as the Dutch do. No two languages have exactly the same sounds, and one of the secrets in learning a language well is to try very hard from the very first to speak the new language with its own sounds, not with those of a language you already know. Careful listening and careful imitation of your Guide will do most of this, and the Hints on Pronunciation will supplement what you get through imitation by giving you a chance to concentrate your attention on one point of pronunciation at a time for special practice.

When you reach even the first **Word Study** you will

already know how to say a good many things in Dutch. The Word Study will explain what is involved in saying those things by showing you how words of different kinds are put, together into sentences, and how some words change in form depending on how they are used. This will make it easier for you to make up new sentences on your own, patterning them after those you have learned.

The **What Would You Say?** sections give you a chance to test yourself on what you should have learned from the Basic Sentences and the Word Study, so that if you have missed anything you can go back and pick it up.

Listening In provides you with a series of short conversations, given orally by the Guide or by the cassette records, which use what you have learned up to that point. It gives you practice in listening to and understanding Dutch as you might overhear it in normal conversation among Dutch speaking people, and provides you with models for your own carrying on of conversation in Dutch.

The **Conversation** practice is the central feature of the entire Unit. You are turned loose with what you have learned, and required to carry on conversation with each other. Topics are suggested, and you are given helps as to what might be said about them, since it is frequently hard to think of things to say conversationally, even in a language one knows well.

The **Finder List** in each Unit is an alphabetical arrangement of the words you have been given in that Unit, for reference when you temporarily forget a particular word. Use the Finder Lists also to check up on whether you have really learned all the individual words of a Unit: cover the definitions and look at the Dutch words, testing your knowledge of each one. Keep in mind, however, that it is the *combinations of words* into useful sentences that are really important; never substitute a study of the Finder List for any other part of the work of a Unit.

4. Dutch writing does not always represent accurately the sounds of the spoken language—though it is better at this than is English writing. Since it is the *sounds* of the language which must concern you primarily, not the spelling of the ordinary written forms, all the Dutch words and sentences in the first part of this manual are given not only in ordinary Dutch writing, but also in a simplified and regularized writing in which each letter or pair of letters stands always for one and the same sound. This *Aid to Listening* will help you because it is completely regular, but it is not something that you can read off like English; it is based on ordinary Dutch spelling, and contains some things that will be unfamiliar at first.

As you are first starting, you should ignore the traditional Dutch spelling in the right-hand column completely. Supplement the Dutch sounds that you get through the ear by following with your eye in the Aids to Listening column. Pay no attention to the regular Dutch spelling until you have mastered at least the first six Units. By then your pronunciation should be very good, and the irregularities of the ordinary writing will not confuse you as they certainly would if you tried to master them earlier in the game. Furthermore, they will be easier to master after you are already able to speak the language a little.

5. This course will give you a valuable tool: the ability to converse with people who know Dutch but do not know English. If there are such people about you as you take the course, then do not wait until you have finished the course before putting what you have learned to work. Even what you get just in the first Unit will be useful in getting along where Dutch is spoken. Conversing in the language, even if you have to limp along at first, gets you just that much closer to your goal. The course itself is simply a systematic arrangement of what you could get, with a hundred times as much effort, from unsystematic conversation with speakers of the language. The more you get, systematically *and* unsystematically, the better.

Nor does your learning of the language by any means cease when you have finished this course. As you have the chance and the need to speak Dutch and to listen to it, you will hear new words which you will want to add to your vocabulary. You will know enough Dutch already that you can ask someone who has spoken the language for a long time to explain to you, *in Dutch*, the meaning of such new words. It is a good idea to carry a little notebook into which you can write any new word or expression you learn, together with what it means. If you do not want to trust the conventional spelling of the new expression, you can write it down in the same Aid to Listening system that is used in this course, and then you will be sure of its pronunciation.

Your job in leading the group consists of the following points:

I. Before the study actually starts:
1. Be sure that all the members of the group read the Introduction which precedes these remarks to you.
2. See that the Guide (if you have one) has this book at the end of which s/he will find instructions in Dutch explaining what s/he is to do in the exercises and tests of the course.

   is to play in the course.

II. Before each meeting of the group:
1. Carefully look over all the material which the group might reasonably be expected to cover in the meeting. Be sure you know exactly in what sequence ·different things are to be done.
2. Tell the Guide what is to be covered, so that he may look it over too. Or, if you have no Guide, be sure that the cassette player is ready and in working condition.

III. During the meeting:
1. Keep order, and keep things moving.
2. If you have to call on different members of the group to recite, vary the order in which you call on them, so that no one of them can guess in advance just what he will be asked to do.
3. Be sure that everyone, always, speaks loudly and clearly, *especially when speaking Dutch.* At all times each member of the group must be able to hear what every other member says.
4. Help the Guide to follow what is happening, and to be ready to do his part as required. He may know no English, in which case the following phrases will be useful in working with him:

ENGLISH EQUIVALENTS	AIDS TO LISTENING	CONVENTIONAL SPELLING
This is where you start. (*show him in the book*)	běGHINT-uu als-t-uu-BLIEFT HIER.	Begint u als 't u blieft hier.
This is where you stop. (*show him in the book*)	tot-HIER.	Tot hier.
Please start.	běGHINT-uu-maar.	Begint u maar.
Wait a minute.	EEN OOghěnblik.	Eén oogenblik.
All right, go on.	JAA, GHAAT-uu-maar VERděr.	Ja, gaat u maar verder.
Please speak slower.	SPREEKT-uu als-t-uu-BLIEFT wat-LANGzaaměr.	Spreekt u als 't u blieft wat langzamer.
Please speak faster.	SPREEKT-uu- als-t-uu-BLIEFT wat-VLUGHěr.	Spreekt u als 't u blieft wat vlugger.
Please speak louder.	SPREEKT-uu als-t-uu-BLIEFT wat-HARDěr.	Spreekt u als 't u blieft wat harder.
Thanks!	DANK-uu!	Dank u!

Take the Guide aside for a few minutes and show him the above expressions; he will teach you to say them.

IV. At the end of this book you will find an answer-book, for the review Units. No one should see it except the Guide and yourself. You should refer to it only when the entire group is stuck on something and the answer cannot be found in this book.

Remember that you are learning the language too. Do everything that the other students are asked to do. If you fall behind, you can no longer function efficiently as Leader.

CONTENTS

PART ONE

PART TWO

GETTING AROUND

Don't start with this until everyone has read the Introduction and you are sure you are starting right.

To the Leader: Read the following to the group before starting in with the Guide or records on the Basic Sentences. Be sure everyone understands what is going to be done.

This Unit is heavier than any of those that follow. This is because you need to learn a certain number of important and useful expressions for getting along in the most practical kinds of situations just as quickly as possible; after you master these you can afford to work a little less intensively. The big dose at the beginning is a sort of 'language first aid'.

A. Basic Sentences

If you have a Guide, the procedure to follow with the material below is this:

1. The Leader reads the first English word or sentence.
2. The Guide says the Dutch equivalent.
3. The whole group repeats what the Guide has said.
4. The Guide says the Dutch again.
5. The whole group repeats again.

If you are using the records, they will give you steps 1, 2, and 4, and there are pauses at the proper places for you to repeat.

Listen carefully to what the Guide says. As you listen, follow with your eyes in the middle column (*not* the column to the right). Repeat in unison, loudly and clearly, imitating as accurately as you can the exact sounds the Guide has made, even to his tone of voice and inflection. *Don't hold back because you are afraid of making mistakes.* You are bound to make mistakes at first, but you can only overcome them by trying *more*, not by trying less.

Note the following points about the Aids to Listening:

1. Syllables written in CAPITAL LETTERS are spoken louder than the rest.

2. *Single vowel letters* represent vowel sounds that are *very short*, while groups of two vowel letters represent vowel sounds that are just slightly longer.

3. The only consonant letters that represent completely unfamiliar sounds are GH and CH. But a few others are used in ways strange for English: J is like English *y* (as in *yes*), and the groups SJ, ZJ, and TJ represent sounds about like the English *sh* in *shoot*, the *si* in *vision*, and the *ch* in *choose*. The sounds themselves will be discussed in detail later on.

1. Basic Sentences

Greetings and General Phrases

ENGLISH EQUIVALENTS	AIDS TO LISTENING	CONVENTIONAL SPELLING
the day	dĕ-DACH	de dag
Good day!	ghoedĕn-DACH![1]	Goeden dag!
the morning	dĕ-MORghĕn	de morgen
Good morning!	ghoedĕn-MORghĕn!	Goeden morgen!
the evening	dĕ-AAvĕnt	de avond

[1] Your Guide may say *ghoedĕ-DACH* or *ghoejĕ-DACH* instead of *ghoedĕn-DACH*. *Any -ĕn* at the end of a word may in fast talking drop the *n*; and a *d* in the middle of a word is sometimes changed to *j* in rapid conversational talking.

Good evening!	ghoedĕn-AAvĕnt!	Goeden avond!
how	HOE	hoe
to go	GHAAN	gaan
goes it	GHAAT-ĕt	gaat het
with you	met-UU	met u
How are you?	hoe-GHAAT-ĕt-met-uu?	Hoe gaat het met u?
Well ('good'), thank you.	GHOET, DANK-uu.	Goed, dank u.
And (with) you?	en-met-UU?	En met u?
Quite well.	HEEL GHOET.	Heel goed.
the gentleman	dĕ-HEER	de heer
sir or *mister*	mĕNEER	mijnheer
Mr. Dekker	mĕneer-DEKKĕr	Mijnheer Dekker
the woman	dè-VROU	de vrouw
ma'am or *Mrs.*	mĕVROU	mevrouw
the young lady	dĕ-JUFrou	de juffrouw
Miss Dekker	jufrou-DEKKĕr	Juffrouw Dekker
Yes, msss.	JAA-jufrou.[2]	Ja, juffrouw.
No, sir.	NEE-mĕneer.	Neen, mijnheer.
Please or *if you please.*	als-t-uu-BLIEFT.	Als 't u blieft.
Thanks a lot. ('thank you well')	dank-uu-WEL.	Dank u wel.
Thank you, ma'am.	dank-uu-WEL-mĕvrou.	Dank u wel, mevrouw.

---

[2] When used without a person's name, in the meaning 'Miss', this word is stressed on the second syllable: *juFROU*. When this happens the vowel of the first syllable is sometimes different; you may hear *jĕFROU*.

You're welcome. (*'nothing to thank'*)	niets-tĕ-DANKĕn.	Niets te danken.
to take	NEEmĕn	nemen
ill or *badly*	KWAAlik	kwalijk
Excuse me. (*'take me not badly'*)	nee-mĕ-niet-KWAAlik.[3]	Neem me niet kwalijk.
So long! (*'until see'*)	tot-ZIENS!	Tot ziens!
Good-by! (*"day!"*)	DACH!	Dag!
to understand	vĕrSTAAN	verstaan
Do you understand me?	vĕrSTAAT-uu-mei?	Verstaat u mij?
to say	ZEGHĕn	zeggen
Do you understand what I say?	vĕrSTAAT-uu-wat-ik-ZECH?	Verstaat u wat ik zeg?
to speak	SPREEkĕn	spreken
slow or *slowly*	LANGsaam	langzaam
Will you please speak slowly?	WILT-uu als-t-uu-BLIEFT LANGsaam-spreekĕn?	Wilt u als 't u blieft langzaam spreken?
I don't understand what you say.	ik-vĕrSTAA-niet wat-uu-ZECHT.	Ik versta niet wat u zegt.
What did you say? (*'what please you?'*)	wat-BLIEFT-uu?[4]	Wat blieft u?

---

[3] The *t* of *niet* 'not' is sometimes dropped in rapid speech.

[4] The *t* of *wat* is often dropped in this expression in rapid speech.

Directions

Where is it?	waar-IS-ĕt?	Waar is het?
the restaurant	hĕt-rĕstoRANG[5]	het restaurant
Where is there a restaurant?	WAAR IS-ĕr ĕn-rĕstoRANG?	Waar is er en restaurant?
Where's the restaurant?	WAAR-is ĕt-rĕstoRANG?	Waar is het restaurant?
the hotel	hĕt-hooTEL	het hotel
Where is there a good hotel?	WAAR IS-ĕr ĕn-GHOET hooTEL?	Waar is er een goed hotel?
Where's the hotel?	WAAR is-ĕt-hooTEL?	Waar is het hotel?
not any or *no*	GHEEN	geen
There's no good hotel here.	ĕr-IS-hier GHEEN GHOET hoo--TEL.	Er is hier geen goed hotel.
the station	hĕt-staaSJON	het station
Where's the station?	WAAR is-ĕt-staaSJON?	Waar is het station?
the toilet	dĕ-wee-SEE	de W. C.
Where's the toilet?	WAAR iz-dĕ-wee-SEE?	Waar is de W. C.?
It's [to the] right.	hĕt-is-RECHS.	Het is rechts.
It's [to the] left.	hĕt-is-LINKS.	Het is links.
straight ahead	rechTUIT	rechtuit
Go straight ahead.	ghaa-rechTUIT.	Ga rechtuit.
It's here.	hĕt-is-HIER.	Het is hier.
Here it is.	HIER IZ-ĕt.	Hier is het.
It's there.	hĕt-iz-DAAR.	Het is daar.

---

[5] The pronunciation *het* will only be heard from someone who is reading and being extra careful. In ordinary speech the form is *always* ĕt.

What is it?	wat-IZ-ĕt?	Wat is het?
What's that?	wat-iz-DAT?	Wat is dat?
What's this?	wat-iz-DIT?	Wat is dit?
to want to	WILLĕn	willen
to have	HEBBĕn	hebben
What do you want?	wat-wilt-uu-HEBBĕn?	Wat wilt u hebben?
I would	ik-ZOU	ik zou
gladly	GHRAACH	graag
the cigarette	dĕ-sieghĕRET	de cigaret
I'd like a cigarette.	ik-zou-GHRAACH ĕn-sieghĕRET-willĕn-hebbĕn.	Ik zou graag en cigaret willen hebben.
cigarettes	sieghĕRETTĕn	cigaretten
I'd like some cigarettes.	ik-zou-GHRAACH sieghĕRETTĕn-willĕn-hebbĕn.	Ik zou graag cigaretten willen hebben.
the match	dĕ-LUUsiefĕr	de lucifer
matches	LUUsiefĕrs	lucifers
I'd like some matches.	ik-zou-GHRAACH LUUsiefĕrs-willĕn-hebbĕn.	Ik zou graag lucifers willen hebben.
I'd like to	ik-WOU	ik wou
something	WAT	wat
to eat	EEtĕn	eten

6 [1–A]

I'd like to eat something.	ik-wou-GHRAACH wat-EEtĕn.	Ik wou graag wat eten.
to drink	DRINKĕn	drinken
I'd like to drink something.	ik-wou-GHRAACH wat-DRINK-ĕn.	Ik wou graag wat drinken.
I'd like a drink.	ik-wou-GHRAACH DRINKĕn.	Ik wou graag drinken.

Foods

bread	BROOT	brood
water	WAAtĕr	water
meat	VLEES	vleesch
potatoes	AARdappĕlĕn	aardappelen
coffee	KOFFie	koffie
milk	MELK	melk
beer	BIER	bier
Do you want coffee?	wilt-uu-KOFFie-drinkĕn?	Wilt u koffie drinken?
I want	ik-WIL	ik wil
I don't want any coffee.	ik-WIL GHEEN KOFFie.	Ik wil geen koffie.
I'd like some milk.	ik-zou-GHRAACH wat-MELK-willĕn-drinkĕn.	Ik zou graag wat melk willen drinken.

Price

much or *many*	VEEL	veel
how much or *how many*	HOE-veel	hoe veel

How much is it?	hoe-veel-IS-ĕt?	Hoeveel is het?
they	ZEI	zij
they are	zei-ZEIN	zij zijn
How much are they?	hoe-veel-ZEIN-zĕ?	Hoeveel zijn zij?
How much is that?	hoe-veel-iz-DAT?	Hoeveel is dat?
One gulden.	EEN GHULdĕn	Een gulden.
That's two gulden.	dat-is-TWEE GHULdĕn.	Dat is twee gulden.
One cent.	EEN SENT.	Een cent.
Ten cents.	TIEN SENT.	Tien cent.

Time

late	LAAT	laat
What time is it?	hoe-LAAT-is-ĕt?	Hoe laat is het?
the hour	hĕt-UUR	het uur
It's one o'clock.	hĕt-is-EEN UUR.	Het is een uur.
It's ten o'clock	hĕt-is-TIEN UUR.	Het is tien uur.
to begin	bĕGHINNĕn	beginnen
the movie	dĕ-biejĕSKOOP	de bioscoop
What time does the movie begin?	hoe-LAAT bĕGHINT dĕ-biejĕ-SKOOP?	Hoe laat begint de bioscoop?

at	OM	om
At eight o'clock	om-ACHT UUR	Om acht uur.
the train	dĕ-TREIN	de trein

What time does the train go?	HOE-laat GHAAT dĕ-TREIN?	Hoe laat gaat de trein?
when	wanNEER	wanneer
to	NAAR	naar
When does the train to Amsterdam go?	wanneer-ghaat-dĕ-TREIN naar--amstĕrDAM?	Wanneer gaat de trein naar Amster-dam?

Numbers

one	EEN	een
two	TWEE	twee
three	DRIE	drie
four	VIER	vier
five	VEIF	vijf
six	ZES	zes
seven	ZEEvĕn	zeven
eight	ACHT	acht
nine	NEEghĕn	negen
ten	TIEN	tien
eleven	ELF	elf
twelve	TWAALF	twaalf

Before going through these sentences a second time, read the following Hints on Pronunciation.

Note: Cues for the Guide to Hints on Pronunciation and other exercises throughout the book are given in the Key at the end of the book.

2. Hints on Pronunciation

To the Leader: Read the following to the group, or have another student read it to them for you. When you come to a set of Dutch words, the Guide or the records will give them for the group to repeat. Don't hesitate to go over each group several times, and give those of the group who so desire a chance to repeat them alone, instead of just in chorus with the rest. If the group seems to tire of pronunciation practice, take them back over the Basic Sentences again after having done about half of the present section, and then come back and complete it.

Syllables in English or Dutch which sound louder than others in a phrase or sentence are said to be *stressed*. In the Aids to Listening the stressed syllables are written with capital letters, everything else in small letters. For example, in the expression meaning 'Good day!': *ghoedĕn-DACH!*, *DACH* is loudly stressed, *ghoe-* and *-dĕn* are softer.

Words joined together in the Aids to Listening with hyphens (-) are pronounced in ordinary speech as though they were just one longer word, with no pause between them.

Short Vowels. There are six short vowels in Dutch: *a, e, i, o, u,* and *ĕ*. The last of these occurs only in syllables that are completely unstressed, and is about like the English *e* of *water, fasten,* or the *o* of *bottom, button*. The *i* is practically the same as the English *i* of *pin, pit, tick, rim,* but shorter. The other four are all a little different from anything in English and need practice.

a is shorter than the vowel of English *hot*; it is really something between the vowel of *hot* and the vowel of *cut*:

PRACTICE 1

MAN	'man'
DACH	'day'
WAT	'what'
DAT	'that'
DANKĕn	'thank'

e is something like the vowel of English *pet*, but tends a little towards the vowel of English *pat*:

PRACTICE 2

MET	'with'
EN	'and'
ZEGHĕn	'say'
RECHS	'right'

o is shorter than the vowel of an English word like *caught*; it is something between the vowel of *caught* and the vowel of *cut*:

PRACTICE 3

KOP	'cup'
KOM	'come'
VOL	'full'
KOFFie	'coffee'
OM	'at, about'

Before *m* and *n* the Dutch *o* has with many speakers a slightly different sound, with the lips slightly puckered. Some speakers have this second kind of *o* in some other words too, but it is not marked specially since Dutch speakers differ as to the words in which they use the second variety. You should follow whatever model your Guide's pronunciation gives you for this.

u is quite different from any English sound. The nearest thing to it is the vowel of an English word like *cut*. But in the Dutch sound the lips are slightly puckered; at the same time the tongue is raised at the middle, as though you were going to say the *e* of *met*:

PRACTICE 4

BUS	'bus'
ZUStĕr	'sister'
KUNNĕn	'can'
ZULLĕn	'should'
JUfrou	'Miss'

To remind you of the shortness of short vowels, the consonant letters after them are sometimes written doubled, as we do in English writing and as is done frequently in conventional Dutch spelling. Note that this does not indicate any difference in the consonant itself; the *f*-sound of *KOFFie* is no longer than that of *STOF* 'dust'.

Long Vowels. There are seven long vowels in Dutch. In the Aids to Listening they are written with pairs of vowel letters: *aa, ee, ie, oo, oe, eu, uu*. They are only a little longer than the short vowels; they are certainly much shorter than English long vowels, as in *far, say, see, go, do*. Especially when the Dutch long vowels are not stressed, they seem quite short to our way of hearing.

aa sounds something like the English vowel in *father*, but the Dutch sound is shorter, and the tongue is pushed just a trifle further forward:

PRACTICE 5

WAAtĕr	'water'
GHAAN	'go'
KWAAlik	'badly'
WAAR	'where'

ee sounds like the English vowel in *day*, but the Dutch vowel is shorter, and the corners of the mouth are slightly drawn back, as if you were smiling:

PRACTICE 6

PEER	'pear'
HEER	'gentleman'
NEEmĕn	'take'
SPREEkĕn	'speak'

oo sounds like the English vowel in *boat*, but the Dutch vowel is shorter:

PRACTICE 7

BOOT	'boat'
BROOT	'bread'
ZOON	'son'
KOOmĕn	'come'

oe sounds like the English vowel in *shoot*, but the Dutch vowel is much shorter:

PRACTICE 8

BOEK	'book'
GHOET	'good'
HOE	'how'
BROER	'brother'
MOEtĕn	'have to'

ie sounds like the English vowel in *beet*, but the Dutch vowel is shorter and the corners of the mouth are slightly drawn back, as if you were smiling:

PRACTICE 9

DIEP	'deep'
VRIENT	'friend'
NIETS	'nothing'
HIER	'here'

eu is not like any English sound. Pucker up your lips almost as if you were going to say *Oh!* and keep them that way but try to pronounce the English vowel of *day*:

PRACTICE 10

DEUR	*'door'*
MEUBĕl	*'piece of furniture'*
KLEUR	*'color'*
NEUS	*'nose'*
KEUkĕn	*'kitchen'*

uu is not like any English sound. Pucker up your lips as if you were going to say *Ooh!* and keep them that way but try to pronounce the English vowel of *see*:

PRACTICE 11

DUUR	*'dear'*
LUUsiefĕr	*'match'*
stuuDENT	*'student'*
naaTUURlik	*'naturally'*

Diphthongs. Diphthongs are close combinations of two vowels. In Dutch there are three diphthongs: *ei, ou, ui.*

ei sounds something like the English diphthong in *bite* (written with the single vowel-letter *i*); more exactly, it is somewhere between the sound in *bite* and the sound in *bait*:

PRACTICE 12

TREIN	*'train'*
MEI	*'me'*
VEIF	*'five'*
ZEI	*'she'*
ZEIN	*'are'*

ou sounds something like the English diphthong in *bout*; more exactly, it is somewhere between the sound in *bout* and the sound in *boat*:

PRACTICE 13

NOU	*'now'*
VROU	*'woman, wife'*
ik-ZOU	*'I should'*
ik-WOU	*'I would'*

ui is different from any English sound. It differs from the diphthong in an English word like *house* in that the tongue moves more in the front of the mouth. The lips are puckered up:

PRACTICE 14

HUIS	*'house'*
MUIS	*'mouse'*
UIT	*'out'*
TUIN	*'garden'*
TUICH	*'harness'*

Now go back to **1**, the Basic Sentences, and go through them again exactly as before. Keep in mind particularly the sounds you have been practicing, and make your imitation of the Guide more accurate because of this practice.

Then go through once or twice more, in the same way as before except that instead of repeating after the Guide in chorus, the members of the group should take turns repeating individually. Continue until everyone has had plenty of chance.

3. Check Yourself

Did you go through the Basic Sentences at least twice with group repetition and at least once more individually?

Did you repeat each word and phrase in a loud, clear voice immediately after hearing it?

Were you careful to follow the pronunciation you heard, even if it seemed different from that shown in the book?

Did you keep in mind the meaning of each word and phrase as you heard and spoke the Dutch?

Do not go beyond this point until you are sure you have done everything so far as you should.

B. WORD STUDY

To the Leader: This Section should be read carefully by each student individually. If the members of the group have time for study outside of class, it can be given as an outside assignment. If they do not, then they can sit together at the ordinary class time and each can read it silently to himself.

1. Word Study

Point 1. Meanings. Compare the Dutch and English ways of putting things in the following expressions:

(a) niets-*tĕ*-DANKĕn.　'Nothing *to* thank.' (that is, 'You're welcome.')

　naar-amstĕrDAM　'*to* Amsterdam'

　ghaa-LINKS　'go *to* the left'

　wilt-uu-wat-EEtĕn?　'Do you want something *to* eat?'

(b) *wat*-iz-DAT?　'*What*'s that?'

　ik-wou-GHRAACH　'I'd like *something* to eat.'
　wat-EEtĕn.

In examples (a), where English uses the word *to*, Dutch has sometimes *tĕ*, as in the first example, sometimes *naar*, as in the second, and sometimes no word at all, as in the third and fourth. And the other way round, in (b), the one Dutch word *wat* means sometimes '*what?*,' as in the first example, and sometimes '*something*,' as in the second.

As you see, the two languages do not always agree as to the meanings of words. Since on the surface Dutch words are often very similar to English words and therefore easy to remember, this is a point that calls for special care and attention.

Point 2. Sir, Ma'am, Miss. The simple words *jaa* 'yes' and *nee* 'no' sound rude or cross in Dutch; usually one adds some other word or phrase. People who do not know each other very well mostly add *mĕNEER* 'sir', *mĕVROU* 'ma'am', or *juFROU* 'miss'. This is not unduly polite, but just the ordinary way of speaking.

Quite generally, the Dutch add *mĕNEER, mĕVROU,* or *juFROU* to a sentence, or else the person's name with one of these titles before·it, much oftener than we do. If you fail to do this, you may sound stiff or rude.

In addressing women, *juFROU* is used not only where we use 'Miss', but also to any woman attendant, such as a saleswoman or a waitress, regardless of age or marriage status.

Point 3. Yes, please; No, thanks. If something is offered to you and you want to *accept* it, say *als-t-uu-BLIEFT* 'please', or *JAA, als-t-uu-BLIEFT* 'yes, please'. If you say *dank-uu-WEL* 'thank you', this means that you don't want it, for the polite refusal is this or *NEE, dank-uu-WEL* (or *NEE, DANK-uu*) 'no, thank you'.

Point 4. Stressed and Unstressed Forms. Some Dutch words have a shorter form when they are spoken without stress in a phrase. We do the same thing: compare *I would* with *I'd like to*, or compare *to them* with *I saw 'em*. In Dutch there is often a difference of meaning, to our way of looking at it, between the stressed form and the unstressed form. Here are some examples:

(a) *MEI, mĕ* '*me*':
    met-MEI, niet-met-UU '*with me, not with you*'
    HELP-mĕ '*help me*'

(b) *ZEI, zĕ* '*they*':
    ZEI, niet-UU '*they, not you*'
    hier-ZEIN-zĕ '*here they are*'

(c) *DIE* '*that*', *dĕ* '*the*' (with some nouns):
    DIE VROU '*that woman*'
    dĕ-VROU '*the woman*'

(d) *DAT* '*that*', *ĕt* '*the*' (with other nouns), *it*':
    DAT hooTEL '*that hotel*'
    ĕt-hooTEL '*the hotel*'
    waar-IZ-ĕt? '*Where is it?*'
    ĕt-is-HIER, *or even* t-is-HIER '*it's here*'

(e) *DAAR, ĕr* '*there*':
    ĕt-iz-DAAR, RECHS "*It's there, on the right.*'
    ĕr-IS-hier gheen-hooTEL '*There's no hotel here.*'

(f) *EEN* '*one*', *ĕn* '*a, an*':
    EEN rĕstoRANG '*one restaurant*'
    ĕn-rĕstoRANG '*a restaurant*'

2. Review of Basic Sentences

Turn back to the Basic Sentences and cover the English. Read the Dutch to yourself, and test yourself to see if you know the meaning of each expression. Check the expressions you are uncertain about, and continue to the end before you uncover the English. If you have checked many of them, do the same thing a second time. End by picking the Dutch expressions at random, instead of in the order in which they are given.

C. WHAT WOULD YOU SAY?

To the Leader: **1** below should be gone over by each member of the group individually, either outside of class time or during the class meeting. **2** is group work, and calls for your direction.

1. What Would You Say?

Below are given several groups of Dutch sentences, each group preceded by some remarks in English. Read first the English, then the Dutch, and decide which of the Dutch sentences of a group best fits the situation described in English. When the group works together, you must be ready to tell which one you selected in each group, and why the others are not appropriate. Be sure you know the meaning of *all* the Dutch expressions, not just the ones you choose as correct.

1. *You meet Mr. Dekker one morning about nine o'clock. You say:*
   a. ghoedĕn-AAvĕnt, mĕneer-DEKKĕr.
   b. ghoedĕn-MORghĕn, mĕneer-DEKKĕr.
2. *You offer Mr. Dekker a cigarette:*
   a. ik-zou-GHRAACH ĕn-sieghĕRET-willĕn-hebbĕn.
   b. wilt-uu-ĕn-sieghĕRET?

3. *Mr. Dekker doesn't want to smoke and says politely:*
   a. als-t-uu-BLIEFT.
   b. dank-uu-WEL.
4. *You want to greet Mr. van Dam in the usual way. You say:*
   a. hoe-GHAAT-ĕt-met-uu?
   b. ik-GHAA-met-uu.
5. *You want him to go to the restaurant with you. You say:*
   a. GHAA-met-mĕ naar-ĕt-rĕstoRANG.
   b. ik-GHAA-niet naar-ĕt-rĕstoRANG.
6. *Mr. Dekker asks you what time it is. You answer:*
   a. om-NEEghĕn UUR.
   b. ĕt-is-NEEghĕn UUR.
7. *He asks you the location of the restaurant. He asks:*
   a. WAAR is-ĕt-rĕstoRANG?
   b. IZ-ĕr-hier ĕn-rĕstoRANG?

2. What Did You Say?

The Leader will read the English for each of the groups in **1** and will call on some member of the group to read out his choice in Dutch. Other members of the group will criticize the choices given if they do not agree with them. The Leader will also be sure that you understand the meanings of the wrong answers too.

D. Listening In

Listen to each of the following conversations, which the Guide or the records will give you. First listen to all of them, with your books closed, and without repeating them, to see how well you can follow them with no assistance from what you see. Then open your books and go through each one separately, repeating after the Guide, and checking on anything you do not understand. Finally, the Leader will assign parts and you can go through them with individual repetition. Repeat often enough for everyone to have a chance at a part. Be careful, especially when you are the only one repeating after the Guide, to speak clearly and in a loud voice, so that everyone can hear you.

1. *Asking Information.*

Jan:	nee-mĕ-niet-KWAALIK-mĕneer.	Neem me niet kwalijk, mijnheer.
	WAAR IS-ĕr ĕn-rĕstoRANG?	Waar is er een restaurant?
dĕ-HEER:	ĕr-is-ĕn-hooTEL RECHS,	Er is een hotel rechts,
	en-ĕn-rĕstoRANG rechTUIT.	en een restaurant rechtuit.
JAN:	wat-BLIEFT-uu?	Wat blieft u?
	ik-fĕrSTAA-niet wat-uu-ZECHT.	Ik versta niet wat u zegt.
	WILT-uu als-t-uu-BLIEFT LANGsaam-spreekĕn?	Wilt u als 't u blieft langzaam spreken?

dĕ-HEER: HIER is-ĕn-hooTEL.
HIER RECHS.
en-HIER rechTUIT is-ĕn-rĕstoRANG.
vĕrSTAAT-uu wat-ik-ZECH?
JAN: JAA-mĕneer.
ik-verSTAA-uu.
dank-uu-WEL-mĕneer.
dĕ-HEER: niets-tĕ-DANKĕn. DACH!
JAN: DACH-mĕneer!

Hier is een hotel.
Hier rechts.
En hier rechtuit is een restaurant.
Verstaat u wat ik zeg?
Ja mijnheer.
Ik versta u.
Dank u wel, mijnheer.
Niets te danken. Dag!
Dag, mijnheer!

2. *In the Restaurant.*

dĕ-JUFrou: ghoejĕn-DACH-mĕneer.
JAN: ghoejĕn-DACH-jufrou.
ik-wou-GHRAACH wat-EEtĕn.
dĕ-JUFrou: wat-wilt-uu-HEBBĕn, mĕNEER?
JAN: ik-zou-GHRAACH VLEES en-AARdappĕlĕn-
-willĕn-hebbĕn.
dĕ-JUFrou: wilt-uu-BIER?
JAN: NEE-jufrou.
ik-wil-GHEEN BIER
dĕ-JUFrou: wilt-uu-KOFFie?
JAN: NEE-jufrou.
ik-wou-GHRAACH MELK-drinkĕn.

Goeden dag, mijnheer.
Goeden dag, juffrouw.
Ik wou graag wat eten.
Wat wilt u hebben, mijnheer?
Ik zou graag vleesch en aardappelen willen
hebben.
Wilt u bier?
Neen, juffrouw.
Ik wil geen bier.
Wilt u koffie?
Neen, juffrouw.
Ik wou graag melk drinken.

dĕ-JUFrou: hier-zein-ĕt-VLEES, dĕ-AARdappĕlĕn, dĕ-MELK, BROOT, en-WAAtĕr	Hier zijn het vleesch, de aardappelen, de melk, brood, en water.
JAN: hoe-veel-IS-ĕt?	Hoeveel is het?
dĕ-JUFrou: dat-is-TWEE GHULdĕn.	Dat is twee gulden.
JAN: hier-zein-TWEE GHULdĕn.	Hier zijn twee gulden.
dĕ-JUFrou: dank-uu-WEL-mĕneer.	Dank u wel, mijnheer.

3. *John and the girl talk about the movie.*

JAN: als-t-uu-BLIEFT-jufrou, WAAR is-dĕ-biejĕSKOOP?	Als 't u blieft, juffrouw, waar is de bioscoop?
dĕ-JUFrou: dĕ-biejĕSKOOP is-hier-RECHS.	De bioscoop is hier rechts.
JAN: hoe-laat-bĕGHINT-ĕt?	Hoe laat begint het?
dĕ-JUFrou: dĕ-biejĕSKOOP bĕGHINT om-ACHT UUR.	De bioscoop begint om acht uur.
JAN: dank-uu-WEL-jufrou.	Dank u wel, juffrouw.
WILT-uu met-MEI naar-dĕ-biejĕSKOOP-ghaan, juFROU?	Wilt u met mij naar de bioscoop gaan, juffrouw?
dĕ-JUFrou: jaa-WEL-mĕneer.	Jawel, mijnheer.
JAN: GHOET, uu-GHAAT met-MEI naar-dĕ-biejĕ- -SKOOP.	Goed, u gaat met mij naar de bioscoop.
dĕ-JUFrou: HEEL GHRAACH.	Heel graag.
ik-GHAA met-UU naar-dĕ-biejĕSKOOP.	Ik ga met u naar de bioscoop.
JAN: HIER RECHS.	Hier rechts.
om-ACHT UUR.	Om acht uur.
dĕ-JUFrou: JAA, om-ACHT UUR.	Ja, om acht uur.

JAN:	om-ACHT UUR.	Om acht uur.
	DACH-jufrou.	Dag, juffrouw.
dĕ-JUFrou:	tot-ZIENS, mĕNEER.	Tot ziens, mijnheer.

4. *In a Store.*

JAN:	ghoedĕn-AAvĕnt, juFROU.	Goeden avond, juffrouw.
dĕ-JUFrou:	ghoedĕn-AAvĕnt, mĕNEER.	Goeden avond, mijnheer.
	WAT wilt-uu-HEBBĕn?	Wat wilt u hebben?
JAN:	ik-zou-GHRAACH sieghĕRETTĕn-willĕn-hebbĕn.	Ik zou graag cigaretten willen hebben.
dĕ-JUFrou:	hier-ZEIN-zĕ	Hier zijn ze.
JAN:	dank-uu-WEL.	Dank u wel.
	JUFrou, wat-IZ-dat-hier?	Juffrouw, wat is dat hier?
dĕ-JUFrou:	dat-zein-LUUsiefĕrs.	Dat zijn lucifers.
	wilt-uu-LUUsiefĕrs-hebbĕn?	Wilt u lucifers hebben?
JAN:	JAA-jufrou, als-t-uu-BLIEFT.	Ja, juffrouw, als 't u blieft.
	hoe-veel-IS-ĕt?	Hoeveel is het?
dĕ-JUFrou:	dat-is-EEN GHULdĕn TIEN.	Dat is een gulden tien.
JAN:	hier-IS-ĕt.	Hier is het.
dĕ-JUFrou:	dank-uu-WEL-mĕneer.	Dank u wel, mijnheer.
JAN:	JUFrou, WAAR is-ĕt-staaSJON?	Juffrouw, waar is het station?
	is-ĕt-hier-LINKS?	Is het hier links?
dĕ-JUFrou:	NEE-mĕneer.	Neen, mijnheer.
	ĕt-staaSJON is-NIET LINKS.	Het station is niet links.
	ĕt-IS-hier RECHtuit.	Het is hier rechtuit.

E. Conversation

To the Leader: **1** of the following is individual study, or can be done by the students working in pairs. **2** and **3** is group work.

1. Review of Basic Sentences

Turn back to the Basic Sentences and cover the Dutch. Read the English to yourself, and test yourself to see if you can speak the Dutch corresponding to each English equivalent. Check the expressions you are uncertain about, and continue to the end before you uncover the Dutch to check up. If you have checked many of them, do the same thing again. End by picking the English equivalents at random, instead of in the order in which they are given.

If you can work in pairs, *both* with the Dutch covered, you can ask each other instead of simply testing yourself.

2. Vocabulary Check-up

Close all your books. The Leader will start the ball rolling by addressing one of the others with such a question as 'How do you say *cigarette* in Dutch?' If the first person addressed doesn't know the answer, the Leader will ask someone else. Whoever answers correctly will in turn address such a question to still another member of the group. Continue until everyone has asked and answered several such questions and until most of the words and phrases of this Unit have been asked about.

This will be a group check on your memory of the material of the Unit. Anyone who has too much trouble should go back and go through the Basic Sentences again.

3. Carrying on Conversation

The Leader will assign parts and will ask you to take turns in pairs, carrying on the following conversations. The two persons who are talking should stand up and act out their parts, speaking as smoothly and naturally as possible. The Guide will help you when you slip on pronunciation or use an expression that isn't used.

The Leader will prompt you if you are not sure what might come next in your part. The models given here are only suggestions; vary them as you wish, but keep in mind that fluency within the sentences you already know is more to be desired than ingenuity in making up new sentences which involves a lot of hemming and hawing.

Conversation 1. A asks B (a woman) for information.

A: apologizes for speaking to B and asks where a restaurant is.

B: gives directions—to the right, to the left, or straight ahead.

A: apologizes and explains that he doesn't understand. He asks B to repeat, more slowly.

B: repeats slowly and clearly and asks A if he understands.

A: says he understands and thanks B.

B: says A is welcome.

A: says good-by.

B: says good-by.

Conversation 2. A still can't find the restaurant and speaks to Miss C.

A: apologizes for speaking to C and asks if this is where the restaurant is.

C: says no, and tells where the restaurant is. She says that it's the movie that is right here.

A: asks when the movie begins.

C: tells him.

A: thanks her and says good-by.

Conversation 3. A finds the restaurant and speaks to the waiter, D.

A: says good morning.

D: says good morning. He asks A if he wants something to eat.

A: says no, he wants something to drink.

D: asks what A would like to drink.

A: asks for milk, or beer, or coffee.

D: says OK and brings the milk.

A: thanks D and says he'd like some cigarettes.

D: Brings the cigarettes and says here they are. He asks A what time it is.

A: tells him the time.

D: thanks A.

A: asks the price.

D: gives him the price.

A: says here's such-and-such an amount of money.

D: says thanks.

They say good-by.

dĕ- AARdappĕl 'the potato'
    AARdappĕlĕn̩ 'potatoes'
dĕ- AAvĕnt 'the evening'
    ACHT 'eight'
    ALS 'if'
    als-t-uu-BLIEFT 'please'

    bĕGHINNĕn 'to begin'
    bĕGHINT 'begins'
dĕ- biejĕSKOOP (biejoSKOOP) 'the movie'
ĕt- BIER 'the beer'
    BLIEFT '(it) pleases'
    als-t-uu-BLIEFT 'please'
    wat-BLIEFT-uu? 'What did you say?'
ĕt-BROOT 'the bread'

    DAAR (unstressed ĕr) 'there'
    DAAR is-ĕt-hooTEL. 'There's the hotel.'
    ĕr-IS-hier gheen-hooTEL.
        'There's no hotel here.'
dĕ- DACH 'the day'
    DACH! 'Hello!', 'Goodbye!'
    DANKĕn 'to thank'
    dank-uu-WEL. 'Thank you.'
    niets-tĕ-DANKĕn. 'You're welcome.'

DAT (unstressed ĕt) 'that, the before some nouns;
    compare DIE), it'
    wat-iz-DAT? 'What's that?'
    wat-IZ-ĕt? 'What is it?'
    DAT hooTEL 'that hotel'
    ĕt-hooTEL 'the hotel'
dĕ unstressed for DIE
DIE (unstressed dĕ) 'that, the (before some nouns;
    compare DAT)'
    DIE TREIN, die-TREIN 'that train'
    dĕ-TREIN 'the train'
DIT 'this'
DRIE 'three'
DRINKĕn 'to drink'

EEN (unstressed ĕn) 'one, a, an'
    EEN hooTEL, een-hooTEL 'one hotel'
    ĕn-hooTEL 'a hotel'
EEtĕn 'to eat'
EN 'and'
ĕn unstressed for EEN
ĕr unstressed for DAAR
ĕt unstressed for DAT

GHAAN 'to go'
   ik-GHAA 'I go'
   GHAAT 'goes'
   GHAAT-uu? 'Do you go?', 'Will you go?'
GHEEN 'not any, not a, no (before a noun)'
   gheen-VLEES 'no meat'
GHOET 'good, well'
   heel-GHOET 'quite well'
   ghoedĕn-DACH! 'Good day!'
GHRAACH 'gladly'
   ik-wou-GHRAACH 'I'd like to'
   ik-zou-GHRAACH . . . willĕn 'I should like to'
   heel-GHRAACH 'very gladly'
dĕ- GHULdĕn 'the guilder *or* gulden' (officially worth
     52 cents in American money in May, 1940)

HEBBĕn 'to have'
HEEL 'quite'
   heel-GHOET 'quite well'
dĕ-HEER 'the gentleman'
HIER 'here'
HOE 'how'
hoe-VEEL, HOE-veel 'how much, how many'
   hoe-veel-BIER? 'How much beer?'
   hoe-veel-sieghĕRETTĕn? 'How many cigarettes?'
ĕt-hooTEL 'the hotel'

IK 'I'
IS, IZ 'is'

JAA 'yes'
dĕ-JUFrou 'the young lady'
   jufrou-DEKKĕr 'Miss Dekker'
   JAA-jufrou 'Yes, Miss'

dĕ-KOFFie 'the coffee'
   KWAAlik 'ill, amiss'
   nee-mĕ-niet-KWAAlik. 'Excuse me.'

LAAT 'late'
   hoe-LAAT? 'at what time?'
   hoe-LAAT-is-ĕt? 'What time is it?'
LANGzaam, LANGsaam 'slow, slowly'
LINKS 'to the left, at the left'
dĕ-LUUsiefĕr 'the match'
   LUUsiefĕrs 'matches'

mĕ unstressed for MEI
MEI (unstressed mĕ) 'me'
   nee-mĕ-niet-KWAAlik. 'Excuse me.'
   met-MEI, niet-met-UU. 'With me, not with you.'
   HELP-mĕ 'help me'
dĕ-MELK 'the milk'
   MELK-drinkĕn 'to drink milk'

měNEER 'sir, Mr.'
    měneer-DEKKĕr 'Mr. Dekker'
MET 'with'
měVROU 'ma'am, Mrs.'
    mĕvrou-DEKKĕr 'Mrs. Dekker'
dĕ-MORghĕn 'the morning'

    NAAR 'to'
    naar-amstĕrDAM 'to Amsterdam'
    NEE, NEEN 'no' (answering a question; compare
        GHEEN)
    NEEghĕn 'nine'
    NEEmĕn 'to take'
    nee-mĕ-niet-KWWAlik. 'Excuse me.'
    NIET 'not'
    ik-GHAA-niet. 'I don't go', 'I'm not going.'
    NIETS 'nothing'
    niets-tĕ-DANKĕn. 'You're welcome.'

    OM 'at' (in telling the time)
    om-VIER UUR 'at four o'clock'

    RECHS 'at the right, to the right'
    rechTUIT, RECHTuit 'straight ahead'
ĕt-rĕstoRANG (restoRANG) 'the restaurant'

dĕ-SENT 'the cent' (one hundredth of a guilder)
    TIEN SENT 'ten cents'

dĕ-sieghĕRET (sieghaaRET) 'the cigarette'
    sieghĕRETTĕn 'cigarettes'
    SPREEkĕn 'to speak'
    SPREEK 'speak'
ĕt-staaSJON 'the station'

    tĕ 'to'
    niets-tĕ-DANKĕn. 'You're welcome.'
    TIEN 'ten'
    TOT 'up to, until'
    tot-ZIENS! 'So long!'
dĕ-TREIN 'the train'
    TWAALF 'twelve'
    TWAALV UUR 'twelve o'clock'
    TWEE 'two'

    UU 'you'
ĕt-UUR 'the hour'
    VIER UUR 'four o'clock'
    om-VIER UUR 'at four o'clock'

    VEEL 'much, many'
    hoe-VEEL 'how much, how many'
    VEIF 'five'
    VEIV UUR 'five o'clock'

věrSTAAN 'to understand'
  věrSTAAT-uu? 'Do you understand?'
  ik-věrSTAA 'I understand'
VIER 'four'
ět-VLEES 'the meat'
dě-VROU 'the woman'

WAAR 'where'
ět-WAAtěr 'the water'
  waNEER, WANNeer 'when?'
  WAT 'what?, something, some'
    wat-IS-ět? 'What is it?'
    wat-EEtěn 'to eat something'
    wat-MELK 'some milk'
dě-wee-SEE 'the toilet'
  WEL 'well'
    dank-uu-WEL. 'Thank you.'
  WILLěn 'to want to'
    ik-WIL 'I want to, I want'

WILT-uu? 'Do you want to?', 'do you want?'
WOU 'would like to'
  ik-wou-GRAACH 'I'd like to'

zě unstressed for ZEI
ZEEvěn 'seven'
ZEGHěn 'to say'
  ik-ZECH 'I say'
  uu-ZECHT 'you say'
ZEI (unstressed zě) 'they'
ZEIN 'to be'
  zě-ZEIN 'they are'
ZES 'six'
  ZEZ UUR 'six o'clock'
ZIEN 'to see'
  tot-ZIENS! 'So long!'
ZOU 'would, should'
  ik-zou-GHRAACH 'I'd like to'

PART ONE

MEETING PEOPLE

To the Leader: This Unit is constructed almost exactly like the first. If there is any question in your mind at any point what the proper procedure is, refer back to the corresponding part of Unit I and reread the directions given there. Refresh your memory of the points made in the Introduction too, so that you won't overlook small but important points.

A. BASIC SENTENCES

In this Unit the Basic Sentences are set up in the form of a conversation. Don't worry too much about keeping the various characters of the conversation straight; the important thing is what they say.

1. Basic Sentences

One morning Mr. John Carver, an American who is in Holland, comes across his Dutch friend Mr. Vink, and is introduced to a Mrs. Dekker and her son Peter.

──────ENGLISH EQUIVALENTS──────	──────AIDS TO LISTENING──────	──────CONVENTIONAL SPELLING──────
	Mr. Carver	
Good morning, Mr. Vink.	ghoejě-MORghě, měneer--VINK.	Goeden morgen, Mijnheer Vink.

28   [2–A]

Mr. Vink

Hello, Carver!	dach-KAARvĕr!	Dag, Carver!
the (man) friend	dĕ-VRIENT	de vriend
Mrs. Dekker, this is my friend, Mr. Carver.	mĕvrou-DEKKĕr, dit-is-mĕn-VRIENT, mĕneer-KAARvĕr.	Mevrouw Dekker, dit is mijn vriend, Mijnheer Carver.

Mrs. Dekker

Pleased to meet you, Mr. Carver.	dach-mĕneer-KAARvĕr.	Dag, Mijnheer Carver.

Vink

of	VAN	van
of me or of mine ·	van-MEI	van mij
Mr. Dekker is a good friend of mine.	mĕneer-DEKKĕr is-ĕn-ghoedĕ-VRIENT-van-mei.	Mijnheer Dekker is een goede vriend van mij.
the (woman) friend	dĕ-vrienDIN	de vriendin
also	OOK	ook
Mrs. Dekker is also a friend of my wife's.	mĕvrou-DEKKĕr is-OOK ĕn-vrienDIN van-mĕn-VROU.	Mevrouw Dekker is ook een vriendin van mijn vrouw.

Carver

who	WIE	wie
this	DEEzĕ	deze
young	JONG	jong
And who is this young man?	en-wie-iz-DEEzĕ jongĕ-MAN?	En wie is deze jonge man?

Vink

the son	dĕ-ZOON	de zoon
This young man is Mr. and Mrs. Dekker's son.	DEEzĕ-jongĕ-man iz-dĕ-ZOON van-mĕNEER en-mĕvrou--DEKKĕr.	Deze jonge man is de zoon **van** Mijnheer en Mevrouw **Dekker**.
his	ZEIN	zijn
the name	dĕ-NAAM	de naam
His name is Peter.	zein-naam-is-PIEtĕr.	Zijn naam is Pieter.
he	HEI	hij
to be called	HEEtĕn	heeten
His name is Peter Dekker.	hei-HEET PIEtĕr DEKKĕr.	Hij heet Pieter Dekker.

Peter

your	UUW	uw
What is your name, Sir?	hoe-is-UUW-naam, mĕNEER?	Hoe is uw naam, mijnheer?

Carver

My name is John Carver.	ik-HEET JAN KAARvĕr.	Ik heet Jan Carver.
I am	ik-BEN	ik ben
I'm a friend of Mr. Vink's.	ik-ben-ĕn-VRIENT van-mĕneer--VINK.	Ik ben een vriend van Mijnheer Vink.

	Mrs. Dekker	
you are	uu-BENT	u bent
married	ghĕTROUT	getrouwd
Are you married, Mr. Carver?	bent-uu-ghĕTROUT, mĕneer--KAARvĕr?	Bent u getrouwd, mihnheer Carver?

	Carver	
No, ma'am, I'm not married.	NEE-mĕvrou, ik-ben-niet--ghĕTROUT.	Neen, mevrouw, ik ben niet getrouwd.

	Mrs. Dekker	
to live or *to be alive*	LEEvĕn	leven
still	NOCH	nog
the father	dĕ-VAAdĕr	de vader
the mother	dĕ-MOEdĕr	de moeder
Are your father and mother still living?	LEEvĕn uu-VAAdĕr en-MOEdĕr--noch?	Leven uw vader en moeder nog?

	Carver	
Yes, ma'am; my father and my mother are living.	JAA-mĕvrou; mein-VAAdĕr en--MOEdĕr LEEvĕn-noch.	Ja, Mevrouw; mijn vader en moeder leven nog.

	Mrs. Dekker	
What are your father's and mother's names?	hoe-zein-dĕ-NAAmĕn van-uu- -VAAdĕr en-van-uu-MOEdĕr?	Hoe zijn de namen van uw vader en van uw moeder?

	Carver	
My father's name is Charles. My mother's name is Mary.	mein-VAAdĕr heet-KAArĕl. mein-MOEdĕr heet-maaRIE.	Mijn vader heet Karel. Mijn moeder heet Marie.

	Mrs. Dekker	
you have	uu-HEPT	u hebt
the brother	dĕ-BROER	de broer
or or whether	OF	of
the sister	dĕ-ZUStĕr	de zuster
Have you any brothers or sisters, Mr. Carver?	hept-uu-BROERS of-ZUStĕrs, mĕneer-KAARvĕr?	Hebt u broers of zusters, Mijnheer Carver?

	Carver	
Yes, ma'am, I have a brother and a sister.	JAA-mĕvrou, ik-hep-ĕn-BROER en-ĕn-ZUStĕr.	Ja, mevrouw, ik heb een broer en een zuster.

	Mrs. Dekker	
now	NUU	nu
Where are your brother and your sister now?	WAAR zein-uu-BROER en-uu- -ZUStĕr-nuu?	Waar zijn uw broer en uw zuster nu?

in	IN	in
America	aMEEriekaa	Amerika
My sister is in America.	mein-ZUStĕr is-in-aMEEriekaa.	Mijn zuster is in Amerika.
Holland	HOLLant	Holland
My brother is in Holland.	mein-BROER is-in-HOLLant.	Mijn broer is in Holland.
just or *but*	MAAR	maar
to know	WEEtĕn	weten
exactly	prĕSIES	precies
maybe	miSCHIEN	misschien
But I don't know exactly where he is now;	maar-ik-weet-NIET-prĕsies waar-hei-NUU-is;	Maar ik weet niet precies waar hij nu is;
perhaps in Amsterdam or in Leiden.	mischien-in-amstĕrDAM of-in--LEIdĕn.	misschien in Amsterdam of in Leiden.
the daughter	dĕ-DOCHtĕr	de dochter
Do you have a daughter too, Mrs. Dekker?	hept-uu-ook-ĕn-DOCHtĕr, mĕvrou-DEKKĕr?	Hebt u ook een dochter, Mevrouw Dekker?

Mrs. Dekker

we	WEI	wij
we have	wei-HEBBĕn	wij hebben
No, we have no daughters.	NEE-mĕneer, wĕ-HEBBĕn gheen--DOCHtĕr.	Neen, mijnheer, wij hebben geen dochter.
alone	aLEEN	alleen

[2–A] 33

the child	het-KINT	het kind
our	ONzĕ	onze
My husband and I have only one child, [our son] Peter here.	mein-MAN en-IK hebbĕn-aleen--maar-EEN KINT, PIEtĕr-hier.	Mijn man en ik hebben alleen maar één kind, Pieter hier.

Carver

Are you married, Mr. Vink?	bent-uu-ghĕTROUT, mĕneer--VINK?	Bent u getrouwd, Mijnheer Vink?

Vink

children	KINdĕrĕn	kinderen
Yes, but my wife and I have no children.	JAA, maar-mein-VROU en-IK hebbĕn-GHEEN KINdĕrĕn.	Ja, maar mijn vrouw en ik hebben geen kinderen.

Mrs. Dekker

no doubt	WEL	wel
Mr. Carver would probably like to know whether we have any daughters.	mĕneer-KAARvĕr zou-wel--GHRAACH-willĕ-weetĕ of-wei--DOCHtĕrs-hebbĕn.	Mihnheer Carver zou wel graag willen weten of wij dochters hebben.
So, Mr. Carver, I want to tell you something.	WEL, mĕneer-KAARvĕr, ik-zal--uu-wat-ZEGHĕn.	Wel, Mihnheer Carver, ik zal u wat zeggen.
she	ZEI	zij
she has	zei-HEEFT	zij heeft

34   [2–A]

My friend, Mrs. Jansen, has two daughters.	mein-vrienDIN, mĕvrou-JANsĕn, heeft-TWEE-dochtĕrs.	Mijn vriendin, Mevrouw **Jansen,** heeft twee dochters.
She has five children, three sons and two daughters.	zĕ-heeft-FEIF KINdĕrĕ, DRIE ZOONS en-TWEE DOCHtĕrs.	Zij heeft vijf kinderen, drie zoons en twee dochters.
to have to	MOEtĕn	moeten
Excuse me, gentlemen, (but) I've got to go now.	nee-mĕ-niet-KWAAlik, HEErĕn, maar-NUU moet-ik-GHAAN.	Neem me niet kwalijk, heeren, maar nu moet ik gaan.
Pete and I have to go to the station.	PIET-en-ik moetĕn-naar-het--staaSJON.	Piet en ik moeten naar het station.
Good day, gentlemen.	ghoedĕn-DACH-heerĕ.	Goeden dag, heeren.

Vink and Carver

Goodbye, ma'am.	dach-mĕVROU.	Dag, mevrouw.

Vink

where to	waar-HEEN	waarheen
Where are you going, Mr. Carver?	waar-heen-ghaat-UU, mĕneer--KAARvĕr?[1]	Waarheen gaat u, Mijnheer Carver?

Carver

I'd like to go to a restaurant.	IK-zou-ghraach naar-ĕn--rĕstoRANG-willĕn-ghaan.	Ik zou graag naar een restaurant willen gaan.
Is there a good restaurant here?	IS-ĕr-hier ĕn-GHOET-rĕstorang?	Is er hier een goed restaurant?

---

[1] For most speakers of Dutch a more natural expression would be *waar-ghaat-uu-naar-TOE?* 'where go you to?'. Your Guide may prefer this.

Yes.	JAA-měneer.	Ja, mijnheer.
There's quite a good restaurant here in this hotel.	ěr-is-ěn-HEEL-ghoet rěstoRANG hier-in-dit-hooTEL.	Er is een heel goed restaurant hier in dit hotel.
It's here, at the left.	hět-is-hier-LINKS.	Het is hier links.

2. Hints on Pronunciation

Only two of the Dutch consonant sounds are entirely strange to us: *ch* and *gh*. Some Dutch speakers, including the one who made the records for this course, do not distinguish between these two sounds, pronouncing them both as other Dutch speakers pronounce the *ch*.

ch is a friction sound, made by the passing of breath between the back of the tongue and the roof of the mouth. We sometimes make this sound when we clear our throat to spit. It is the same kind of friction sound as the English sounds *f*, *th*, *s*, *sh* (as in *fin, thin, sin, shin*), only that it is made in the back of the mouth.

gh resembles Dutch *ch*; it is a friction sound, formed between the back of the tongue and the roof of the mouth. It differs from Dutch *ch* in being *voiced*, like the English sounds *v*, *th*, *z*, *zh* (as in *van, then, zoo,*

vision). If you hold your hands on your ears, closing your ears, and then say *fin, van,* or *sin, zoo,* you will hear a buzz for the *v* and *z*, but not for *f* and *s*. This buzz is what is meant by the term *voicing*.

If you are using the records, the following examples of *gh* and *ch* will all sound the same. If you have a Guide, he may pronounce them differently. Imitate whatever model you have; both are perfectly good Dutch.

PRACTICE 1

ZEGHěn	*'say'*
GHAAN	*'go'*
GHEEN	*'none'*

GHULdĕn   *'guilder'*
GRAACH   *'with pleasure'*
SCHIP   *'ship'*
miSCHIEN   *'perhaps'*

(If you have studied German, note with special care that the writing *sch* represents the Dutch *s*-sound followed by the Dutch *ch*-sound, not the *sh*-sound that it stands for in German writing.)

Another tricky thing in Dutch is the difference between the sounds *f*, *v*, and *w*. *f* is about the same as our *f*-sound in *fish*, if anything a little stronger. *v* is a sound similar both to English *f* and to English *v*, as in *van*; *w* is a sound similar both to English *v* and to English *w*, as in *wind*. Try them in the following words, giving particular attention to the difference between *v* and *w*:

3. Check Yourself

Did you go through the Basic Sentences at least twice with group repetition and at least once more individually?

Did you repeat each word and phrase in a loud, clear voice immediately after hearing it?

Were you careful to follow the pronunciation you

PRACTICE 2

FIER, VIER, WIER   *'proud, four, seaweed'*
VONT, WONT   *'found, wound'*
VIS, WIS   *'fish, wipe'*
VANG, WANG   *'catch, cheek'*
VINdĕn, WINdĕn   *'find, wind'*

Now go back to **1**, the Basic Sentences, and go through them again exactly as before. Keep in mind particularly the sounds you have been practicing, but also remember to keep the meaning of each expression in mind as you listen to it and imitate it.

Then go through once or twice more, in the same way as before except with individual repetition, taking turns around the group. Continue until ·everyone has had ample opportunity to repeat the Dutch alone.

heard, even if it seemed different from that shown in the book?

Did you keep in mind the meaning of each word and phrase as you heard and spoke the Dutch?

Do not go beyond this point until you are sure you have done everything so far as you should.

B. Word Study

1. Word Study

Point 1. Meanings. (a) Note that *dĕ-MAN* means both 'the man' and 'the husband'; and that *dĕ-VROU* means both 'the woman' and 'the wife'.

(b) The word *wel* rarely means 'well' in the sense of 'not sick'. Usually it means something like 'nicely', 'no doubt', 'surely', 'I think', 'I guess': *dank-uu-WEL* 'thank you'; *wel-JAA* 'well, yes, I guess so'; *jaa-WEL* 'yes, but . . .'.

(c) The verb *MOEtĕn* means 'to have to': *ik-moet--nuu-GHAAN.* 'I must go now.'; but it often means 'to have to go' to such and such a place: *ik-moet-naar--mĕn-hooTEL.* 'I have to go to my hotel.' But for this meaning you will hear also *ik-moet-naar-mĕn--hooTEL-ghaan.* In this last sentence, notice the order of the words in Dutch.

Point 2. Verbs. You have noticed in the Basic Sentences that verbs change form depending on what words are used with them: *ik-WIL* 'I want, I want to', but *uu-WILT* 'you want, you want to'. In trying to talk you will need to know the different forms of verbs. Here are the most necessary forms:

Form 1, with ending -ĕn or -n

SPREEkĕn	*'to speak'*	WEETĕn	*'to know'*	GHAAN	*'to go'*
wĕ-SPREEkĕn	*'we speak'*	wĕ-WEETĕn	*'we know'*	wĕ-GHAAN	*'we go'*
zĕ-SPREEkĕn	*'they speak'*	zĕ-WEETĕn	*'they know'*	zĕ-GHAAN	*'they go'*
dĕ-HEErĕn		dĕ-HEErĕn		dĕ-HEErĕn	
SPREEkĕn	*'the gentlemen speak'*	WEETĕn	*'the gentlemen know'*	GHAAN	*'the gentlemen go'*

Form 2, with no ending

SPREEK!	*'speak!'*	WEET!	*'know!'*	GHAA!	*'go!'*
ik-SPREEK	*'I speak'*	ik-WEET	*'I know'*	ik-GHAA	*'I go'*

Form 3, with ending -t or nothing

hei-SPREEKT	'he speaks'	hei-WEET	'he knows'	hei-GHAAT	'he goes'
ză-SPREEKT	'she speaks'	ză-WEET	'she knows'	ză-GHAAT	'she goes'
ĕt-SPREEKT	'it speaks'	ĕt-WEET	'it knows'	ĕt-GHAAT	'it goes'
uu-SPREEKT	'you speak'	uu-WEET	'you know'	uu-GHAAT	'you go'
dĕ-HEER		dĕ-HEER		dĕ-HEER	
SPREEKT	'the gentleman speaks'	WEET	'the gentleman knows'	GHAAT	'the gentleman goes'

Form 2, with no ending, is called the *stem*. It is used with *ik* 'I', and when making a request.

If the stem ends in a vowel, as in the third example above (stem *ghaa-*), form *1* adds the ending *-n*. If the stem ends in a consonant, as in the first and second examples (stems *spreek-*, *weet-*), form *1* adds the ending *-ĕn*. This form is used with *wei* 'we', *zei* 'they', and with a noun like *dĕ-HEErĕn* 'the gentlemen' which refers to more than one person or thing. Form *1* is the one listed in the Basic Sentences when a new verb is given; you can find the stem, when you know form *1*, by simply dropping the *-n* or *-ĕn* ending.

If the stem ends in *t*, as in the second example above, then form *3* adds no ending, and is like form *2*. Otherwise, as in the first and third examples, form *3* adds a *-t* to the stem. This form is used with *hei* 'he', *zei* 'she', *ĕt* 'it', *uu* 'you', and with a noun like *dĕ-HEER* 'the gentleman' which refers to a single person or thing.

There are a few verbs that don't go like the above models. Of these you have had two:

Form 1

ZEIN	'to be'	HEBBĕn	'to have'
wĕ-ZEIN	'we are'	wĕ-HEBBĕn	'we have'
ză-ZEIN	'they are'	ză-HEBBĕn	'they have'
dĕ-HEErĕn ZEIN	'the gentlemen are'	dĕ-HEErĕn HEBBĕn	'the gentlemen have'

WEES!   'be!'   HEP!   'have'

ik-BEN   'I am'   ik-HEP   'I have'

hei-IS   'he is'   hei-HEEFT   'he has'
zě-IS   'she is'   zě-HEEFT   'she has'
ět-IS   'it is'   ět-HEEFT   'it has'
dě-HEER IS   'the gentleman is'   dě-HEER HEEFT   'the gentleman has'

uu-BENT 'you are'   uu-HEPT   'you have'

2. Review of Basic Sentences

Turn back to the Basic Sentences and cover the English. Read the Dutch to yourself, and test yourself to see if you know the meaning of each expression. Check the expressions you are uncertain about, and continue to the end before you uncover the English to check up. If you have missed many of them, do the same thing a second time. End by picking the Dutch expressions at random, instead of in the order in which they are given.

C. What Would You Say?

1. What Would You Say?

Look over the following groups of Dutch sentences, practicing them to yourself, making sure you know the meaning of them all, and selecting the one of each group which fits the requirements given in English.

1. *Your acquaintance suddenly starts to leave you and you want to know where he is bound for. You say:*
   a. hoe-GHAAT-ĕt met-uuw-VAAdĕr?
   b. waar-ghaat-uu-naar-TOE?
   c. hept-uu-ĕn-DOCHtĕr?

2. *You like the beer you are drinking. You say:*
   a. dit-BIER is-heel-GHOET.
   b. hoe-veel-IZ-dit-bier?
   c. dit-BIER is-niet-GHOET.

3. *You want to explain why you are leaving. You say:*
   a. ik-wou-GHRAACH wat-EEtĕn.
   b. ik-zou-GHRAACH ĕn-sieghĕRET-willĕn-hebbĕn.
   c. ik-MOET-nuu naar-ĕt-staaSJON-ghaan.

4. *You want to tell your sister's name. You say:*
   a. mĕn-ZUStĕr is-noch-NIET ghĕTROUT.
   b. mĕn-ZUStĕr heet-ANNie.
   c. mĕn-ZUStĕr is-noch-JONG.

5. *You want to ask when your train goes:*
   a. wanneer-ghaat-mĕn-TREIN?
   b. iz-DIT dĕ-trein-naar-amstĕrDAM?
   c. ghaan-wĕ-met-DEEzĕ-trein?

6. *You want to ask a young lady whether she is married. You say:*
   a. is-uuw-MAN hier-in-ĕt-hooTEL?
   b. hoe-veel-KINdĕrĕn-hept-uu, mĕVROU?
   c. bent-uu-ghĕTROUT-jufrou?

7. *Mrs. Dekker asks you whether your father and mother are living. She says:*
   a. zein-uuw-VAAdĕr en-uuw-VROU in-HOLLant?
   b. leevĕn-uuw-VAAdĕr en-uuw-ZUStĕr-noch?
   c. leevĕn-uuw-VAAdĕr en-uuw-MOEdĕr-noch?

8. *Mrs. Jansen offers you a cup of coffee. You want to accept it. You say:*
   a. dank-uu-WEL-mĕvrou.
   b. ik-DRINK gheen-KOFFie-mĕvrou.
   c. als-t-uu-BLIEFT-mĕvrou.

9. *Someone asks you where Annie Jansen is. You don't know, so you say:*
   a. ik-WEET-niet waar-zĕ-IS.
   b. ik-WEET-niet of-zĕ-ghĕTROUT-is.
   c. ik-WEET-niet of-zĕ-noch-JONG-is.

2. What Did You Say?

The Leader will read the English for each of the groups in **1** and will call on some member of the group to read out his choice in Dutch. Other members of the group will criticize the choices given if they do not agree with them. The Leader will also be sure that you understand the meanings of the wrong answers too.

D. Listening In

Listen to each of the following conversations, which the Guide or the records will give you. First listen to all of them, with your books closed, and without repeating them, to see how well you can follow them with no assistance from what you see. Then open your books and go through each one separately, repeating after the Guide, and checking on anything you do not understand. Finally, the Leader will assign parts and you can go through them with individual repetition. Repeat often enough for everyone to have a chance at a part. Be careful, especially when you are the only one repeating after the Guide, to speak clearly and in a loud voice, so that everyone can hear you.

1. *Mr. Carver meets Mrs. Mulder and her children.*

mĕvrou-MULdĕr: hoe-GHAAT-ĕt-met-uu, mĕneer-KAARvĕr?	Hoe gaat het met u, Mijnheer Carver?
Mr. Carver: heel-GHOET, dank-uu-WEL-mĕvrou.	Heel goed, dank u wel, mevrouw.
en-met-UU?	En met u?
mĕvrou-MULdĕr: heel-GHOET, dank-uu-WEL.	Heel goed, dank u wel.
mĕneer-KAARvĕr, dit-zein-mĕn-KINdĕrĕn.	Mijnheer Carver, dit zijn mijn kinderen.
dit-is-mein-DOCHtĕr ANNie,	Dit is mijn dochter Annie,
en-dit-is-mein-DOCHtĕr maaRIE,	en dit is mijn dochter Marie,
en-deezĕ-JONGĕns zein-mein-ZOONS, PIET en-JAN.	en deze jongens zijn mijn zoons, Piet en Jan.

Mr. Carver:	dach-ANNie, dach-maaRIE.	Dag, Annie; dag, Marie.
	dach-PIET en-JAN.	Dag, Piet en Jan.
	IK-heet OOK-jan.	Ik heet ook Jan.
	mein-NAAM-is JAN KAARvĕr.	Mijn naam is Jan Carver.
	waar-heen-GHAAT-uu, mĕvrou-MULdĕr?	Waarheen gaat u, Mevrouw Mulder?
mĕvrou-MULdĕr:	ik-ghaa-met-dĕ-KINdĕrĕn naar-dĕ-biejĕ--SKOOP	Ik ga met de kinderen naar de bioscoop.
	mein-MAN GHAAT-niet-ghraach naar-dĕ--biejĕSKOOP.	Mijn man gaat niet graag naar de bioscoop.
Mr. Carver:	hoe-LAAT bĕGHINT dĕ-biejĕSKOOP?	Hoe laat begint de bioscoop?
mĕvrou-MULdĕr:	die-bĕGHINT om-ZEEvĕn-uur.	Die begint om zeven uur.
	hoe-LAAT is-ĕt-NUU?	Hoe laat is het nu?
Mr. Carver:	het-is-prĕSIES ZEEvĕn-uur.	Het is precies zeven uur.
mĕvrou-MULdĕr:	dan-MOEtĕn-wĕ wel-GHAAN.	Dan moeten we wel gaan.
	tot-ZIENS mĕneer-KAARvĕr.	Tot ziens, Mijnheer Carver.

2. *Mr. Vos asks Mr. Carver about his family.*

mĕneer-VOS:	ZECH, mĕneer-KAARvĕr, hoe-GHAAT-ĕt met--uu-VAAdĕr?	Zeg Mijnheer Carver, hoe gaat het met uw vader?
Mr. Carver:	heel-GHOET, dank-uu-WEL.	Heel goed, dank u wel.
mĕneer-VOS:	en-met-uu-MOEdĕr?	En met uw moeder?
Mr. Carver:	OOK-ghoet, dank-uu-WEL.	Ook goed, dank u wel.
mĕneer-VOS:	en-uu-ZUStĕr, maaRIE?	En uw zuster, Marie?
	is-zĕ-ghĕTROUT?	Is zij getrouwd?

Mr. Carver:	JAA-mĕneer, mĕn-zustĕr-maaRIE is-ghĕTROUT.	Ja, mijnheer, mijn zuster Marie is getrouwd.
	zĕ-heet-NUU mĕvrou-BEL.	Zij heet nu Mevrouw Bell.
mĕneer-VOS:	heeft-zĕ-KINdĕrĕn?	Heeft zij kinderen?
Mr. Carver:	JAA, zĕ-heeft-ĕn-ZOON.	Ja, zij heeft een zoon.
	hei-HEET KAArĕl.	Hij heet Karel.
mĕneer-VOS:	en-uu-broer-TEDDie?	En uw broer Teddie?
Mr. Carver:	TEDDie is-nuu-OOK in-HOLLant.	Teddie is nu ook in Holland.
	hei-is-in-amstĕrDAM of-mischien-in-LEIdĕn.	Hij is in Amsterdam of misschien in Leiden.
	ik-weet-NUU niet-prĕSIES of-hei-in-amstĕrDAM of-in-LEIdĕn-is.	Ik weet nu niet precies of hij in Amsterdam of in Leiden is.

3. *Mr. Whitney asks Mr. Vos about the Dekkers.*

Mr. Whitney (WITnie):	WEET-uu wie-mĕneer-DEKKĕr-is?	Weet u wie Mijnheer Dekker is?
mĕneer-VOS:	JAA, alfred-DEKKĕr is-ĕn-ghoedĕ-VRINT-van--mei.	Ja, Alfred Dekker is een goede vriend van mij.
Mr. Whitney:	HOE is-zĕn-NAAM?	Hoe is zijn naam?
	ik-vĕrSTAA-uu-niet-ghoet.	Ik versta u niet goed.
mĕneer-VOS:	ALfret.	Alfred.
	zĕn-NAAM is-ALfret.	Zijn naam is Alfred.
	hei-HEET ALfret DEKKĕr.	Hij heet Alfred Dekker.
Mr. Whitney:	hoe-iz-dĕ-NAAM van-zein-VROU?	Hoe is de naam van zijn vrouw?
mĕneer-VOS:	mĕvrou-DEKKĕr heet-maaRIE.	Mevrouw Dekker heet Marie.
Mr. Whitney:	hebbĕn-mĕNEER en-mĕvrou-DEKKĕr KINdĕrĕn?	Hebben Mijnheer en Mevrouw Dekker kinderen?

mĕneer-VOS:	JAA, zĕ-hebbĕn-EEN-kint.	Ja, zij hebben één kind.
Mr. Whitney:	is-ĕt-ĕn-ZOON of-ĕn-DOCHtĕr?	Is het een zoon of een dochter?
mĕneer-VOS:	het-is-ĕn-ZOON.	Het is een zoon.
	hei-is-noch-HEEL JONG.	Hij is nog heel jong.

E. CONVERSATION

1. Review of Basic Sentences

Turn back to the Basic Sentences and cover the Dutch. Read the English to yourself, and test yourself to see if you can speak the Dutch corresponding to each English equivalent. Check the expressions you are uncertain about, and continue to the end before you uncover the Dutch to check up. If you have missed many of them, do the same thing again. End by picking the English equivalents at random, instead of in the order in which they are given.

If you can work in pairs, both with the Dutch covered, you can ask each other instead of simply testing yourself.

2. Vocabulary Check-up

Close all your books. The Leader will start the ball rolling by addressing one of the others with such a question as 'How do you say *cigarette* in Dutch?' If the first person addressed doesn't know the answer, the Leader will ask someone else. Whoever answers correctly will in turn address such a question to still another member of the group. Continue until everyone has asked and answered several such questions and until most of the words and phrases of this Unit and the first Unit have been asked about.

Anyone who has too much trouble at this should go back and review the Basic Sentences again.

3. Carrying on Conversation

The Leader will assign parts and will ask you to take turns in pairs, carrying on the following conversations. The two persons who are talking should stand up and act out their parts, speaking as smoothly and naturally as possible. The Guide will help you when you slip on pronunciation or put the words together wrong. The models given here are only suggestions; vary them as you wish. Try to avoid *ums* and *ers* as much as possible; say something familiar fluently rather than something clever more slowly.

Here are some Dutch names that you might give yourselves for these conversations: van-DOOrĕn, TERPstraa, van-AALST, BEK, HULST.

Conversation 1. A and B meet on the street.

A: greets B and asks him how he is today.

B: thanks A and says he is well. He asks about A's son Dirk (DIRK), and if Dirk is here too.

A: says no, his son is in Delft (DELFT).

B: asks where A's daughter Emma (EMMaa) is now.

A: says she may still be at the movies.

B: excuses himself, saying he has to go to the station, to see his wife at eleven o'clock.

A: says goodbye.

B: says so long.

Conversation 2. A and his son Tom meet Mr. B.

B: says good evening to A and to Tom.

A: says hello.

Tom: says how do you do.

B: says he is well. He asks where the others are going.

A: says they are going to a restaurant to have something to drink.

B: says he is going to the station, because he and his wife have to go to Bussum (BUSSĕm).

Tom: asks when the train goes.

B: says exactly at ten o'clock.

A: says good evening.

Tom: says good evening.

B: says goodbye.

Conversation 3. Mrs. A. meets an American, Mr. B.

A: says good morning and asks how B is.

B: says he is fine, and asks A the same.

A: says she is fine. She asks where B's father is.

B: says his father is still in America, but would like to come to Holland too.

A: asks if B's mother is still living.

B: says no, but that he still has a sister who is in America.

A: asks if B's sister is married.

B: says yes, and that she has three children, two sons and a daughter.

FINDER LIST

aLEEN 'alone'
  aLEEN-maar 'only'
aMEEriekaa (aaMEEriekaa) 'America'

BEN see ZEIN
BENT see ZEIN
dĕ-BROER 'the brother'
  BROERS 'brothers'

DAN 'then'
DEEzĕ 'this'
  deezĕ-HEER 'this gentleman'
DIT 'this'
  dit-is-mĕn-ZOON 'this is my son'
  dit-hooTEL 'this hotel'
dĕ-DOCHtĕr 'the daughter'
  DOCHtĕrs 'daughters'

ei unstressed for HEI

ghĕTROUT 'married'
  is-zĕ-ghĕTROUT? 'is she married?'
  niet-ghĕTROUT 'not married'

HEBBĕn 'to have'
  ik-HEP 'I have'
  uu-HEPT 'you have'
  hei-HEEFT 'he has'
  wĕ-HEBBĕn 'we have'
HEEFT see HEBBĕn
HEErĕn 'gentlemen'
HEEtĕn 'to be called'
  ik-heet-JAN 'I am called John'
  hei-heet-JAN 'he is called John'
HEI (unstressed ei, ie) 'he'
  hei-is-HIER 'he is here'
  waar-IS-ie? 'where is he?'
HEP see HEBBĕn
HEPT see HEBBĕn
HOLLant 'Holland'

ie unstressed for HEI
IN 'in'

JONG 'young'
dĕ-JONGĕ 'the boy'
JONGĕns, JONGĕs 'boys'

ĕt-KINT 'the child'
KINdĕrĕn 'children'

LEEvĕn 'to live, to be alive'
hei-LEEFT 'he lives'

MAAR 'but'
aLEEN-maar 'only'
dĕ-MAN 'the man, the husband'
MEIN (unstressed mĕn) 'my'
mĕn-ZOON 'my son'
mĕn unstressed for MEIN
miSCHIEN 'maybe, perhaps'
dĕ-MOEdĕr 'the mother'
MOEtĕn 'to have to, to have to go'
ik-moet-naar-ĕt-staaSJON 'I have to go to the
station'

dĕ-NAAM 'the name'
NAAmĕn 'names'
NAAR 'to'
naar-TOE 'to'

waar-ghaat-uu-naar-TOE? 'where are you going
(to)?'
NOCH 'still, yet, besides'
noch-NIET 'not yet'
NOCH-ĕn-zoon 'another son'
nou unstressed for NUU
NUU (unstressed nuu, nou) 'now'

OF 'or, whether'
DOCHtĕrs of-ZOONS 'daughters or sons'
WEET-uu of-ie-HIER-is? 'Do you know whether
he is here?'
ONzĕ 'our'
OOK 'also'

prĕSIES 'exactly'

UUW (unstressed uuw, uu) 'your'
uuw-ZOON, uu-ZOON 'your son'

dĕ-VAAdĕr 'the father'
VAN 'of'
dĕ-KINdĕrĕn van-die-MAN 'that man's children'
ĕn-VRIENT-van-mĕ 'a friend of mine'
dĕ-VRIENT 'the (male) friend'
VRIENdĕn '(male) friends'

děvrienDIN 'the (female) friend'
vrienDINNĕn '(female) friends'
VRINT same as VRIENT
dĕ-VROU 'the woman, the wife'
mĕn-VROU 'my wife'

waar-HEEN, waar-heen 'where to'
waar-heen-GHAAT-uu? 'Where are you going?'
wĕ unstressed for WEI
WEEtĕn 'to know'
ik-WEET-niet waar-ĕt-IS 'I don't know where
it is'
WEI (unstressed wĕ) 'we'
WEL 'probably, I think'
ĕt-is-wel-HIER 'It's probably here'
WIE 'who'

zĕ unstressed for ZEI
ZEI (unstressed zĕ) 'she'
zĕ-GHAAT 'she goes'
ZEIN (unstressed zĕn) 'his'
zĕn-ZOON 'his son'
ZEIN 'to be'
wĕ-ZEIN 'we are'
ik-BEN 'I am'
uu-BENT 'you are'
hei-IS 'he is'
WEES! 'be!'
zĕn unstressed for ZEIN 'his'
dĕ-ZOON 'the son'
ZOONS 'sons'
dĕ-ZUStĕr 'the sister'
ZUStĕrs 'sisters'

WHAT'S YOUR TRADE?

A. BASIC SENTENCES

1. Basic Sentences

In a café, John Carver gets acquainted with the Pietersen brothers and their friends.

ENGLISH EQUIVALENTS	AIDS TO LISTENING	CONVENTIONAL SPELLING
	Mr. Pietersen	
What is your name, Sir?	wat-is-uu-NAAM, mĕNEER?	Wat is uw naam, mijnheer?
	Mr. Carver	
My name is John Carver.	IK-heet JAN KAARver.	Ik heet Jan Carver.
	Mr. Pietersen	
you come	uu-KOMT	u komt
from	VAN	van
where from	WAAR van-DAAN	waar vandaan
Where do you come from?	waar-KOMT-uu van-DAAN?	Waar komt u vandaan?

Mr. Carver

I come from America.	IK-kom uit-aMEEriekaa.	Ik kom uit Amerika.
the American (man)	dĕ-ameerieKAAN	de Amerikaan
I'm an American.	ik-ben-ĕn-ameerieKAAN.	Ik ben een Amerikaan.

Mr. Pietersen

to do	DOEN	doen
What are you doing now here in Holland?	wat-DOET-uu nuu-hier-in-HOLL--ant?	Wat doet u nu hier in Holland?

Mr. Carver

the sailor	dĕ-maTROOS	de matroos
I'm a sailor.	ik-ben-maTROOS.	Ik ben matroos.
the ship	hĕt-SCHIP	het schip
My ship is here in Rotterdam now.	mein-SCHIP is-nuu-hier-in-rottĕr--DAM.	Mijn schip is nu hier in Rotterdam.
And you, sir, what is your name?	en-UU-meneer, hoe-is-UUW-naam?	En u, Mijnheer, hoe is uw naam?

Mr. Pietersen

My name is Charles Pietersen.	IK-heet KAArĕl PIEtĕrsĕn.	Ik heet Karel Pietersen.
the carpenter	dĕ-TIMMĕrman	de timmerman
I'm a carpenter.	ik-ben-TIMMĕrman.	Ik ben timmerman.
to come	KOOmĕn	komen
come	KOM	kom

once	EENS	eens
Herman! Come here!	HERman! kom-ĕns-HIER!	Herman! Kom eens hier!
This gentleman is an American.	DEEzĕ HEER is-ĕn-ameerie- -KAAN.	Deze heer is een Amerikaan.
American	ameerieKAANS	Amerikaansch
He's an American sailor.	hei-iz-ĕn-ameerieKAANS ma- -TROOS.	Hij is een Amerikaansch matroos.
Mr. Carver, this is my brother Her- man Pietersen.	mĕneer-KARvĕr, dit-is-mĕn- -BROER, HERman PIEtĕrsĕn.	Mijnheer Carver, dit is mijn broer, Herman Pietersen.
the barber	dĕ-barBIER	barbier
He's a barber.	hei-iz-barBIER.	Hij is barbier.

Herman Pietersen

Pleased to meet you, sir.	dach-mĕneer-KAARvĕr.	Dag, Mijnheer Carver.
These gentlemen here are our friends.	deezĕ-heerĕ-HIER zein-onzĕ- -VRIENdĕn.	Deze heeren hier zijn onze vrienden.
the mechanic	dĕ-meekaanieSJENG	de mecanicien
to work	WERkĕn	werken
the garage	dĕ-gaaRAAzjĕ	de garage
Mr. Jansen is a mechanic.	mĕneer-JANsĕn is-meekaanie- -SJENG.	Mijnheer Jansen is mecanicien.
He works in a garage.	hei-WERKT in-ĕn-gaaRAAzjĕ.	Hij werkt in een garage.
to repair	reepaaREErĕ	repareeren ·
the auto	dĕ-OOtoo	de auto
He repairs autos.	hei-reepaaREERT OOtoos.	Hij repareert autos.

Mr. Carver

Pleased to meet you Mr. Jansen.	dach-měneer-JANsěn.	Dag, Mijnheer Jansen.
My sister's husband in America is a mechanic too.	dě-MAN van-mein-ZUStěr in--aMEEriekaa is-OOK meekaanie--SJENG.	De man van mijn zuster in Amerika is ook mecanicien.

Mr. Pietersen

And this gentleman is my friend Joe Klinker	en-DEEzě-heer is-mein-VRIENT, JOOS KLINKěr.	En deze heer is mijn vriend, Joost Klinker.
the store	dě-WINkěl	de winkel
clothes	KLEErěn	kleeren
the clothing store	dě-KLEErěn-winkěl	de kleerenwinkel
He works in a store, in a clothing store.	HEI WERKT in-ěn-WINKěl, in-ěn-KLEErěn-winkěl.	Hij werkt in een winkel, in een kleerenwinkel.

Herman Pietersen

And here is our friend Paul Edelmans.	en-HIER is-onzě-VRIENT, POUL EEdělmans.	En hier is onze vriend, Paul Edelmans.
the factory	dě-faBRIEK	de fabriek
He works in a factory.	HEI WERKT in-ěn-faBRIEK.	Hij werkt in een fabriek.
the workman	dě-WERK-man	de werkman
the piece of furniture	hět-MEUběl	het meubel
the furniture factory	dě-MEUběl-fabriek	de meubelfabriek
He's a workman in a furniture factory.	hei-is-WERK-man in-ěn--MEUběl-fabriek.	Hij is werkman in een meubelfabriek.

Mr. Carver

Beg pardon?	wat-BLIEFT-uu?	Wat blieft u?
to understand	běGHREIpěn	begrijpen
I don't understand you very well.	ik-běGHREIP-uu niet-GHOET.	ik begrijp u niet goed.

Mr. Pietersen

to make	MAAkěn	maken
He is a workman in a furniture factory.	hei-is-WERK-man in-ěn--MEUběl-fabriek.	Hij is werkman in een meubelfabriek.
In a factory where they make furniture.	in-ěn-faBRIEK waar-zě--MEuběls-maakěn.	In een fabriek, waar ze meubels maken.

Mr. Edelmans

the farmer	dě BOER	de boer
Yes, I'm a workman, but my father is a farmer.	JAA, IK-ben-WERK-man, maar--měn-VAAděr iz-BOER.	Ja, ik ben werkman, maar mijn vader is boer.
the farm	dě-boerděREI	de boerderij
He has a farm.	HEI heeft-ěn-boerděREI.	Hij heeft een boerderij.
on	OP	op
the land	hět-LANT	het land
He works on the land.	HEI-werkt op-ět-LANT.	Hij werkt op het land.
My brother Nicholas doesn't work.	mein-broer-KLAAS werkt-NIET.	Mijn broer Klaas werkt niet.
the student.	dě-stuuDENT	de student
He's a student.	HEI is-stuuDENT.	Hij is student.

to study	stuuDEErĕn	studeeren
for	VOOR	voor
the doctor	dĕ-DOKtĕr	de dokter
He's studying to be a doctor.	hei-stuuDEERT foor-DOKtĕr.	Hij studeert voor dokter
who	DIE	die
And I have a sister who works here in Rotterdam too.	en-IK heb-ĕn-ZUStĕr die-OOK hier-in-rottĕrDAM-werkt.	En ik heb een zuster die ook hier in Rotterdam werkt.
the typist	dĕ-tiePIStĕ	de typiste
She's a typist.	zei-is-tiePIStĕ.	Zij is typiste.
the bank	dĕ-BANK	de bank
She works in a bank	zei-WERKT in-ĕn-BANK.	Zij werkt in een bank.
the youngest	dĕ-JONGstĕ	de jongste
the (female) student	dĕ-stuuDENtĕ	de studente
My youngest daughter is a student too.	mein-JONGstĕ-dochtĕr is-OOK-stuudentĕ.	Mijn jongste dochter is ook studente.

2. Hints on Pronunciation

Vowels. It is tricky for speakers of English to learn the Dutch vowel sounds, particularly because so many words sound like English words except for the vowel sounds. For this reason it is important to work hard on getting them right. Here are some exercises that will show you the difference between the 'short' vowels and the 'long' vowels of Dutch. The words 'short' and 'long' are put in quotation marks to remind you that the terms are only relative; they are all shorter than the long vowels of English.

PRACTICE 1

MAN, MAAN	'man, moon'
STAT, STAAT	'city, state'
RAS, RAAS	'race, roar'

PRACTICE 2

MET, MEET	'with, measure'
HET, HEET	'it (reading form only), hot'
HEL, HEEL	'hell, whole'

PRACTICE 3

VIS, VIES	'fish, dirty'
MIS, MIES	'amiss, (girl's name)'
LIGHĕn, LIEghĕn	'to lie, to tell a lie'

PRACTICE 4

ROT, ROOT	'rotten, red'
MOT, MOOT	'moth; slice of fish'
ROS, ROOS	'steed, rose'

PRACTICE 5

LUS, LEUS	'loop, slogan'
RUS, REUS	'Russian, giant'

Consonants. Before going back over the Basic Sentences again, note the following points that you should watch for carefully:

(a) Dutch r is a "rolled' or 'trilled' r-sound. Some Dutch speakers make it with the tip of the tongue and others make it in the back of the mouth. If you use an American English r-sound, you will be understood, but your speech will not sound very pleasing to Dutch ears. But *never leave off the r-sound*, as we do in the South and around Boston: wherever the Aid to Listening has an r, be sure to pronounce an r-sound, as much like the Dutch as you can.

(b) Dutch l is much like the English l in *well*. If you have studied German or French, be sure not to use the German or French 'light' l that you may have learned.

(c) When Dutch r or l comes before another consonant, there is often a little vowel glide between the r or l and the following consonant. In English, some speakers make a glide sound of this kind in words like elm, saying something like *ellum*; in Dutch this is a normal form of pronunciation, and you should imitate it when you hear it.

(d) Dutch *s* is like the English *s* in *see, miss*. The letter *s* in the Aids to Listening always means a real *s*-sound, and never the *z*-sound. The *z*-sound is always written *z* in the Aid to Listening.

(e) The Dutch *ng*-sound is like the English *ng*-sound in words like *sing, singer*, and not like the English sound in *finger*. If you come from New York City or nearby and the words *singer* and *finger* sound the same as you say them to yourself, then give particular attention to the Dutch *ng*-sound. It may be exactly like the sound you have in both words, in which case you will have no trouble. Or it may be different, in which case you will have to be especially careful.

Now go back, as usual, to **1**. Follow the same plan that you followed in Units 1 and 2, and be sure to check up carefully, before going on to Section B, to see whether you have done everything that you should.

B. Word Study

1. Word Study

Point 1. Meanings. Compare the following expressions in English and Dutch:

(a) dě-NAAM *van*-měn-ZUStěr 'the name *of* my sister' —that is, 'my sister's name'

(b) ik-KOM *van*-zein-HUIS 'I'm coming *from* his house.'

(c) waar-komt-uu-*van-DAAN?* 'Where are you coming *from?*'

In (a) the Dutch word *van* is like the English word *of*, but in (b) it is like the English word *from*. The English word *from*, on the other hand, is not always equivalent to the Dutch *van*, for in (c) the Dutch sentence has *van-DAAN*. In short, the words in different languages just don't match up together.

Point 2. He's a sailor. Note that in Dutch one says *hei-is-maTROOS* 'he is sailor', not 'he is *a* sailor'. In telling one's trade in Dutch, one does not say '*a* sailor' or the like, but just the name of the trade, 'sailor'.

Point 3. EENS. Compare these two:

kom-HIER!   'Come here!'

kom-ĕs-HIER! 'Come here, won't you please?'

The word EENS 'once', in the unstressed form ĕns or ĕs, is often used in requests and commands; it makes them less abrupt.

Point 4. VOOR. The Dutch say *ik-stuuDEER voor-DOKtĕr*, literally 'I study *for* doctor' to mean 'I'm studying to be a doctor'. The word *voor* is used in many ways, usually meaning something like 'for' or 'in front of'.

Point 5. Who. Compare these two sentences:

wie-IZ-dat? 'Who is that?'

ik-hep-ĕn-VRIENT *die*-nuu-in-rottĕrDAM-is. 'I have a friend *who* is in Rotterdam now.'

Who in asking a question is *WIE*; but *who* in starting a *clause* (a short sentence that is included in a longer sentence, as in the second example), is *DIE*. Once again, where English uses a single word Dutch uses two different words.

Point 6. The verb 'to come'. The verb KOOmĕn is irregular: form *2* is *KOM*, as in *ik-KOM* 'I come';

form *3* is *KOMT*, as in *uu-KOMT* 'you come'. That is, the stem is *koom-*, with a long *oo*, in form *1*, but *kom-*, with a short *o*, in forms *2* and *3*.

Point 7. Unstressed Forms of Words in Fast Speech. In the Word Study of Unit I it was pointed out that in rapid speech words which are not stressed frequently have shorter forms. Here are some more examples:

(a) *HEI, hei, ei, ie* 'he':
   niet-HEI, maar-ZEI *'not he, but she'*
   hei-GHAAT *'he goes, he's going'*
   GHAAT-ie? *'Is he going?'*

(b) *ZEI, zei, zĕ* 'she':
   niet-HEI, maar-ZEI *'not he, but she'*
   zei-GHAAT, zĕ-GHAAT *'she goes, she is going'*
   GHAAT-zĕ? *'Is she going?'*

(c) *WEI, wei, wĕ* 'we':
   niet-WEI, maar-ZEI *'not we, but they'*
   wĕ-GHAAN *'we are going'*

(d) *ZEI, zei, zĕ* 'they':
   niet-WEI, maar-ZEI *'not we, but they'*
   zĕ-GHAAN *'they're going'*

(e) *MEIN, mĕn* 'my':
   dat-is-niet-MEIN-ootoo *'that's not my auto'*
   dit-is-mĕn-ZOON *'this is my son'*

Point 8. Other Changes in Rapid Speech.
There are some other changes that are apt to take place when people are speaking rapidly, whatever words are involved. They are mainly changes in words that are run together rapidly—indicated in the Aids to Listening by hyphens between the words concerned.

(a) Final *n*. Any word that ends in *-ĕn* may in rapid speech drop the *n*. Thus you may hear *WEEtĕ* for *WEEtĕn* 'to know', *EEtĕ-en-DRINKĕ* for *EEtĕn-en--DRINKĕn* 'to eat and drink', *ĕ-WINKĕl* or *ĕ-BANK* for *ĕn-WINKĕl* 'a store', and *ĕn-BANK* 'a bank'; *mĕ-VRIENT* for *mĕn-VRIENT* 'my friend'.

Before a word beginning with a *p* or *b*, such a final *n* may not drop, but change into *m* instead, giving *ĕm--BANK* 'a bank', *ĕm-PEN* 'a pen'.

(b) Double consonants. When two like consonants come together within a word, or in two words that are run together in rapid speech, frequently only a single consonant is spoken. Thus *TIEN* 'ten' and *NACHtĕn* 'nights' when put together may sound either *tien--NACHtĕn* or *tie-NACHtĕn* 'ten nights'.

Point 9. Mutes. There is one more type of change in the form of words which is very important. Twelve of the Dutch consonants are particularly subject to change. These twelve are called *mutes*. Six are called *unvoiced* mutes and six are called *voiced*:

Mutes

unvoiced	p	t	k	f	s	ch
voiced	b	d	g	v	z	gh

The mutes go in pairs, unvoiced and voiced. That is, *p* interchanges with *b*; *t* with *d*; *ch* with *gh*; and so on. The *ng* sound (as in *ring*) does not count as a mute.

Final Mutes. At the end of a word that is not run together with the next word, *only unvoiced mutes* are used.

If a word contains an *unvoiced* mute, this sound will not change when it comes at the end of the word:

STOPPĕn : STOP! '*to stop* : *stop!*'
solDAAtĕn : dĕ-solDAAT '*soldiers* : *the soldier*'
DRINkĕn : ik-DRINK '*to drink* : *I drink*'
BLUFFĕn : BLUF-niet '*to boast* : *don't boast*'
MESSĕn : ĕt-MES '*knives* : *the knife*'
LACHĕn : ik-LACH '*to laugh* : *I laugh*'

(Remember that the double writing of consonant letters is only a reminder that the preceding vowel is short: the *s*-sound is the same in *MES* and *MESSĕn*.)

But if a word contains a *voiced* mute, and this sound

comes to the end of the word, it will be replaced by the corresponding unvoiced mute: *b* will be replaced by *p*, and so on:

HEBBĕn : ik-HEP *'to have : I have'*
VRIENdĕn : ĕn-VRIENT *'friends : a friend'*
LEEvĕn : ik-LEEF *'to live : I live'*
maTROOzĕn : ĕn-maTROOS *'sailors : a sailor'*
ZEGHĕn : ik-ZECH *'to say : I say'*

There are no examples for the sound *g*.

The voiced mute is often kept if the word is run together with a following word that begins with a vowel, though speakers differ greatly as to this habit:

ik-HEB-ĕt, ik-HEP-ĕt *'I have it'*
dĕ-maTROOZ-is-hier, dĕ-maTROOS-is-hier. *'The sailor is here.'*
dat-ZEGH-ik-niet, dat-ZECH-ik-niet. *'I don't say that.'*

Since your Guide may keep the voiced mutes or change them in these conditions, the Aid to Listening gives them as the voice on the records gives them. If your Guide does it one way where the Aid to Listening writes it the other way, imitate your Guide and ignore the Aid to Listening.

Clusters of Mutes. When two or three mutes come together within a word, they are either all voiced or all unvoiced. In rapid speech, when words are run together, many speakers make a group of mutes either all voiced or all unvoiced even when some are at the end of one word and others are at the beginning of the next word. The voice on the records does not do this, but your Guide may, particularly if he comes from the western part of the Netherlands.

If the last mute of the sequence is *b* or *d*, the whole sequence is voiced:

ĕd-BIER (d-b) *for* ĕt-BIER (t-b) *'the beer'*
ĕt-smaagd-BITTĕr (gd-b) *for* ĕt-smaakt-BITTĕr (kt-b) *'it tastes bitter'*
wat-IZ-dat? (z-d) *for* wat-IS-dat? (s-d) *'What is that?'*
ig-ben-HIER (g-b) *for* ik-ben-HIER (k-b) *'I'm here.'*

The *d* of the words *dĕ, die, dat, DEEzĕ, dit* is often changed to *t* instead:

ik-HEB-dat (b-d) *or* ik-HEP-tat (p-t) *for* ik-HEP--dat (p-d) *'I have that'*

hei-heev-dĕ-OOtoo (v-d) *or* hei-heef-tĕ-OOtoo (ft)-
for hei-heeft-dĕ-OOtoo (ft-d) '*He has the auto.*'

If the last mute of the sequence is not *b* or *d*, the
whole sequence is unvoiced:

ĕt-FLEES (t-f) *for* ĕt-VLEES (t-v) '*the meat*'
ik-SECH (k-s) *for* ik-ZECH (k-z) '*I say*'
ĕt-smaakt-SOET (kt-s) *for* ĕt-smaakt-ZOET (kt-z)
    '*it tastes sweet*'

There are many fluctuations and irregularities in the
use of voiced and unvoiced mutes:

ZES : SEStich : ZEZ UUR *or* ZES UUR '*six :
    sixty : six o'clock*'

Some words, especially *NIET* 'not', often lose final *t*
in rapid speech:

wat-BLIEFT-uu? *or* wa-BLIEFT-uu? '*What did
    you say?*'
ik-HEB-ĕt-niet, ik-HEB-ĕt-nie '*I haven't got it.*'

When this happens, a following mute is treated as if the
t were still there:

da-s-CHOET *for* dat-s·CHOET *for* dat-is-GHOET
    '*that's good*'
da-s-niet-CHOET *or* da-s-nie-CHOET *for* dat-s-
    -niet-GHOET '*that's not good*'
nie-FEEL *or* NIE-fĕl *or* niet-FEEL *for* niet-VEEL
    '*not much*'

These possible changes could not all be marked in
the Aid to Listening because the voice on the record
does not make many of them, and because your Guide
also may not.   But if he does, be sure to imitate what
he says.

2. Review of Basic Sentences

Review the Basic Sentences with the English covered; be sure you can recognize the meaning of every Dutch
phrase or sentence instantly.

C. What Would You Say?

1. What Would You Say?

1. *Mrs. Dekker wants to meet your friend, who is not yet in town. You say:*
   a. měn-VRIENT is-noch-niet-HIER.
   b. měn-vrienDIN is-noch-niet-ghěTROUT.
   c. měn-vrienDIN is-tiePISTě.

2. *Your car needs repairs. You go to a garage and say:*
   a. wilt-uu-měn-OOtoo-reepaareerěn?
   b. ik-sou-GHRAACH ěn-OOtoo-willě-hebběn.
   c. in-aMEEriekaa zein-veel-OGtoos.

3. *Someone asks you the time, but you haven't the exact time. You say:*
   a. ik-weet-NIET hoe-laat-dě-TREIN-ghaat.
   b. WEET-uu wanneer-dě-TREIN-ghaat?
   c. ik-weet-NIET-prěsies hoe-LAAT-ět-is.

4. *You want to invite a young lady to go to the movies. You say:*
   a. ik-ghaa-niet-GHRAACH naar-dě-biejěsKOOP.
   b. WILT-uu-met-mě naar-dě-biejěSKOOP-ghaan?
   c. ik-ghaa-NUU naar-dě-biejěSKOOP.

5. *A lady has fainted in the hotel, and you want to help by getting a doctor. You ask the clerk:*
   a. hept-uu-ghoet-BIER in-dit-hooTEL?
   b. hoe-LAAT běghint-dě-biejěSKOOP?
   c. is-ěr-ěn-DOKtěr in-ět-hooTEL?

6. *Someone asks about your father's calling. You say:*
   a. ik-wil-voor-DOKtěr-stuudeerěn.
   b. ik-ben-maTROOS op-ěn-ameerieKAANS SCHIP.
   c. měn-VAAděr is-TIMMěrman.

7. *You want to excuse your leaving, because you have to catch your train. You say:*
   a. ik-moet-naar-ět-staaSJON.
   b. ik-wou-GHRAACH wat-EEtěn.
   c. ik-wil-voor-DOKtěr-stuudeerěn.

8. *Mrs. Dekker asks how many brothers and sisters you have. You say:*
   a. dank-uu-WEL, ik-DRINK gheen-BIER.
   b. ik-heb-ěn-BROER en-ěn-ZUSTěr.
   c. měn-ZUStěr is-tiePIStě.

2. What Did You Say?

Go over **1** working as a group, under the Leader's direction, and check up on anything which is not clear.

D. LISTENING IN

First listen to all of the following conversations with your books closed, to see how well you can understand the Dutch without following it with your eyes at the same time. Then open your books and go through each one separately, repeating after the Guide, and checking on anything you don't understand. Then the Leader will assign parts and you can go through them with individual repetition.

1. *Mr. Smits, Mr. van Dam, and Mr. Hettema are discussing their work.*

Smits: ghoejĕn-AAvĕnt, mĕneer.   Goeden avond, mijnheer.
            hoe-GHAAT-ĕt-met-uu?   Hoe gaat het met u?
van Dam: HEEL GHOET, dank-uu-WEL.   Heel goed, dank u wel.
            en-met-UU?   En met u?
Smits: HEEL GHOET, dank-uu-WEL.   Heel goed, dank u wel.
            hier-is-mĕn-VRIENT, HENdrik van-DAM.   Hier is mijn vriend, Hendrik van Dam.
            mĕn-VRIENT, FRANS HETTĕmaa.   Mijn vriend, Frans Hettema.
Hettema: dach-mĕneer-van-DAM.   Dag, Mijnheer van Dam.
            werkt-uu-OOK in-dĕ-BANK, mĕneer-van-DAM?   Werkt u ook in de bank, Mijnheer van Dam?
van Dam: Nee-mĕneer.   Neen, mijnheer.
            ik-ben-barBIER.   Ik ben barbier.
            mĕ-BROER werkt-in-dĕ-BANK.   Mijn broer werkt in de bank.

Hettema:	ik-heb-ĕn-VRIENT die-OOK barBIER-is.	Ik heb een vriend die ook barbier is.
	ik-werk-in-dĕ-BANK-hier.	Ik werk in de bank hier.
	en-wat-doet-UU, mĕneer SMITS?	En wat doet u, Mijnheer Smits?
	uu-ben-TIMMĕrman?	u bent timmerman?
Smits:	NEE-mĕneer.	Neen, mijnheer.
	ik-ben-GHEEN TIMMĕrman.	Ik ben geen timmerman.
	ik-ben-meekaanieSJENG.	Ik ben mecanicien.
Hettema:	dan-is-ĕt-uu-VAAdĕr die-TIMMĕrman-is?	Dan is het uw vader die timmerman is?
	is-uu-VAAdĕr TIMMĕrman?	Is uw vader timmerman?
Smits:	NEE-mĕneer.	Neen, mijnheer.
	mĕn-VAAdĕr is-GHEEN TIMMĕrman.	Mijn vader is geen timmerman.
	hei-is-WERKman in-ĕn-faBRIEK.	Hij is werkman in een fabriek.
	maar-ik-heb-ĕn-BROER die-TIMMĕrman-is.	Maar ik heb een broer die timmerman is.

2. *Mr. de Jong and Mr. Kalvers join the discussion.*

de Jong:	WAAR WERKĕn PIET en-KLAAS MULdĕr?	Waar werken Piet en Klaas Mulder?
	WERKĕn-zĕ op-ĕ-SCHIP?	Werken zij op een schip?
Kalvers:	NEEN, zĕ-werkĕ-NIET op-ĕn-SCHIP.	Neen, zij werken niet op een schip.
	zĕ-zein-GHEEN maTROOzĕ.	Zij zijn geen matrozen.
	zĕ-zein-meekaanieSJENGS.	Zij zijn mecaniciens.
de Jong:	en-WAAR werkt-uu-ZOON?	En waar werkt uw zoon?
Kalvers:	mein-ZOON is-noch-JONG.	Mijn zoon is nog jong.
	hei-WERKT noch-NIET.	Hij werkt nog niet.

de Jong: is-uu-ZOON stuuDENT?   Is uw zoon student?
Kalvers: JAA, hei-is-stuuDENT.   Ja, hij is student.
        stuuDENtĕn WERkĕn-niet.   Studenten werken niet.
de Jong: wat-doet-uu-BROER?   Wat doet uw broer?
Kalvers: mein-BROER werkt-op-ĕt-LANT.   Mijn broer werkt op het land.
        hei-iz-BOER.   Hij is boer.

3. *Mr. Jansen and Mr. Mulder ask each other for information.*

Jansen: om-HOE-laat bĕghint-ĕ-biejĕSKOOP?   Om hoe laat begint de bioscoop?
Mulder: dĕ-biejĕsKOOP bĕghint-om-ACHT-uur.   De bioscoop begint om acht uur.
Jansen: ghaat-uu-OOK naa-dĕ-biejĕSKOOP, mĕneer-MULdĕr?   Gaat u ook naar de bioscoop, Mijnheer Mulder?

Mulder: NEE-mĕneer.   Neen, mijnheer.
        ik-ghaa-NIET naar-dĕ-biejĕSKOOP.   Ik ga niet naar de bioscoop.
        ik-MOET naar-ĕt-staaSJON.   Ik moet naar het station.
Jansen: wanneer-ghaat-uu-TREIN?   Wanneer gaat uw trein?
Mulder: mein-TREIN ghaat-om-NEEghĕn-UUR.   Mijn trein gaat om negen uur.
        en-HOE-laat is-ĕt-NUU?   En hoe laat is het nu?
Jansen: ĕt-is-SEEvĕn UUR.   Het is zeven uur.
Mulder: ZEEvĕn UUR?   Zeven uur?
        ĕt-is-LAAT.   Het is laat.
        ik-MOET-noch naar-mein-hooTEL, en-DAN-moet-ik--naar-ĕt-staasSJON.   Ik moet nog naar mijn hotel, en dan moet ik naar het station.

E. Conversation

1. Review of Basic Sentences

Turn back to the Basic Sentences and review them with the Dutch covered. Work alone or in pairs. Be sure that you can rattle off the Dutch the instant you hear the English Equivalent.

2. Vocabulary Check-up

Review the vocabulary of this Unit in the usual manner. This time, however, cover also the points taken up in the Word Study, Section B. Thus a question might be 'What is queer about the verb *to come* in Dutch?' The answer would be simply the statement that it is irregular in the simplest forms, with examples.

Remember, whenever asking questions like this, that it is only the *how* of a language that counts; no one knows *why*. The only real answer to a question like '*Why* do the Dutch say such-and-such?' is simply that that is the way they do it.

3. Carrying on Conversation

Here are some models for your free conversation for this Unit. Remember once again that the models are only intended to be suggestive. The conversations of Section D of this Unit and of the first two can be used as models too.

If you have time for work outside of the class meeting, you can get together in pairs and rehearse a conversation, which you can then act out for the rest of the group when the class meets.

Here are some more Dutch names for you to use: VALK-hof, STRUIK, van-VEEN, GHEEvĕrs, KUI--tĕrs, van-BEMMĕlĕn. Also some first names; for men: WILLĕm, DIRK, KLAAS; for women: GHREET, KLAARtjĕ.

Conversation 1. A addresses B, whose name he thinks he knows, though B has not met A.
A: asks B if his name is such-and-such.
B: says yes, and asks A his name.

A: identifies himself, tells where he is from, and says he has a furniture factory there.

B: asks if a certain friend of his works in A's factory.

A: says maybe, he doesn't know for sure. Someone else with the same last name works in a clothing store in A's town.

B: says that that's the first person's brother, and that his youngest sister is a typist in the American bank in Amsterdam.

A: asks if the girl is married.

B: says yes, and gives her married name.

Conversation 2.   Two sailors, A and B, can't find their ship.

A: asks B where their ship is.

B: says he doesn't know. He says that if they have another beer he'll know it, maybe. He asks where they should go.

A: suggests that they go visit C.

B: asks where D (another sailor) is now.

A: says he was probably in his garage fixing his car.

B: asks what after the car is fixed.

A: suggests that then they go with D to a movie, and then have some beer.

B: says he has to be at the ship by such and such an hour.

A: says OK, they'll go there too.

Conversation 3.   A calls his daughter, B:

A: says come here, B, we're going to the barber.

B: says what?

A: repeats.

B: says but she had wanted to go to the movies with her mother.

A: asks when the movie starts.

B: says she doesn't know, but probably at such and such an hour.

A: says OK. He tells B to go to the movie first, then with him to the barber. Right now he is going to the garage to see the mechanic who is fixing their car.

FINDER LIST

dĕ: ameerieKAAN (aameerieKAAN)
'the (male) American'
ameerieKAANS (aameerieKAANS) 'American'

dĕ- BANK 'the bank'
dĕ- barBIER 'the barber'
bĕGHREIpĕn 'to understand'

dĕ- BOER 'the farmer'
    dĕ-boerdĕREI 'the farm'

DIE 'who'
    ik-hep-ĕn-BROER die-OOK-stuudent-is.   'I have
      a brother who is also a student.'
DOEN 'to do'
dĕ- DOKtĕr 'the doctor'

    EENS (unstressed ĕns, ĕs) 'once, just'
      kom-ĕs-HIER 'come here, won't you please?'

dĕ- gaaRAAzjĕ (ghaaRAAzjĕ) 'the garage'

    JONG 'young'
    dĕ-JONGstĕ 'the youngest'

    KLEErĕn 'clothes'
    dĕ-KLEErĕn-winkĕl 'the clothing store'
    KOOmĕn 'to come'
    ik-KOM 'I come'
    uu-KOMT 'you come'

ĕt- LANT 'the land, the country'

    MAAkĕn 'to make'
dĕ- maTROOS 'the sailor'
    maTROOzĕn 'sailors'
dĕ- meekaanieSJENG 'the mechanic'

ĕt- MEUbĕl 'the piece of furniture'
    MEUbĕls 'pieces of furniture, furniture'
    dĕ-MEUbĕl-fabriek 'the furniture factory'

OP 'on'
    op-ĕn-SCHIP 'on a ship'
dĕ- OOtoo (OUtoo) 'the automobile'

    reepaaREErĕn (rĕpaaREErĕn) 'to repair'

ĕt- SCHIP 'the ship'
    stuuDEErĕn 'to study'
    dĕ-stuuDENT 'the (male) student'
    dĕ-stuuDENtĕ 'the (female) student'

dĕ- tiePIStĕ 'the (female) typist'
dĕ- TIMMĕrman 'the carpenter'

    UIT 'out, from'
    ik-kom-uit-aMEEriekaa 'I come from America'

    VAN 'from'
    van-DAAN 'from a place'

    VOOR 'before, in front of, for'
    hei-stuuDEERT voor-DOKtĕr 'he is studying to
      be a doctor'

    WERkĕn 'to work'
    dĕ-WERKman 'the workman'
dĕ- WINkĕl 'the store'

PART ONE

 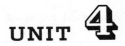

WHERE ARE YOU FROM?

A. BASIC SENTENCES

1. Basic Sentences

A group of American sailors, including John Carver, meet a Mr. Olpers, who asks them about themselves.

─ENGLISH EQUIVALENTS─	─AIDS TO LISTENING─	─CONVENTIONAL SPELLING─
	Mr. Olpers	
all (of us, of you, of them)	allĕMAAL	allemaal
Good evening, gentlemen.	ghoedĕn-AAvĕnt, HEErĕn.	Goeden avond, heeren.
I guess you're all American sailors?	bent-uu-ALLĕmaal ameerie--KAANsĕ maTROOzĕ?	Bent u allemaal Amerikaansche matrozen?
	Mr. Carver	
Yes, sir.	JAA-mĕneer.	Ja, mijnheer.
We're all of us American sailors.	wĕ-zein-ALLĕmaal ameerieKAANsĕ maTROOzĕ.	Wij zijn allemaal Amerikaansche matrozen.

And where are you from?	**Mr. Olpers** en-WAAR bent-UU van-DAAN?	En waar bent u vandaan?

Mr. Carver

naturally *the United States* *Where from? From America, of course.* *We come from the United States.*	naaTUURlik dĕ-vĕREEnighdĕ STAAtĕn waar-van-DAAN? van--aMEEriekaa, naaTUURlik. wĕ-KOOmĕn van-dĕ-vĕREEnighdĕ STAAtĕn.	natuurlijk de Vereenigde Staten Waar vandaan? Van Amerika, natuurlijk. Wij komen van de Vereenigde Staten.

Mr. Olpers

which *the city* *Yes, but from which city?*	WELK dĕ-STAT JAA, maar-van-WELkĕ-stat?	welk de stad Ja, maar van welke stad?

Mr. Carver

oh *all* *cities* *the part* *Oh, we come from all cities and from all parts of the country.* *new*	OO ALLĕ STEEdĕn ĕt-DEEL OO, wĕ-KOOmĕn van-allĕ--STEEdĕn en-van-allĕ--DEElĕn van-ĕt-LANT. NIEW	oh alle steden het deel O, wij komen van alle steden en van alle deelen van het land. nieuw

I come from Chicago, and my friend here comes from New York.	IK-kom van-sjiKAAghoo, en-měn--VRIENT-hier komt-van-niew--JORK.	Ik kom van Chicago, en mijn vriend hier komt van Nieuw-York.

Mr. Olpers

the cousin or *the nephew*	dě-NEEF	de neef
to live in a place	WOOněn	wonen
I have a cousin who lives in Chicago.	ik-hep-ěn-NEEF die-in-sjiKAA-.ghoo-woont.	Ik heb een neef die in Chicago woont.
already	AL	al
the year	hět-JAAR	het jaar
He's been in America twelve years now.	hei-is-al-TWAALF JAAR in--aMEEriekaa.	Hij is al twaalf jaar in Amerika.
the American (woman)	dě-ameerieKAANsě	de Amerikaansche
He's married to an American girl.	hei-is-met-ěn-ameerieKAANsě--ghětrout.	Hij is met een Amerikaansche getrouwd.

Mr. Carver

What's his name?	hoe-HEET-ie?	Hoe heet hij?

Mr. Olpers

His name is Walter Olpers.	hei-HEET WOUtěr OLpěrs.	Hij heet Wouter Olpers.

| And what does your cousin do in Chicago? | en-wa-DOET uu-NEEF in-sjiKAA-ghoo? | En wat doet uw neef in Chicago? |

He's a mechanic.	hei-is-meekaanieSJENG.	Hij is mecanicien.
to fly	VLIEghĕn	vliegen
the machine	dĕ-maSJIEnĕ	de machine
He works in a factory where they make airplanes.	hei-WERKT in-ĕn-faBRIEK waar-zĕ-VLIECH-masjienĕs--maakĕn.	Hij werkt in een fabriek waar zij vliegmachines maken.
to know a person or place	KENNĕn	kennen
him	HEM	hem
You don't know him, do you?	uu-KENT-ĕm-niet, WEL?	U kent hem niet, wel?

No, I don't know him.	NEE-mĕneer, ik-KEN-ĕm-niet.	Neen, mijnheer, ik ken hem niet.
of course you know	IMMĕrs	immers
large	GHROOT	groot
Of course you know Chicago is a big city.	sjiKAAghoo is-IMMĕrs ĕn-GHROOtĕ STAT.	Chicago is immers een groote stad.

	Mr. Olpers	
the (female) cousin or the niece	dĕ-NICHT	de nicht
And then too, I have a girl cousin who is married to an American.	en-dan-heb-ik-OOK ĕn-NICHT, die-met-ĕn-ameerieKAAN--ghĕtrout-is.	En dan heb ik ook een nicht, die met een Amerikaan getrouwd is.
small	KLEIN	klein
the state	dĕ-STAAT	de staat
She lives in a small town in the state of Michigan.	zĕ-WOONT in-ĕn-kleinĕ-STAT in-dĕ-STAAT MISJighĕn.	Zij woont in een kleine stad in de staat Michigan.

Mr. Carver

her	HAAR	haar
What's her name?	wat-is-ĕr-NAAM?	Wat is haar naam?

Mr. Olpers

Her husband's name is Al Jones.	haar-MAN heet-EL DZJOONS.	Haar man heet Al Jones.
He's a carpenter.	hei-is-TIMMĕrman.	Hij is timmerman.
He works in a furniture factory.	hei-WERKT in-ĕn-MEUbĕl--fabriek.	Hij werkt in een meubelfabriek.

Mr. Carver

Yes, I know they make lots of good furniture in Michigan.	JAA, ik-WEET dat-zĕ-in--MISJighĕn VEEL ghoedĕ--MEUbĕls-maakĕn.	Ja, ik weet dat zij in Michigan veel goede meubels maken.
There are lots of furniture factories there.	DAAR-zein veel-MEUbĕl--fabriekĕn.	Daar zijn veel meubelfabrieken.

Do you know my cousin who is married to Mr. Jones?	KENT-uu mĕn-NICHT die-met--mĕneer-DZJOONS-ghĕtrout-is?	Kent u mijn nicht die met Mijnheer Jones getrouwd is?

No, I don't know her.	NEE-mĕneer, ik-ken-ĕr-NIET.	Neen, mijnheer, ik ken haar niet.
Where are you from, Mr. Olpers?	WAAR bent-UŲ-van-daan, mĕneer-OLpĕrs?	Waar bent u vandaan, Mijnheer Olpers?

the Dutchman	dĕ-HOLLandĕr	de Hollander
I'm a Dutchman.	ik-ben-ĕn-HOLLandĕr.	Ik ben een Hollander.
I'm from Rotterdam, but I've been living here in the Hague four years now.	ik-kom-van-rottĕrDAM, maar-ik--woon-al VIER-jaar in-dĕn--HAACH.	Ik kom van Rotterdam, maar ik woon al vier jaar in den Haag.

always	AL-teit	altijd
you have lived	uu-hept-ghĕWOONT	u hebt gewoond
Then [I guess] you've always lived in Holland.	dan-hept-uu-ALteit in-HOLLant--ghĕwoont.	Dan hebt u altijd in Holland gewoond.
ever	OOJT	ooit
you have been	uu-bent-ghĕWEEST	u bent geweest

Have you ever been in America?	bent-uu-OOJT in-aMEEriekaa--ghĕweest?	Bent u ooit in Amerika geweest?

Mr. Olpers

never	NOOJT	nooit
No, I've never been in America.	NEE, ik-ben-NOOJT in--aMEEriekaa-ghĕweest.	Neen, ik ben nooit in Amerika geweest.
England	ENGĕlant	Engeland
a little	ĕn-BEEtjĕ	een beetje
English	ENGĕls	Engelsch
But I've been in England, and I speak a little English.	maar-ik-ben-in-ENGĕlant--ghĕweest; ik-SPREEK ĕn--beetjĕ-ENGĕls.	Maar ik ben in Engeland geweest; ik spreek een beetje Engelsch.

Mr. Carver

why	waaROM	waarom
us	ONS	ons
Then why don't you speak English with us?	WAArom SPREEKT-uu-dan niet-ENGĕls-met-ons?	Waarom spreekt u dan niet Engelsch met ons?

Mr. Olpers

Hollandish or *Dutch*	HOLLants	Hollandsch
Why, I see you speak Dutch quite well.	ik-ZIE-immĕrs dat-uu-HEEL--ghoet HOLLants-spreekt, mĕNEER.	Ik zie immers dat u heel goed Hollandsch spreekt, mijnheer.

	Mr. Carver	
Oh, I only speak it a little.	OO, ik-SPREEK-ĕt aLEEN- -maar ĕn-BEEtjĕ.	O, ik spreek het alleen maar een beetje.

	Mr. Olpers	
few or *little*	WEInich	weinig
Lots of Dutch people speak English, but not many Americans speak Dutch.	VEEL HOLLandĕrs spreekĕn- -ENGĕls, maar-WEInich ameerieKAAnĕn spreekĕn- -HOLLants.	Veel Hollanders spreken Engelsch, maar weinig Amerikanen spreken Hollandsch.

2. Hints on Pronunciation

The Dutch vowel-sounds need constant practice.   Try the most difficult of them again now.

Go back to Cassette 1A, page 13 for these 5 PRACTICES.

PRACTICE 1

DEUR	*'door'*	NEUS	*'nose'*
MEUbĕl	*'piece of furniture'*	KEUkĕn	*'kitchen'*
KLEUR	*'color'*		

PRACTICE 2

DUUR	*'dear'*	stuuDENT	*'student'*
LUUsiefĕr	*'match'*	naaTUURlik	*'naturally'*

PRACTICE 3

TREIN	*'train'*	ZEI	*'she'*
MEI	*'me'*	ZEIN	*'are'*
VEIF	*'five'*		

PRACTICE 4

NOU	*'now'*	ik-ZOU	*'I should'*
VROU	*'woman, wife'*	ik-WOU	*'I would'*

PRACTICE 5

HUIS	*'house'*	TUIN	*'garden'*
MUIS	*'mouse'*	TUICH	*'harness'*
UIT	*'out'*		

B. WORD STUDY

1. Word Study

Point 1. Pronunciation of Words from Other Languages. Dutch words that are taken into the language from French or English, or other languages, sometimes are pronounced in different ways by different speakers of the language. Here are some examples:

(a) 'cigarette', borrowed from French, and pronounced either *sieghĕRET* or *sieghaaRET*.

(b) 'match', also borrowed from French, pronounced usually *LUUsiefĕr*, but sometimes *LUUsiefer*.

(c) 'restaurant', from French; pronounced *rĕsto-*

-RANG or *restoRANG* usually, but people who see the word in its written form may say *rĕstoRANT* or *resto--RANT*.

(d) 'station', from French, may similarly end in either *-ON* or *-ONG*.

(e) 'America', from the English word, is pronounced either *aMEEriekaa* or *aaMEEriekaa*. Similarly the derived word 'American' is either *ameerieKAAN* or *aameerieKAAN*.

(f) 'garage', from French, is pronounced *gaaRAAzjĕ* or *ghaaRAAzjĕ*. The *g*-sound of other languages is usually changed to *gh* in Dutch, though some speakers keep it unchanged.

(g) 'repair', from French, is *rĕpaaREErĕn* or *reepaa--REErĕn*.

These variations don't make much trouble, because the words involved are mainly words that we have in English too. You should use whatever pronunciation your Guide gives you.

Point 2. Meanings. One of the things one has to master in any foreign language is the strange *coverage* of the words. Many Dutch words seem to do the work of several English words, but if we turn this around, we find that many English words are matched by more than

one Dutch word. We have just met two instances of this sort:

(a) haar-VAAdĕr *LEEFT*-noch. 'Her father is still *living*.'
haar-VAAdĕr *woont*-in-dĕn-HAACH. 'Her father *lives* in The Hague.'

Where we say 'to live', the Dutch say *LEEvĕn* in the meaning of 'to be alive', but *WOOnĕn* in the sense of 'to live in a place, reside, dwell'.

(b) uu-*WEET*-immĕrs dat-amstĕrDAM in-HOLL--ant-is. 'You *know*, of course, that Amsterdam is in Holland.'
ik-*WEET*-niet waar-ie-WOONT. 'I don't *know* where he lives.'
WEET-uu of-zĕ-KOMT? 'Do you *know* whether she is coming?'
ik-*KEN* amstĕrDAM. 'I *know* Amsterdam.'
kent-uu-mĕn-NEEF? 'Do you *know* my cousin?'
ik-*KEN* gheen-ENGĕls. 'I don't *know* any English.'

Where we say 'to know', the Dutch say *WEEtĕn* in the meaning 'to know a fact', but *KENNĕn* in the sense of 'to be acquainted with a person, a thing, a place'.

No one could remember all the statements of this

sort that would have to be made. The way to master a foreign language is to learn how to say things, lots of things, without worrying about the differences in the coverage of words.

Point 3. Has lived, has been. In the same way, we were not quite accurate when we said that *HEBBĕn* means 'to have' and *ZEIN* means 'to be'. The coverage of the Dutch words is different. Just now we have met with the following difference:

> hei-*heeft*-NOOJT in-sjiKAAghoo-ghĕwoont. 'He *has* never lived in Chicago.'
> hei-*is*-NOOJT in-sjiKAAghoo-ghĕweest. 'He *has* never been in Chicago.'

Point 4. That, This, The. The Dutch word for 'that' is *DIE* with some nouns and *DAT* for others:

> die-VORK   'that fork'
> dat-MES   'that knife'

We shall need names for these two kinds of nouns. We shall call them *die*-nouns and *dat*-nouns.

> die-VORkĕn   'those forks'
> die-MESSĕn   'those knives'

In the *plural*, all nouns take *DIE*.

The word for 'this' with *die*-nouns is *DEEzĕ*; with *dat*-nouns 'this' is *DIT*; with nouns in the plural, 'these' is *DEEzĕ* for all nouns:

> deezĕ-VORK   'this fork'
> dit-MES   'this knife'
> deezĕ-VORkĕn   'these forks'
> deezĕ-MESSĕn   'these knives'

The words for 'the' are the unstressed forms of *DIE* and *DAT*, as in the following examples:

> dĕ-VORK   'the fork'
> ĕt-MES   'the knife'
> dĕ-VORkĕn   'the forks'
> dĕ-MESSĕn   'the knives'

Most words that mean persons are *die*-nouns, but there are a few exceptions: *ĕt-KINT* 'the child' is one.

Point 5. Other Uses of DIE and DAT.

(a) ik-hep-ĕn-BROER   *die*-in-dĕn-HAACH-woont.
     'I have a brother *who* lives in The Hague.'
     dit-hooTEL *dat*-uu-hier-ZIET is-heel-GHOET.
     'This hotel *that* you see here is quite good.'

In sentences like the two above *DIE* and *DAT* are used for 'who, which, that'.

(b) *DAT* iz-měn-ZOON. '*That* is my son.'
DAT zein-měn-ZOONS. '*Those* are my sons.'
DIT iz-ons-KINT. '*This* is our child.'
DIT zein-onzě-KINděrěn. '*These* are our children.'

In sentences like these four, *DAT* is used where English would use either *that* or *those*, and *DIT* is used where English would use either *this* or *these*.

(c) hei-ZECHT *dat*-zěn-ZUStěr in-sjiKAAghoo-woont. 'He says *that* his sister lives in Chicago.

ik-WEET *dat*-sjiKAAghoo ěn-ghrootě-STAT-is. 'I know *that* Chicago is a big city.'

In sentences like these two *DAT* is used like the English *that*. (Notice also the order of words here—verb last.)

Point 6.   Plural of Nouns.

(a) dě-OOtoo : OOtoos   '*the auto   :   autos*'
dě-gaaRAAzjě : gaaRAAzjěs   '*the garage   :   garages*'
dě-LUUsiefěr : LUUsiefěrs   '*the match   :   matches*'
dě-WINkěl : WINkěls   '*the store   :   stores*'

Nouns ending in a vowel, or in the syllables *-ěr, -ěl*, take *-s* in the plural.   Note that this is a real *s*-sound (never a *z*-sound).

(b) dě-faBRIEK : faBRIEkěn   '*the factory   :   factories*'
dě-sieghěRET : sieghěRETTěn '*the cigarette   :   cigarettes*'

Nouns ending in a consonant add *-ěn*.   The final *n* of such words can, of course, drop off, like the final *n* of any *-ěn* ending.   Notice that the ending is really just *-ěn*.   When the consonant before it is written double, this is only to remind you that the preceding vowel stays short.

(c) dě-maTROOS : maTROOzěn   '*the sailor   :   sailors*'
ět-MES : MESSěn   '*the knife   :   knives*'

A voiced mute (*b*, *d*, *v*, *z*, *gh*) will show up before the ending -*ĕn*. When there is no ending, it is replaced by an unvoiced mute. An unvoiced mute, on the other hand, stays put.

(d) dĕ-VROU : VROUwĕn   *'the woman : women'*
    dĕ-boerdĕREI : boerdĕREIjĕn *'the farm : farms'*
    dĕ-UI : UIjĕn   *'the onion : onions'*

Nouns ending in the diphthong *ou* add *w* before the -*ĕn* ending, and nouns ending in the diphthongs *ei* or *ui* add *j*.
   The rules given above cover most nouns. But there are quite a few nouns that make the plural in other ways. Whenever the plural form of a noun is irregular, it will be listed specially in the Finder List; if it forms the plural according to the above rules, only the singular form will be listed in the Finder List.

Some nouns use either -*s* or -*ĕn*, and some use one when you would expect the other:

    dĕ-BROER : BROERS   *'the brother : brothers'*
    dĕ-ZOON : ·ZOONS   *'the son : sons'*
    dĕ-APPĕl : APPĕls, APPĕlĕn   *'the apple : apples'*
    dĕ-AARdappĕl : AARdappĕls, AARdappĕlĕn   *'the potato : potatoes'*
Some make other changes:
    dĕ-DACH : DAAghĕn   *'the day : days'*
    ĕt-SCHIP : SCHEEpĕn   *'the ship : ships'*
    dĕ-STAT : STEEdĕn   *'the city : cities'*
Some take longer endings:
    ĕt-KINT : KINdĕrĕn   *'the child : children'*
    ĕt-EI : EIjĕrĕn   *'the egg : eggs'*

Point 7. Nouns after Numbers.

(a) dĕ-GHULdĕn *'the guilder'* : GHULdĕns *'one-guilder coins'* : VEIF GHULdĕn *'five guilders'*
ĕt-JAAR *'the year'* : JAArĕn *'years'* : TIEN JAAR *'ten years'*

(b) dĕ-DACH *'the day'* : VEIV DAAghĕn *'five days'*
dĕ-WEEK *'the week'* : ZES WEEkĕn *'six weeks'*

After numbers, some nouns that are very often counted (units of measure) take no plural ending, as in (a). But other such words do take a plural ending, as in (b).

2. Review of Basic Sentences

Review the Basic Sentences with the English covered.

C. WHAT WOULD YOU SAY?

1. What Would You Say?

1. *You want to explain that New York City is in New York State. You say:*
   a. niew-JORK is-EEN STAAT van-dĕ-vĕREE-nighdĕ-staatĕn.
   b. dĕ-STAT-niew-jork is-in-dĕ-STAAT-niew-jork.
   c. niew-JORK is-ĕn-ghrootĕ-STAT in-aMEErie-kaa.

2. *You want to say that your friend's father lives in New York. You say:*
   a. dĕ-VAAdĕr van-mĕn-VRIENT woont-in-niew-JORK.

b. dĕ-VAAdĕr van-mĕn-VRIENT heeft-NOOJT in-niew-JORK-ghĕwoont.

c. dĕ-VAAdĕr van-mĕn-VRIENT is-ĕs-in-niew-JORK-ghĕweest.

3. *A Dutchman wants to say that his cousin is married to an American. He says:*
   a. ik-heb-ĕn-NICHT die-in-aMEEriekaa-woont.
   b. mĕn-NICHT is-ghĕTROUT met-ĕn-ameerie-KAAN.
   c. mĕn-NICHT is-al-TIEN-jaar ghĕTROUT.

4. *You and Mr. Dekker both know that your friend Smits*

drinks a lot, and the matter has come up in your conversation. You say:

   a. hei-DRINKT-mischien gheen-BIER.

   b. hei-DRINKT-imměrs veel-BIER.

   c. hei-zou-GHRAACH wat-BIER-willěn-drinkěn.

5. *You want to call Mr. Dekker's attention to an airplane that is overhead. You say:*

   a. WILT-uu-ěs met-ons-FLIEghěn?

   b. ZEIN-ěr-hier veel-VLIECH-masjieněs?

   c. ZIET-uu dě-VLIECH-masjieně?

6. *You want to explain that you understand only a little Dutch. You say:*

   a. ik-věrSTAA maar-ěn-KLEIN-beetjě HOLLants.

   b. ik-věrSTAA HEEL-ghoet HOLLants.

   c. ik-věrSTAA GHEEN HOLLants.

7. *You want to way that your brother wants to study medicine. You say:*

   a. měn-BROER wou-ghraach-op-ět-LANT--werkěn.

   b. měn-BROER wil-in-ěn-faBRIEK-werkěn.

   c. měn-BROER wil-voor-DOKtěr-stuudeerěn.

8. Here is a list of the nouns which you have learned so far. See if you know which ones are *die*-nouns and which ones are *dat*-nouns. When you are not sure, check in the Finder List of this Unit or of the three preceding units. When the group meets, the Leader will have each in turn read off one of the following words with *DIE* or *DAT* before it. You must also know what the plural form of each one is.

VROU	NACHT
HEER	UUR
ZOON	MELK
ZUStěr	VLEES
stuuDENT	staaSJON
MAN	gaaRAAzje (ghaaRAAzjě)
BOER	wee-SEE
LANT	TREIN
AAvěnt	GHULděn
JAAR	STAT
BROOT	JUFrou
BIER	MOEděr
LUUsiefěr	BROER
hooTEL	vrienDIN
WINkěl	meekaanieSJENG
ŎOtoo (OUtoo)	HOLLanděr
maSJIEně	MORghěn
STAAT	WAAtěr
KINT	APPěl
VAAděr	KOFFie

DOCHtĕr	sieghĕRET	maTROOS	biejĕSKOOP
VRIENT	rĕstoRANG	ameerieKAAN	SCHIP
stuuDENtĕ	faBRIEK	DACH	DEEL

2. What Did You Say?

D. LISTENING IN

1. *An American, Mr. Cooper, and a Hollander, Mr. Olpers, tell each other about themselves.*

Olpers: van-welkĕ-STAT BENT-uu, mĕneer-KOEpĕr?
Van welke stad bent u, Mihnjeer Cooper?

Cooper: IK-ben van-sjiKAAghoo.
Ik ben van Chicago.

en-UU, mĕneer-OLpĕrs?
En u, Mijnheer Olpers?

Olpers: IK-ben ĕn-HOLLandĕr.
Ik ben een Hollander.

IK-woon hier-in-dĕn-HAACH.
Ik woon hier in den Haag.

ik-hep-ĕn-NEEF in-sjiKAAghoo.
Ik heb een neef in Chicago.

Cooper: wat-DOET-uu-neef in-sjiKAAghoo?
Wat doet uw neef in Chicago?

Olpers: mĕn-NEEF WERKT in-ĕn-VLIECH-masjienĕ-fabriek.
Mijn neef werkt in een vliegmachinefabriek.

HEI is-meekaanieSJENG.
Hij is mecanicien.

Cooper: WAAR-iz die-faBRIEK?
Waar is die fabriek?

Olpers: in-sjiKAAghoo, naaTUURlik.
In Chicago, natuurlijk.

waar-is-uu-BROER-nuu, mĕneer-KOEpĕr?
Waar is uw broer nu, Mijnheer Cooper?

Cooper: mein-BROER is-maTROOS.
Mijn broer is matroos.

hei-WERKT op-ĕn-SCHIP, maar-hei-WOONT in-niew-
-JORK.
Hij werkt op een schip, maar hij woont in
Nieuw-York.

Olpers: en-JUFrou KOEpĕr, uu-ZUStĕr, werkt-die-OOK?	En Juffrouw Cooper, uw zuster, werkt die ook?
Cooper: JAA, zĕ-WERKT in-ĕn-MEUbĕl-fabriek. zei-is-tiePIStĕ.	Ja, zij werkt in een meubelfabriek. Zij is typiste.
Olpers: dat-is-GHOET. ik-ZIE dat-ALLĕ ameerieKAAnĕn WERkĕn.	Dat is goed. Ik zie dat alle Amerikanen werken.
Cooper: JAA, ĕr-zein-maar-WEInich ameerieKAAnĕn die- -NIET-werkĕn.	Ja, er zijn maar weinig Amerikanen die niet werken.

2. *Mr. van Dam and Mr. Bell discuss their friends Mr. Olpers and Mr. Carver.*

van Dam: van-welk-DEEL van-dĕ-vereenighdĕ-STAAtĕn is- -mĕneer-KAARvĕr?	Van welk deel van de Vereenigde Staten is Mijnheer Carver?
Bell: hei-komt-van-sjiKAAghoo.	Hij komt van Chicago.
van Dam: WAT, NIET van-niew-JORK?	Wat, niet van Nieuw-York?
Bell: NEE-mĕneer. mĕneer-KAARvĕr is-NIET van-niew-JORK. mĕneer-KAARvĕr komt-van-sjiKAAghoo. van-welk-DEEL van-HOLLant is-mĕneer-OLpĕrs?	Neen, mijnheer. Mijnheer Carver is niet van Nieuw-York. Mijnheer Carver komt van Chicago. Van welk deel van Holland is Mijnheer Olpers?
van Dam: mĕneer-OLpĕrs komt-van-rottĕrDAM. maar-NUU woont-hei-HIER in-dĕn-HAACH. bent-uu-ghĕTROUT, mĕNEER?	Mijnheer Olpers komt van Rotterdam. Maar nu woont hij hier in den Haag. Bent u getrouwd, mijnheer?

Bell:	JAA-měneer.	Ja, mijnheer.
	měn-VROU en-měn-DOCHtěr zein-naaTUURlik in-aMEEriekaa.	Mijn vrouw en mijn docter zijn natuurlijk in Amerika.
	zě-ZEIN in-niew-JORK.	Zij zijn in Nieuw-York.
van Dam:	in-dě-STAAT niew-JORK?	In de staat Nieuw-York?
Bell:	JAA, in-dě-STAAT niew-JORK, en-in-dě-STAT niew-JORK.	Ja, in de staat Nieuw-York en in de stad Nieuw-York.
	dě-STAT niew-JORK is-imměrs-in-dě-STAAT niew--JORK.	De stad Nieuw-York is immers in de staat Nieuw-York.

3. *Mr. Cooper tries to get a date.*

Cooper:	wilt-uu-met-MEI naar-dě-biejěSKOOP-ghaan, juFROU?	Wilt u met mij naar de bioscoop gaan, juffrouw?
Annie:	NEE, dank-uu-WEL-měneer.	Neen, dank u wel, mijnheer.
	ik-wil-NIET met-uu-naar-dě-biejěSKOOP-ghaan.	Ik wil niet met u naar de bioscoop gaan.
Cooper:	WAArom wilt-uu-NIET met-mě-naar-dě-biejěSKOOP--ghaan?	Waarom wilt u niet met mij naar de bioscoop gaan?
Annie:	ik-KEN-uu-imměrs-niet, měNEER.	Ik ken u immers niet, mijnheer.
Cooper:	ik-heet-KAArěl KOEpěr.	Ik heet Karel Cooper.
	ik-ben-ěn-ameerieKAANsě maTROOS.	Ik ben een Amerikaansche matroos.
	mein-SCHIP is-nuu-in-rottěrDAM.	Mijn schip is nu in Rotterdam.
	ik-KOM van-sjiKAAghoo.	Ik kom van Chicago.
Annie:	sjiKAAghoo?	Chicago?
	waar-iz-DAT-nuu?	Waar is dat nu?

Cooper: sjiKAAghoo is-ĕn-GHROOtĕ-stat in-aMEEriekaa, in--dĕ-vĕreenighdĕ-STAAtĕn. nuu-KENT-uu-mei-wel, juFROU. wilt-uu-NUU met-mei-naar-dĕ-biejĕSKOOP-ghaan?	Chicago is een groote stad in Amerika, in de Vereenigde Staten. Nu kent u mij wel, juffrouw. Wilt u nu met mij naar de bioscoop gaan?

E. CONVERSATION

1. Review of Basic Sentences

Cover the Dutch.

2. Vocabulary Check-up

3. Carrying on Conversation

Some more Dutch names: van-DUIN, BRAAM, ·KOOL, van-dĕr-PLAS, FRUIN, dĕ-HAAS.

Conversation 1. A and B meet in a small town named Laren (LAArĕn), but A does not know the town's name.

A: asks B where they are.

B: tells him they are in a small town named Laren.

A: asks if B comes from this part of the country.

B: says yes, he has been (or lived) here now for five years.

A: asks B if he knows Mr. so-and-so who comes from Laren.

B: says of course, the man is his cousin. B says that

Mr. so-and-so's wife speaks English very well, and comes from Springfield, USA.

A: asks if it is Springfield Massachusetts.

B: says no, Springfield Illinois.

A: asks what she is doing now.

B: says she is studying to be a doctor, but that her husband still works on the farm, and their son Fred is a sailor.

A: says he's never before (noch-NOOJT) been in Laren.

Conversation 2. A wants to take B to visit an airplane factory in which A works.

A: asks B why B can't go with A to the airplane factory.

B: says that he has to work, but suggests that A take B's brother.

A: objects that B's brother is always working too and has no time. He says that he'd also like to go flying with B.

B: asks if there are many planes in the factory.

A: says yes, and asks if B has never been there.

B: says no, never. He has always lived in a small town and has never visited an airplane factory.

Conversation 3. A meets B, an Englishman, and speaks to him without having been introduced.

A: says that he knows B is from the United States.

B: says how does A know, when he hasn't met B.

A: says that it is because B speaks English and he knows that all Americans of course speak English.

B: says yes, but he comes from England, not from America.

A: says Oh.

B: asks A if A understands him when he speaks English.

A: says yes, he understands B quite well He says that obviously he himself is Dutch, but that he speaks a little English.

B: asks what part of the country A is from.

A: says from Groningen (GHROOningĕn). He asks B if he knows the city.

B: says of course, since after all Groningen is a large city.

FINDER LIST

AL 'already'

ALLĕ 'all'

   allĕ-OOtoos 'all autos'

   ALLĕmaal 'all of us, of you, of them'

   dĕ-OOtoos zein-allĕmaal-HIER. 'The autos are all here.'

al-TEIT, AL-teit 'always'

aMEEriekaa (aaMEEriekaa) 'America'

   dĕ-ameerieKAAN 'the (male) American'

   ameerieKAANS 'American'

   ameerieKAANsĕ OOtoos 'American autos'

   dĕ-ameerieKAANsĕ 'the (female) American'

ĕt-BEEtjĕ 'the little bit'
   ĕn-BEEtjĕ 'a little, a bit'
ĕt-DEEL 'the part'
   ĕm unstressed for HEM
   ENGĕlant 'England'
   ENGĕls 'English'
   ĕr unstressed for HAAR

ghĕWEEST 'been'
   ik-ben-ĕr-ghĕWEEST 'I've been there.'
ghĕWOONT 'lived (in a place), resided, dwelt'
   ik-hep-ĕr-EEN-jaar ghĕWOONT. 'I lived there
      for one year.'
GHROOT 'large'

HAAR (unstressed ĕr) 'her'
HEM (unstressed ĕm) 'him'
HOLLant 'Holland'
   dĕ-HOLLandĕr 'the Hollander'
   HOLLants 'Hollandish, Dutch'

IMMĕrs 'of course, as you know'
   niew-JORK is-immĕrs-ĕn-ghrootĕ-STAT. 'Of
      course New York is a big city.'

ĕt-JAAR 'the year'
   TIEN JAAR 'ten years'

   KENNĕn 'to know a person or a place'
      ik-KEN-ĕm-niet. 'I don't know him.'
      hei-KENT rottĕrDAM. 'He knows Rotterdam.'
   KLEIN 'small'

dĕ-maSJIEnĕ (maaSJIEnĕ) 'the machine'

   naaTUURlik 'naturally, of course'
dĕ-NEEF 'the nephew *or* male cousin'
dĕ-NICHT 'the niece *or* female cousin'
   NIEW 'new'
   NOOJT 'never'

   ONS 'us'
   OO 'Oh!'
   OOJT 'ever'
      bent-uu-ĕr-OOJT ghĕWEEST? 'Have you ever
      been there?'

dĕ-STAAT 'the state'
   dĕ-vĕREEnighdĕ STAAtĕn 'the United States'
dĕ-STAT 'the city'
   STEEdĕn, STEEjĕn 'cities'

věREEnicht 'united'
  dě-věREEnighdě STAAtěn 'the United States'
VLIEghěn 'to fly'
  dě-VLIECH-masjiěně 'the airplane'

WAArom 'why'
WEInich 'little, few'

weinich-MELK 'little milk'
weinich-OOtoos 'few autos'
WELK 'which'
  welkě-STAT? 'which city?'
WOOněn 'to live (in a place), reside, dwell'
  waar-WOONT-ZĚ? 'Where does she live?'

LET'S TALK ABOUT THE WEATHER

A. BASIC SENTENCES

1. Basic Sentences

Mr. Carver is talking with Mrs. Dekker and Mrs. Jansen.

ENGLISH EQUIVALENTS	AIDS TO LISTENING	CONVENTIONAL SPELLING
	Mrs. Dekker	
Betty, here's our American friend, Mr. Carver.	BETje, hier-is-onzĕ-ameeriekaansĕ-VRIENT, mĕneer-KAARvĕr.	Betje, hier is onze Amerikaansche vriend, Mijnheer Carver.
Mr. Carver, Mrs. Jansen.	Mĕneer-KAARvĕr, mĕvrou-JAN-sĕn.	Mijnheer Carver, Mevrouw Jansen.
	Mrs. Jansen	
the acquaintance	dĕ-KENNis	de kennis
Pleased to meet you, sir.	AANghĕnaam KENNis-tĕ-maakĕn, mĕnEER.	Aangenaam kennis te maken, mijnheer.

Pleased to meet you, Mrs. Jansen.	AANghĕnaam KENNis-tĕ-maakĕ, mĕvrou-JANsĕn.	Aangenaam kennis te maken, Mevrouw Jansen.
I already know Mr. Jansen.	mĕNEER JANsĕn KEN-ik-al.	Mijnheer Jansen ken ik al.

Mrs. Jansen

warm or *hot*	WARM	warm
My, it's hot!	WAT IS-ĕt WARM!	Wat is het warm!
to be going to	ZULLĕn	zullen
it's going to	hĕt-SAL	het zal
again	WEER	weer
to rain	REEghĕnĕn	regenen
I guess it's going to rain	hĕt-SAL wel-weer ghaan-REE-ghĕnĕn.	Het zal wel weer gaan regenen.

Mrs. Dekker

hot	HEET	heet
Oh! but it's so hot.	OO, wat-is-ĕt-HEET!	O, wat is het heet!
the weather	hĕt-WEER	het weer
What weather!	wat-ĕn-WEER!	Wat een weer!
by or *with*	BEI	bij
so	ZOO	zoo
such a	ZOO-ĕn	zoo een
to be able	KUNNĕn	kunnen
I can	ik-KAN	ik kan

In weather like this I can't do a thing.	bei-ZOO-ĕn-weer kan-ik-NIETS--doen.	Bij zoo'n weer kan ik niets doen.
Aren't you warm, Betty?	hep-JEI-ĕt-niet-warm, BETjĕ?	Heb jij het niet warm, Betje?
Aren't you warm, Mr. Carver?	hept-UU-ĕt-niet-warm, mĕneer--KAARvĕr?	Hebt u het niet warm, Mijnheer Carver?

Mrs. Jansen

sure or *surely*	ZEEkĕr	zeker
Yes, of course I feel warm, Mary.	jaa-ZEEkĕr heb-ik-ĕt-WARM, ma--RIE.	Ja zeker heb ik het warm, Marie.
very	ERCH	erg
today	van-DAACH	vandaag
It's very warm today.	ĕt-is-ERCH WARM van-DAACH.	Het is erg warm vandaag.
Is it as hot as this in America too, Mr. Carver?	is-ĕt-OOK-soo-warm in-aMEErie--kaa, mĕneer-KAARvĕr?	Is het ook zoo warm in Amerika, Mijnheer Carver?

Mr. Carver

the summer	dĕ-ZOOmĕr	de zomer
often	DIKwĕls	dikwijls
Yes, ma'am; in summer it's often hot.	JAA-mĕvrou; in-dĕ-ZOOmĕr-is-ĕt--DIKwĕls HEET.	Ja, mevrouw; in de zomer is het dikwijls heet.

Mrs. Dekker

cold	KOUT	koud
the winter	dĕ-WINtĕr	de winter
And it is cold in winter too?	en-is-ĕt-OOK KOUT in-dĕ-WIN--tĕr?	En is het ook koud in de winter?

Mr. Carver

Certainly, ma'am. In winter it's very cold.	jaa-ZEEkĕr-mĕvrou. in-dĕ-WIN--tĕr is-ĕt-ERCH-kout.	Ja zeker, mevrouw. In de winter is het erg koud.
But in Florida and in California it's warm.	maar-in-FLOOriedaa en-in-kalie--FORniejĕ is-ĕt-WARM.	Maar in Florida en in Californië is het warm.
How is winter here in Holland?	hoe-is-dĕ-WINtĕr hier-in-HOLLant?	Hoe is de winter hier in Holland?

Mrs. Dekker

Here in Holland it's probably not as cold as it is in Chicago or in New York.	hier-in-HOLLant is-ĕt-mischien--NIET-soo-kout als-in-sjiKAA--ghoo ov-in-niew-JORK.	Hier in Holland is het misschien niet zoo koud als in Chicago of in Nieuw-York.
But I always feel cold in winter.	maar-IK-heb-ĕt alTEIT-kout in--dĕ-WINtĕr.	Maar ik heb het altijd koud in de winter.

Mrs. Jansen

the spring	hĕt-VOOR-jaar	het voorjaar
beautiful	MOOJ	mooi

But spring is quite beautiful here.	maar-ĕt-VOOR-jaar is-hier HEEL-MOOJ.	Maar het voorjaar is hie heel mooi.
The weather is always nice here in the spring.	ĕt-WEER is-hier-alTEIT mooj in-ĕt-VOOR-jaar.	Het weer is hier altijd mooi in het voorjaar.

Mr. Carver

the fall	hĕt-NAA-jaar	het najaar
In America the weather is nicest in the fall.	in-aMEEriekaa is-ĕt-weer-ĕt-MOO-JST in-ĕt-NAA-jaar.	In Amerika is het weer het mooist in het najaar.

Mrs. Jansen

the rain	dĕ-REEghĕn	de regen
too much	tĕ-VEEL	te veel
In the fall we have too much rain here.	in-ĕt-NAA-jaar hebbĕ-wĕ-HIER tĕ-veel-REEghĕn.	In het najaar hebben we hier te veel regen.
the snow	dĕ-SNEEW	de sneeuw
Have you much snow in America?	hept-uu-veel-SNEEW in-aMEE-riekaa?	Hebt u veel sneeuw in Amerika?

Mr. Carver

Yes, indeed; in winter we have a lot of snow.	jaa-ZEEkĕr-mĕvrou, in-dĕ-WINtĕr hebbĕn-wĕ ERCH feel-SNEEW.	Ja zeker, mevrouw, in de winter hebben we erg veel sneeuw.
to snow	SNEEwĕn	sneeuwen
rarely	ZELdĕn	zelden

But in Florida and in California it only snows once in a while.	maar-in-FLOOrieđaa en-in-kalie--FORniejě sneewt-ět-maar-ZEL--děn.	Maar in Florida en in Californië sneeuwt het maar zelden.

so Does it rain in America as much as it does here, Mr. Carver?	ZOO REEghěnt-ět-in-aMEEriekaa OOK-soo-veel als-hier, měneer--KAARvěr?	zoo Regent het in Amerika ook zooveel als hier, Mijnheer Carver?

Mr. Carver

Yes, ma'am; I guess there are parts of the country where it rains as much as it does here in Rotterdam.	JAA-měvrou; er-zein-WEL DEELě van-ět-LANT, waar-ět-OOK soo--veel REEghěnt als-hier-in-rot--těrDAM.	Ja, mevrouw, er zijn wel deelen van het land waar het ook zoo veel regent als hier in Rotterdam.
But in Chicago or in New York it doesn't rain as much as it does in Holland.	maar-in-sjiKAAghoo ov-in-niew--JORK reeghent-ět-NIET-soo--veel als-in-HOLLant.	Maar in Chicago of in Nieuw-York regent het niet zoo veel als in Holland.

Mrs. Jansen

whole *the week* Here it often rains a whole week.	HEEL dě-WEEK HIER REEghěnt-ět-DIKwěls ěn--HEElě WEEK.	heel de week Hier regent het dikwijls een heele week.

Well, Betty, it's late and we still have to go to the (clothing) store.

NUU, BETjĕ, hĕt-is-LAAT, en--wĕ-MOEtĕ-noch naar-dĕ-KLEE--rĕ-winkĕl.

Nu, Betje, het is laat en wij moeten nog naar de kleerenwinkel.

Excuse me, Mr. Carver.

nee-mĕ-niet-KWAAlik, mĕneer--KAARvĕr.

Neem me niet kwalijk, Mijnheer Carver.

to seek or *to look for*
to look up or *to visit*
Come and look us up sometime, Mr. Carver.

ZOEkĕn
OP-zoekĕn
kom-ons-eens-OP-soekĕn, mĕneer-KAARvĕr.

zoeken
opzoeken
Kom ons eens opzoeken, Mijnheer Carver.

this evening
with us or *at our house*
Come and have dinner with us to-night, Mr. Carver.
glad
I know that my husband will be very glad to see you at our house.

van-AAvĕnt
bei-ONS
kom-van-AAvĕnt bei-ons-EEtĕ, mĕneer-KAARvĕr.
BLEI
ik-WEET-dat-mein-man-ergh--BLEI-zal-zein uu-BEI-ons-tĕ--zien.

vanavond
bij ons
Kom vanavond bij ons eten, Mijnheer Carver.
blij
Ik weet dat mijn man erg blij zal zijn u bij ons te zien.

Thank you, ma'am. I shall be very glad to come to your home.

dank-uu-WEL-mĕvrou, ik-sal--HEEL-ghraach BEI-uu-koomĕn.

Dank u wel, mevrouw, ik zal heel graag bij u komen.

	Mrs. Dekker	
Yes, please do, Mr. Carver.	JAA, DOE-dat-maar, mĕneer--KAARvĕr.	Ja, doe dat maar, Mijnheer Carver.
Maybe you don't know yet that Mrs. Jansen has two pretty daughters.	uu-WEET mischien-noch-NIET dat-mĕvrou-JANsĕn TWEE moojĕ-DOCHtĕrs-heeft.	U weet misschien nog niet dat Mevrouw Jansen twee mooie dochters heft.
the girl	hĕt-MEIsjĕ	het meisje
to marry	TROUwĕn	trouwen
hers	dĕ-HAArĕ	de hare
If you want to marry a Dutch girl, then I guess you can take one of hers.	als-uu-met-ĕn-hollants-MEIsjĕ wilt-TROUwĕn, dan-KUNT-uu--wel een-van-dĕ-HAArĕ-neemĕn.	Als u met een Hollandsch meisje wilt trouwen, dan kunt u wel een van de hare nemen.
	Mrs. Jansen	
joke	GHRAPJĕ	grapje
There she is again with her little jokes!	daar-heb-jĕ-HAAR-weer met-ĕr--GHRAPjĕs!	Daar heb je haar weer met haar grapjes!
We have dinner at seven o'clock, Mr. Carver.	wĕ-EEtĕn om-ZEEvĕn UUR, mĕneer-KAARvĕr.	Wij eten om zeven uur, Mijnheer Carver.
See you this evening!	tot-fan-AAvĕnt!	Tot vanavond!
	Mrs. Dekker	
Good Bye, Mr. Carver.	dach-mĕneer-KAARvĕr!	Dag, Mijnheer Carver!

2. Hints on Pronunciation

Go through the following five exercises again, and then review anything else which you think might need more special practice. Vowels are discussed in the Hints on Pronunciation in Units I and III, consonants in those in Units II and III.

Go back to Cassette 2A, page 56 for these 5 PRACTICES.

PRACTICE 1

MAN, MAAN	'man, moon'	RAS, RAAS	'race, roar'
STAT, STAAT	'city, state'		

PRACTICE 2

MET, MEET	'with, measure'	HEL, HEEL	'hell, whole'
HET, HEET	'it (reading form only), hot'		

PRACTICE 3

VIS, VIES	'fish, dirty'	LIGHĕn, LIEghĕn	'to lie, to tell a lie'
MIS, MIES	'amiss, (girl's name)'		

PRACTICE 4

ROT, ROOT	'rotten, red'	ROS, ROOS	'steed, rose'
MOT, MOOT	'moth, slice of fish'		

PRACTICE 5

LUS, LEUS   *'loop, slogan'*

This is the last Unit in which there is a special section called 'Hints on Pronunciation'. But that does not mean that your learning of pronunciation is over. Remember *always*, no matter how far you have gone, that there are points of pronunciation that call for

RUS, REUS   *'Russian, giant'*

constant practice and careful listening. Come back to the Hints on Pronunciation of the first few Units whenever you feel the need to, and remember to imitate carefully *whenever* you are speaking Dutch, even when you have finished the course itself.

B. WORD STUDY

1. Word Study

Point 1. Meanings. a. The Dutch often say WARM 'warm' where in English one would say 'hot'.

b. Here are some new uses of the word *WAT*:

wat-ĕn-MOOJ MEIsjĕ!   *'What a pretty girl!'*
wat-iz-ĕt-KOUT!   *'How cold it is!'*

c. Notice that *ZOO* and *ALS* go together:

hei-is-*zoo*-GHROOT *als*-IK.   *'He is as big as I.'*
ik-ben-NIET *zoo*-GHROOT *als*-HEI.   *'I am not as big as he.'*

Notice also the combination *ZOO-ĕn* (English *such a*):

zoo-ĕn-OOtoo   zou-ik-OOK   ghraach-willĕn--HEBBĕn.   *'I'd like to have a car like that too.'*

d. Notice that the Dutch use the word *the* when they

say 'in summer' and so on: *in-dĕ-ZOOmĕr, in-dĕ--WINtĕr, in-ĕt-VOOR-jaar, in-ĕt-NAA-jaar* 'in summer, in winter, in spring, in autumn'.

e. The Dutch say *ik-heb-ĕt-KOUT* and *ik-heb-ĕt--WARM* 'I have it cold' and 'I have it warm', for 'I feel cold' and 'I feel warm'.

f. Notice that in *van-DAACH*, literally 'of day', meaning 'today', the vowel of 'day' is like the vowel it has in the plural *DAAGHĕn* 'days', and not like the vowel it has in the singular, *DACH* 'day'.

Point 2. New Irregular Verbs. In the Basic Sentences are three more verbs that do not go according to the regular scheme:

ZULLĕn	*'to be going to'*	KUNNĕn	*'to be able'*	WILLĕn	*'to want to'*
wĕ-ZULLĕn	*'we're going to'*	wĕ-KUNNĕn	*'we can'*	wĕ-WILLĕn	*'we want to'*
	etc.				

ik-*ZAL*	*'I'm going to'*	ik-*KAN*	*'I can'*	ik-WIL	*'I want to'*

hei-*ZAL*	*'he's going to'*	hei-*KAN*	*'he can'*	hei-*WIL*	*'he wants to'*
	etc.				

uu-ZULT	*'you're going to'*	uu-KUNT	*'you can'*	uu-WILT	*'you want to'*

The irregular forms are in italics.

Point 3. Diminutives. Mrs. Dekker calls her good friend Mrs. Jansen *BETjĕ*, and is in turn called *maaRIEtjĕ*. Probably Mrs. Jansen's full name is *eeLIEzaabet*; Mrs. Dekker's is *maaRIE*. But since they know each other well, they use affectionate or familiar *diminutive* forms. These end in *-jĕ*, *-tjĕ*, or *-ĕtjĕ* and are made from names and from all kinds of nouns. These diminutives are all *dat*-nouns, and they all make their plural with *-s*. They mean *small* things:

dĕ-MAN, MANNĕn : ĕt-MANNĕtjĕ, MANNĕtjĕs *'the man, men : the little man, little men'*
dĕ-GHRAP, GHRAPPĕn : ĕt-GHRAPjĕ, GHRAPjĕs *'the joke, jokes : the little joke, little jokes'*

The words *ĕt-BEEtjĕ* 'the little bit' and *ĕt-MEIsjĕ* 'the girl' are diminutives, but there are no simple nouns to match them.

Point 4. Pronouns. Here is a summary of the pronouns you have learned.

a. The forms of the pronouns are as follows:

IK	*'I'*	MEI (měn)	*'me'*	MEIN (měn)	*'my'*
UU	*'you'*	UU	*'you'*	UUW (uu)	*'your'*
JEI (jě)	*'you'*	JOU (jě)	*'you'*	JOU (jě)	*'your'*
WEI (wě)	*'we'*	ONS	*'us'*	ONzě	*'our'*
HEI (hei, ie)	*'he'*	HEM (ěm)	*'him'*	ZEIN (zěn)	*'his'*
ZEI (zě)	*'she'*	HAAR (ěr, děr, zě)	*'her'*	HAAR (ěr, děr)	*'her'*
ZEI (zě)	*'they'*	HUN (un, zě)	*'them'*	HUN (un, ěr, děr)	*'their'*

b. The forms in the first column are used when the word names the person or people who are doing the thing, as in *ik-DENK* 'I am thinking', *zě-GHAAT* 'she goes', *GHAAN-zě?* 'are they going?' The forms in the second column are used when the word names the person or people who are the object of the action (object form), as in *met-ONS* 'with us', *met-MEI* 'with me'. The forms in the third column are used just as we use the possessive forms like *my*: *měn-BROER* 'my brother'. The forms in parentheses are used in rapid speech when the word is not stressed. In this situation, *ie* is the form of *HEI* used when it follows another word: *KENT-ie-ěr?* 'Does he know her?'

c. The forms *JEI* and *JOU* for 'you' are used between near relatives and close friends, or in speaking to children up to the age of sixteen or seventeen. Elsewhere the forms *UU* and *UUW* are used. Thus Mrs. Dekker and Mrs. Jansen address each other with *JEI* and *JOU*, but both, in speaking to Mr. Carver, say *UU*.

d. Before a *dat*-noun, 'our' is ONS; before a *die*-noun, including plurals, 'our' is ONzě:

dat-is-ONzě-ootoo, en-NIET HAAR-ootoo. 'That's *our* auto, and not *her* auto.'

e. There are also longer forms of all the possessive pronouns; these longer forms are used after *dě* and *ět* when no noun follows: *een-van-dě-HAArě* 'one of hers'; *als-ie-gheen-GHELT-heeft, neemt-ie-ět-HAArě*. 'When he has no money, he takes hers.'

f. Here are some sentences which illustrate most of the forms just discussed:

UU hept-ět-ghěDAAN, en-NIET IK. *'You did it not I.'*

ZEI heeft-ět-ghěDAAN, en-NIET HEI. *'She did it, not he.'*

ZEI hebběn-ět-ghěDAAN, en-NIET WEI. *'They did it, not we.'*

hei-ZOEKT MEI, en-NIET UU. *'He's looking for me, not you.'*

ik-ZOEK HAAR, en-NIET HEM. *'I'm looking for her, not him.'*

zě-ZOEKT ONS, en-NIET HUN. *'She's looking for us, not them.'*

ik-KEN-ěm. *'I know him.'*

uu-KENT-ěr. *'You know her.'*

hei-KENT-mě. *'He knows me.'*

zě-KENT-ons. *'She knows us.'*

wě-KENNěn-zě, wě-KENNěn-hun. *'We know them'.*

zě-KENNěn-uu. *'They know you.'*

dat-is-MEIN-ghelt, en-NIET UUW-ghelt. *'That's my money, not yours.'*

dat-is-HAAR-ghelt, en-NIET ZEIN-ghelt. *'That's her money, not his.'*

dat-is-ONS-ghelt, en-NIET HUN-ghelt. *'That's our money, not theirs.'*

ik-zoek-měn-GHELT. *'I'm looking for my money.'*

wě-zoekěn-ons-GHELT. *'We're looking for our money.'*

wě-zoekěn-onzě-OOtoo. *'We're looking for our car.'*

ZOEKT-uu uuw-OOtoo? *'Are you looking for your car?'*

hei-zoekt-zěn-GHELT. *'He's looking for his money.'*

zě-zoekt-ěr-OOtoo. *'She's looking for her auto.'*

zě-zoekěn-hun-OOtoo. *'They're looking for their car.'*

Point 5. It. The word for 'it' is *DAT*, unstressed ět (*hět*):

> ik-WEET-ět. *'I know it.'*
>
> dat-WEET-ik-al. *'I already know it.'*
>
> WAAR is-ět-GHELT? ik-HEB-ět. *'Where's the money? I have it.'*
>
> dat-HEB-ik-al. *'I've got it all right.'*

However, if the thing talked about is a *die*-noun, they rarely use these forms. Instead, they use *DIE* for the stressed form, and for the unstressed forms *hei, ei, ie* 'he' and *ěm* 'him', or *zě* 'she' and *zě, ěr* 'her'. As to the choice between 'he, him' and 'she, her', in talking about some things they will favor 'he, him', and in talking about others they will favor 'she, her'. But there is great variation in this between different speakers and between different parts of the country. Very often they will turn the sentence so as to use the stressed form, *DIE*:

HIER iz-dĕ-MELK, maar-zĕ-is-niet-GHOET, en--ik-KAN-zĕ niet-DRINKĕn. *'Here's the milk, but it's not good, and I can't drink it.'*

HIER iz-dĕ-WEIN, maar-ie-is-tĕ-ZUUR, en-ik--KAN-ĕm niet-DRINKĕn. *'Here's the wine, but it's too sour, and I can't drink it.'*

In either case, they might often say

die-kan-ik-niet-DRINKĕn. *'I can't drink that.'*

The plural 'they', in talking about things (as opposed to persons), is stressed *DIE* and unstressed *zĕ*:

HIER zein-dĕ-AARdappĕlĕ, maar-zĕ-zein-al--KOUT, en-ik-WIL-zĕ niet-EEtĕn. *'Here are the potatoes, but they're already cold, and I don't want to eat them.'*

DIE zein-WARM en-ik-wil-zĕ-WEL EEtĕn. *'Those are warm and I want to eat them.'*

2. Review of Basic Sentences with English Covered

C. What Would You Say?

1. What Would You Say?

1. *You want to ask your friend whether he thinks it's going to rain. You say:*
a. ghaat-ĕt-SNEEwĕn?
b. ghaat-ĕt-REEghĕnĕn?
c. is-ĕt-mooj-WEER?

2. *You want to tell a visitor that the winters are very cold. You say:*
a. in-dĕ-WINtĕr is-ĕt-erch-KOUT-hier.
b. in-dĕ-WINtĕr heb-ik-ĕt-ALteit KOUT.
c. ĕt-is-KOUT van-DAACH.

3. *You feel very cold. You say:*
a. in-dĕ-WINtĕr is-ĕt-KOUT.
b. deezĕ-KOFFie is-KOUT.
c. ik-heb-ĕt-ERCH KOUT.

4. *Mr. Dekker asks you to come and see him. He says:*
a. ik-WOON-hier in-rottĕrDAM.

b. KOM-ons OP-soekĕn.

c. AANghĕnaam KENNis-tĕ-maakĕn.

5. *You want to tell him that you'll come this week. You say:*

a. ik-wou-GHRAACH wat-EEtĕn.

b. kunt-uu-mĕ-ZEGHĕn waar-ik-wat-EEtĕn-kan?

c. ik-sal-uu-DEEzĕ-week OP-soekĕn.

6. *You want to explain that it does not snow much in California. You say:*

a. in-kaalieFORniejĕ is-ĕt-niet-KOUT.

b. in-kaalieFORniejĕ REEghĕnt-ĕt-VEEL.

c. in-kaalieFORniejĕ SNEEWT-ĕt maar-WEInich.

7. *You want to say that you don't know a certain man. You say:*

a. ik-KEN-ĕm-niet.

b. ik-WEET-ĕt-niet.

c. ik-WEET-niet waar-ie-WOONT.

8. *You want to say that you have never been in a certain restaurant. You say:*

a. DAAR heb-ik-NOOJT ghĕwOONT.

b. in-dat-rĕstoRANG ben-ik-NOOJT ghĕWEEST.

c. in-dat-rĕstoRANG wil-ik-niet-EEtĕn.

2. What Did You Say?

D. Listening In

1. *Mr. Holmes talks with Mr. Renkema.*

Holmes:	mooj-WEER-van-daach!	Mooi weer vandaag!
Renkema:	JAA, HEEL MOOJ!	Ja, heel mooi!
	maar-hĕt-IS ĕn-beetjĕ-WARM.	Maar het is een beetje warm.
Holmes:	jaa-ZEEkĕr, WARM is-ĕt-WEL.	Ja zeker, warm is het wel.
	miSCHIEN zal-ĕt-fan-DAACH noch-ghaan--REEghĕnĕ.	Misschien zal het vandaag nog gaan regenen.
Renkema:	JAA, hĕt-sal-wel-ghaan-REEghĕnĕ.	Ja, het zal wel gaan regenen.
Holmes:	hier-in-rottĕrDAM REEghĕnt-ĕt alTEIT.	Hier in Rotterdam regent het altijd.

Renkema: aLEEN-maar in-ĕt-NAA-jaar.
Holmes: bei-ons-in-sjiKAAghoo reeghĕnt-ĕt-NIET-soo-veel als--HIER.

Alleen maar in het najaar.
Bij ons in Chicago regent het niet zooveel als hier.

2. *Mrs. Dekker urges Mr. Carver to visit her.*

Mevrouw Dekker: OO, ghoedĕn-AAvĕnt, mĕneer-KAARvĕr!
ik-ben-BLEI uu-weer-tĕ-ZIEN.
Carver: hoe-GHAAT-ĕt-met-mĕNEER-dekkĕr, en--met-PIETjĕ?
Mevrouw Dekker: HEEL-GHOET, dank-uu-WEL.
KOM-ons-eens OP-zoekĕn.
mein-MAN zal-HEEL-blei-zein uu-tĕ-ZIEN.
wĕ-SPREEkĕn DIKwĕls-oovĕr-UU.
PIETjĕ zecht-alTEIT:
wanneer-komt-dĕ-ameeriekaansĕ-HEER bei--ONS?
ik-zou-ĕm-GHRAACH WEER willĕ-ZIEN.

O, goeden avond, Mijnheer Carver!
Ik ben blij u weer te zien.
Hoe gaat het met Mijnheer Dekker, en met Pietje?
Heel goed, dank u wel.
Kom ons eens opzoeken.
Mijn man zal heel blij zijn u te zien.
Wij spreken dikwijls over u.
Pietje zegt altijd:
"Wanneer komt de Amerikaansche heer bij ons?
Ik zou hem graag weer willen zien."

3. *Little Peter Dekker can't go to the movies.*

Mevrouw Dekker: NEEN, PIEtjĕ, bei-DIT-weer kun-jĕ-NIET naar-dĕ-biejĕSKOOP-ghaan.
Pieter: WAArom NIET?

Neen, Pietje, bij dit weer kun je niet naar de bioscoop gaan.
Waarom niet?

Mevrouw Dekker:	hět-REEghěnt-imměrs!	Het regent immers!
Pieter:	maar-ik-BEN-ghraach in-dě-REEghěn.	Maar ik ben graag in de regen.
Dekker:	waar-wil-jě-naar-TOE, PIET?	Waar wil je naar toe, Piet?
Pieter:	naar-dě-biejěsKOOP.	Naar de bioscoop.
Mevrouw Dekker:	en-ik-ZECH dat-hei-bei-dit-WEER NIET naar-dě-biejěSKOOP-kan-ghaan.	En ik zeg dat hij bij dit weer niet naar de bioscoop kan gaan.
Dekker:	PIEtěr, als-jě-moeděr-ZECHT dat-jě-NIET naar-dě-biejěSKOOP-kunt-ghaan, dan-kun--jě-NIET-chaan.	Pieter, als je moeder zegt dat je niet naar de bioscoop kunt gaan, dan kun je niet gaan.

4. *Mr. Carver is talking with Mr. Dekker.*

Carver:	ik-zou-GHRAACH wat-willě-DRINKěn. zullěn-wě in-DIT-rěstorang ghaan?	Ik zou graag wat willen drinken. Zullen we in dit restaurant gaan?
Dekker:	in-DIT-rěstorang is-ět-BIER NIET erch-GHOET. DAAR, in-ět-hootel-LINKS hebběn-zě-GHOET-bier.	In dit restaurant is het bier niet erg goed. Daar in het hotel links hebben zij goed bier.
Carver:	wat-IS-ět-warm!	Wat is het warm!
Dekker:	JAA, ět-is-WARM-van-daach. ik-heb-ět-OOK heel-WARM. bei-DIT-weer kan-ik-NIET-ghoet-WERkěn.	Ja, het is warm vandaag. Ik heb het ook heel warm. Bij dit weer kan ik niet goed werken.
Carver:	hept-uu-VEEL-tě-doen in-uuw-faBRIEK?	Hebt u veel te doen in uw fabriek?
Dekker:	NEE, in-dě-ZOOměr is-ěr-NIET-zoo-veel tě-DOEN. maar-in-ět-NAA-jaar en-in-dě-WINtěr moet-ik-VEEL WERkěn.	Nee, in de zomer is er niet zoo veel te doen. Maar in het najaar en in de winter moet ik veel werken.

dan-moet-ik-dĕ-heelĕ-DACH WERkĕn.
en-DIKwĕls werk-ik-ZEEvĕn-daaghĕn in-dĕ-WEEK.
maar-in-dĕ-ZOOmĕr HEBBĕn-wei-maar-WEInich-tĕ-
-doen.

Dan moet ik de heele dag werken.
En dikwijls werk ik zeven dagen in de week.
Maar in de zomer hebben wij maar weinig te
doen.

E. Conversation

1. Review of Basic Sentences with Dutch Covered

2. Vocabulary and Word Study Check-up

Try not only to review all the new words of this unit, but also the points made in the word study. For example, one question might be 'What is irregular about the verb ZULLĕn?'; another might be 'What is a diminutive? What does it end in? Is a diminutive a *die*-noun or a *dat*-noun?'; or 'When do you use *JEI* for "you", and when *UU*?'

3. Carrying on Conversation

Some more Dutch names: dĕ-GHROOT, VOLkĕrs, ENGĕrs, dĕ-REIkĕ.

Conversation 1. A speaks to his son, B.

A: says he can't go to the factory today because it's too hot.

B: says how come? He's not hot. (He addresses his father as 'father'.)

A: asks B if he would want to go to work in weather like this.

B: says sure.

A: asks when B would want to go.

B: says at nine o'clock.

A: says that's too late. He wants B to go now.

B: says very well, but asks A if A won't go with him.

A: says no, B should go alone.

Conversation 2. Two men who know each other by reputation but haven't met before meet each other.

A: asks B if his name is such-and-such.

B: says yes, and that A's name is probably such-and-such.

A: says yes, and that he is pleased to meet B.

B: says the same to A.

A: says he already knows B's wife.

B: asks A if he is married too.

A: says yes, but that his wife is not here. He says she lives in Gouda (GHOUdaa). He says they have a small farm.

B: comments on the beauty of the weather today.

A: agrees, but says that it often rains here.

B: agrees, but says that it rarely snows.

A: says that a little rain is good for his farm.

Conversation 3. Mr. A and his wife B are talking.

A: says that in the winter they'll go to England, perhaps to the United States.

B: says she'd like to go to the United States in the fall. There the weather is nicest in the fall, but England has nicer weather in the summer and she'd prefer to go to England then.

A: says OK. He says they'll stay here in Holland in the spring, since it's quite warm and beautiful here in that season.

B: asks if they should look up the van Berkums (dĕ--van-BERkums) this evening. She suggests that the girls (their daughters) might like to go too.

A: says that's a good joke, since the van Berkums wouldn't know they were coming, and usually have dinner at eight, he thinks.

FINDER LIST

AANghĕnaam 'pleased, agreeable'
  AANghĕnaam KENNis-tĕ-maakĕn 'Pleased to make (your) acquaintance.'

dĕ-AAvĕnt 'the evening'
  van-AAvĕnt 'this evening'
  ALS 'as'
  zoo-GHROOT als-HEI 'as big as he'

BEI 'by, at, with, at the house of'
  bei-ONS 'with us, at our house, in our country'
BLEI 'glad'

dĕ-DACH 'the day'
  van-DAACH 'today'
  dĕr unstressed for HAAR or HUN
  DIKwĕls 'often'

ERCH 'very'
ĕm unstressed for HEM
ĕr unstressed for HAAR or HUN

dĕ-GHRAP 'the joke'
    ĕt-GHRAPjĕ 'the little joke'
    HAAR (unstressed ĕr, dĕr) 'her, hers'
      ik-ZIE-ĕr 'I see her'
      haar-MAN 'her husband'
      dĕ-HAArĕ, ĕt-HAArĕ 'hers'
    HEEL 'whole'
      dĕ-heelĕ-DACH 'the whole day'
    HEET 'hot'
    HEM (unstressed ĕm) 'him'
    HUN (unstressed un, ĕr, dĕr) 'them, their'

jĕ unstressed for JEI or JOU
JEI (unstressed jĕ) 'you' (intimate form)
JOU (unstressed jĕ) 'you, your' (intimate form)

dĕ-KENNis 'the acquaintance'
    KENNis-tĕ-maakĕn 'to get acquainted'
    KOUT 'cold'
    KUNNĕn 'to be able'
      ik-KAN 'I can'
      hei-KAN 'he can'
      uu-KUNT 'you can'

ĕt-MEIsjĕ 'the girl'
    MOOJ 'beautiful, pretty'
      ĕt-MOOJST 'the prettiest, the nicest'

ĕt-NAA-jaar 'the autumn, fall'

    OP 'up'
      OP-zoekĕn 'to look (someone) up, to pay a call on'

dĕ-REEghĕn 'the rain'
    REEghĕnĕn 'to rain'

dĕ-SNEEW 'the snow'
    SNEEwĕn 'to snow'

    tĕ (before an adjective) 'too'
      tĕ-WEInich 'too little'
    TROUwĕn 'to get married'
      zĕ-TROUT met-ĕn-ameerieKAAN 'she is marrying an American'

    un unstressed for HUN

ĕt-VOOR-jaar 'the spring (season)'
    in-ĕt-VOOR-jaar 'in spring'

    WARM 'warm, hot'
dĕ-WEEK 'the week'
    WEER 'again'

ĕt-WEER 'the weather'
dĕ-WINtĕr 'the winter'
　in-dĕ-WINtĕr 'in winter'

　ZEEkĕr 'sure, surely'
　ZELdĕn 'seldom'
　zĕ unstressed for HUN
　ZOEkĕn 'to seek, to look for'
　　OP-zóekĕn 'to look (someone) up, to pay a call on'
　ZOO 'so'

zoo-GHROOT als-HEI 'as big as he'
　zoo-ĕn-OOtoo 'such an auto'
dĕ-ZOOmĕr 'the summer'
　in-dĕ-ZOOmĕr 'in summer'
　ZULLĕn 'to be going to'
　　ik-ZAL 'I shall'
　　hei-ZAL 'he will'
　　uu-ZULT 'you will'

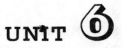
REVIEW

To the Leader: This Review Unit is not organized like the five preceding Units, so you must be especially careful to look it over in advance and be sure of what is to be done.

This Unit will furnish you with a thorough review of all the work done to date. Pronunciation should be the object of attention whenever any of you are talking; if you have no Guide, then correct each other's pronunciation as well as you can, and go back to the records for authority when necessary.

A. TRUE-FALSE TEST

Each student is to take a sheet of paper and write down along the side the numbers from 1 through 80. Then the Guide, or the records, will give you a series of eighty statements, repeating each one twice. You should have no trouble understanding these statements if you have done the work properly up to this point. Each statement is either *obviously* true, or else *usually* false. If the statement is obviously true, mark a T by the corresponding number on your paper; if it is usually false, mark an F by the corresponding number on your paper. Don't go into particular cases in deciding whether a particular statement is true or false; the thing that counts is whether it is *generally* true or *generally* false.

The Leader will stop the Guide, or stop the tape recorder and rewind, after the first statement, and you can check up with each other to see that everyone understands what is to be done.

After you have gone through the test, the Leader will go through the answers with you as a group and tell you in each case whether the statement is true or false. If you come out pretty well on this quiz—65 or 70 correct answers—it means that you have a good understanding of the material covered to date.

To the Leader: The True-False Statements, together with their English translations and the indication of whether they are true or false, are in the Key to exercises and tests at the end of the book.

B. Putting It into Dutch

1. Individual Study

Go through the following English sentences and prepare to say the equivalents for the English when the group is working together. *Don't write anything down,* but practice the Dutch sentences to yourself aloud until you have them down cold and can fire them out the moment the English is given to you.

I

1. Good evening, sir.
2. What time is it?
3. It's four o'clock.
4. It's raining again.
5. It's snowing today.
6. I don't understand what you say.
7. Speak slowly, please.
8. Where is there a restaurant?
9. There's a restaurant to the left.
10. Go to the left.

II

11. I'd like to eat something.
12. I should like a cigarette.
13. I should like meat and potatoes.

14. How much is it?
15. Do you want some matches?
16. That's three guilder.
17. At what time does the movie begin?
18. The movie begins at eight o'clock.
19. When does the train go?
20. Does this train go to Amsterdam?

III

21. What's your name?
22. What's your friend's name?
23. His name is Alfred Dekker.
24. Where does he live?
25. Where does his sister live?
26. She lives in this hotel.
27. Is his father still living?
28. Are his brothers still in America?
29. Yes, they're in America.
30. Her father works in a factory.

IV

31. I must go to the station.
32. My train goes at four o'clock.

33. I guess it's going to snow.
34. In this weather I can't work.
35. Do you speak English?
36. I can't repair the auto.
37. I don't know where our friend is.
38. I don't know whether he's coming.
39. He's coming this evening.
40. I must call on Mr. Vos.

V

41. Is she married?
42. How many children have they?
43. They have no children.
44. They have only one child.
45. They have four children, two sons and two daughters.
46. Farmers work on the land.

47. I'm going to the farm.
48. She's a typist.
49. Her brother is a sailor.
50. Our son is studying to be a doctor.

VI

51. He's as big as his father.
52. In winter it's very cold here.
53. I feel cold.
54. In California it snows only rarely.
55. It often rains a whole week.
56. Have you ever been in America?
57. I've never been in The Hague.
58. What did you say?
59. Excuse me.
60. So long until this evening.

2. How Do You Say It?

This is the group drill on the above sentences. The Leader will call on one or another of the members of the group for the Dutch equivalent of each of the English sentences in §1. All the rest should keep their books closed. If the Guide is present, he will listen and check on how you say the Dutch.

C. More Putting It into Dutch

1. Individual Study

Prepare here, working individually, just as in Section B.

I

1. This coffee is cold.
2. In winter it's cold.
3. We still have to go to the clothing store.
4. It's late.
5. The spring is quite beautiful here.
6. Pleased to make your acquaintance, ma'am.
7. Mr. Jansen I already know.
8. Many Dutchmen speak English.
9. Do you speak English?
10. I speak it only a little.

II

11. Do you understand what I say?
12. I've already been living in the Hague five years.
13. I have a niece who is married to a Dutchman.
14. She lives in a small town in Holland.
15. Where are you from?
16. I come from the United States.
17. From what city do you come?

18. Do you drink beer or water?
19. I don't drink beer.
20. He has a wife and four children.

III

21. My wife and my daughter are in America, of course.
22. My wife and I have been married ten years already.
23. There are only a few Americans who don't work.
24. My daughter is still young.
25. She's a student.
26. My sister is a good typist.
27. Come and have dinner with us tonight.
28. Who is that man?
29. I don't know him.
30. I don't know who that is.

IV

31. I'm glad that you're coming.
32. Thank you, ma'am.
33. You're welcome, sir.

34. We are all of us American sailors.
35. I can't drink that milk.
36. Where are the potatoes?
37. Here they are.
38. These are my friends.
39. Will you go to the movie with me?
40. No, sir; with you I shan't go to the movie.

V

41. Why won't you go to the movie with me?

42. I don't know you, you see.
43. I can't eat that.
44. I can't drink that beer.
45. He works in this factory.
46. Are you coming this evening?
47. We're going to the movie this evening.
48. What does he say?
49. What does she say?
50. What do they say?

2. How Do You Say It?

Go over the above sentences under the direction of the Leader, as in Section B.

D. Conversation

The members of the group are to carry on short conversations, lasting not more than one or two minutes, which use the entire contents of the first five Units. Everyone in the group should have a chance to take part as many times as possible. The situations of the conversations should be varied and combined as much as possible. Each conversation should begin with the usual polite greetings and inquiries about health, and should end with polite leave-taking. Here are a few of the many possibilities:

1. Meeting friends on the street. Include questions about each other's health, health of parents, children.

2. Meeting a stranger and introducing oneself. Include statement of names, nationalities, occupations.

3. Welcoming friends and speaking of the weather. Include questions about health, and statements of rain, snow, and so forth.

4. Asking for directions and the time the train leaves. Include questions and answers on the whereabouts of hotel, restaurant, movies, or toilet; question and answer on the whereabouts of railroad station; question and answer about the time a train leaves.

5. Exchanging information about one's home. Include questions about each other's origin, where born and brought up, answers about locations of homes, and city from which one comes.

6. Conversing about the weather in different cities and countries. Include questions about the type of weather in summer and winter in the various cities from which the soldiers come, complaints about the weather, etc. Also compare the Dutch climate with that of the United States.

7. Talking about one's relatives and their whereabouts. Include identification of relatives, their homes in various countries, languages they speak, professions.

8. Asking about a movie and how to get to it. Include mention of the place, the time, whether it is good or not, whether the person wants to go.

9. Conversing about trades. Include questions about the type of work one does, the work of one's friends.

FINDING ROOMS

A. BASIC SENTENCES

1. Basic Sentences

Mr. Kuypers, Mr. Carver, and Mr. Molenaer speak to a landlady about some rooms.

ENGLISH EQUIVALENTS	AIDS TO LISTENING	CONVENTIONAL SPELLING

Mr. Kuypers

Good morning, ma'am.	ghoeden-MORghĕn mĕVROU.	Goeden morgen, mevrouw.
the room	dĕ-KAAmĕr	de kamer
the rent	dĕ-HUUR	de huur
for rent	tĕ-HUUR	te huur
You have rooms for rent?	hept-uu-KAAmĕrs-tĕ-huur?	Hebt u kamers te huur?

Landlady

Yes, sir.	JAA-mĕneer.	Ja, mijnheer.
the person	dĕ-perSOON	de persoon
For how many (persons?)	voor-HOE-veel pĕrSOOnĕn?	Voor hoeveel personen?

For three (persons).	voor-DRIE-pĕrsoonĕn.	Voor drie personen.

the bed — hĕt-BET — het bed

beds — BEDDĕn — bedden

I have one room with two beds and one room with one bed. — ik-hep-EEN-kaamĕr me-TWEE--beddĕn, en-EEN-kaamĕr met--EEN-bet. — Ik heb een kamer met twe bedden en een kamer met een bed.

inside — BINNĕn — binnen

to let — LAAtĕn — laten

to let see or *to show* — laatĕn-ZIEN — laten zien

Come inside, please, and I'll show you the rooms. — kom-BINNĕn als-t-uu-BLIEFT, en--ik-sal-uu-dĕ-KAAmĕrs laatĕn--ZIEN. — Kom binnen, alst u blieft, en ik zal u de kamers laten zien

the stairs — dĕ-TRAP — de trap

high — HOOCH — hoog

the second — dĕ-TWEEdĕ — de tweede

floor higher than the first — dĕ-vĕrDIEping — de verdieping

They're two flights up, on the second floor. — hĕt-is-TWEE-trappĕn HOOCH, op--dĕ-TWEEdĕ vĕrdIEping. — Het is twee trappen hoog, op de tweede verdieping.

just — EEvĕn — even

above or *upstairs* — BOOvĕn — boven

Will you please come upstairs, gentlemen? — wilt-uu-EEvĕn naar-BOOvĕn--koomĕn, HEErĕn? — Wilt u even naar boven komen, heeren?

Mr. Kuypers

to cost
How much do these rooms cost, ma'am?

KOStĕn
hoe-veel-KOStĕn-deezĕ-kaamĕrs
mĕVROU?

kosten
Hoeveel kosten deze kamers,
mevrouw?

Landlady

twenty
per person
*The room with two beds is two guilder
twenty-five per person.*

TWINtich
per-pĕrSOON
dĕ-KAAmĕr met-TWEE-beddĕn is
TWEE-ghuldĕn VEIV-en-
-TWINtich per-pĕrSOON.

twintig
per persoon
De kamer met twee bedden is twee
gulden vijf en twintig per persoon.

other
fifty
*The other, with one bed is two guilder
fifty.*

ANdĕr
FEIFtich
dĕ-ANdĕrĕ, met-EEN-bet, is-
-TWEE-ghuldĕn FEIFtich.

ander
vijftig
De andere, met één bed, is twee
gulden vijftig.

Mr. Kuypers

cheap
*Can't you make it a bit cheaper,
ma'am?*

ghoetKOOP
kan-ĕt-NIET wat-choetKOOpĕr-
-mĕVROU?

goedkoop
Kan het niet wat goedkooper,
mevrouw?

Landlady

expensive or *dear*	DUUR	duur
It isn't expensive, sir.	ĕt-IS-niet-duur, mĕNEER.	Het is niet duur, mijnheer.
the house	hĕt-HUIS	het huis
everything	ALLĕs	alles
clean	SCHOON	schoon
The furniture is good and in my house everything is always clean.	dĕ-MEUbĕls-zein-ghoet en-bei--MEI-in-huis is-ALLĕs ALteit SCHOON.	De meubels zijn goed en bij mij in huis is alles altijd schoon.

Mr. Kuypers

the light	hĕt-LICHT	het licht
the heating	dĕ-vĕrWARming	de verwarming
included	IN-bĕghreepĕn	inbegrepen
Is light and heat included?	is-LICHT en-vĕrWARming IN--bĕghreepĕn?	Is licht en verwarming inbegrepen?

Landlady

the breakfast	hĕt-ontBEIT	het ontbijt
Yes, sir, and breakfast too.	JAA-mĕneer, en-ook-ĕt-ont-BEIT.	Ja, mijnheer, en ook het ontbijt.

How much do the rooms cost by the week, ma'am?	hoe-veel-KOStěn-dě-kaaměrs per--WEEK měVROU?	Hoeveel kosten de kamers per week, mevrouw?

Landlady

fourteen	VEERtien	veertien
sixteen	ZEStien	zestien
The big one is fourteen guilder a person and the small one sixteen.	dě-GHROOtě is-FEERtien-ghulděn per-pěrSOON en-dě KLEIně ZEStien.	De groote is veertien gulden per persoon en de kleine zestien.
to get	WORděn	worden
in advance	voorUIT	vooruit
to pay	běTAALěn	betalen
paid	běTAALT	betaald
The rent is always paid in advance.	dě-HUUR wort-ALteit fooRUIT--bětaalt.	De huur wordt altijd vooruit betaald.

Mr. Kuypers

Shall we take the rooms?	ZULLěn-wě dě-KAAměrs-neeměn?	Zullen we de kamers nemen?

Mr. Carver

to think	DENkěn	denken
I think so.	IK-denk van-JAA.	Ik denk van ja.

Mr. Molenaer

Yes, let's take them.	JAA, LAATĕn-wĕ zĕ-NEEmĕn.	Ja, laten we ze nemen.
the number	hĕt-NUMMĕr	het nummer
The big room is number seven.	dĕ-GHROOtĕ-kaamĕr is-nummĕr--ZEEvĕn.	De groote kamer is nummer zeven.
And the other room is number nine.	en-dĕ-ANdĕrĕ-kaamĕr is-nummĕr--NEEghĕn.	En de andere kamer is nummer negen.

Mr. Kuypers

Well, all right, ma'am. We'll take the rooms.	nuu-GHOET-mĕvrou. wĕ--NEEmĕn dĕ-KAAmĕrs.	Nu, goed, mevrouw. Wij nemen de kamers.

Landlady

Very well, gentlemen.	heel-GHOET HEErĕn.	Heel goed, heeren.
to be permitted	MOOghĕn	mogen
I am permitted	ik-MACH	ik mag
May I know your name?	mach-ik-uuw-NAAmĕn-weetĕn?	Mag ik uw namen weten?

Mr. Kuypers

My name is Kuypers. This gentleman is Mr. Carver, and this is Mr. Molenaer.	ik-heet-KUIpĕrs. DEEzĕ-heer is--mĕneer-KAARvĕr, en-dit-is mĕneer-MOOlĕnaar.	Ik heet Kuypers. Deze heer is Mijnheer Carver, en dit is Mijnheer Molenaer.

Landlady

Pleased to know you.	AANghĕnaam-heerĕn.	Aangenaam, heeren.
the key	dĕ-SLEUtĕl	de sleutel
to give	GHEEvĕn	geven
Now I still have to give you the keys.	nuu-MOET-ik-uu-noch dĕ--SLEUtĕls-gheevĕn.	Nu moet ik u nog de sleutels geven.
That key is for the big room, and this one is for the small one.	DIE-sleutĕl is-fan-dĕ-GHROOtĕ--kaamĕr, en-DEEzĕ is-fan-dĕ--KLEInĕ.	Die sleutel is van de groote kamer, en deze is van de kleine.
the bath	hĕt-BAT	het bad
at	an	aan
the end	hĕt-EINT	het eind
the hall	dĕ-GHANG	de gang
The bathroom and the toilet are here at the end of the hall.	dĕ-BAT-kaamĕr en-dĕ-wee-SEE zein-HIER an-ĕt-EINT van--dĕ-GHANG.	De badkamer en de W.C. zijn hier aan het eind van de gang.

Mr. Kuypers

the baggage	dĕ-baaGHAAzjĕ	de bagage
Our baggage will probably (still) come today.	onzĕ-baaGHAAzjĕ zal-van-DAACH noch-wel-KOOmĕ.	Onze bagage zal vandaag nog wel komen.

at once	DAAdĕlik	dadelijk
to bring	BRENGĕn	brengen
Very well, gentlemen. When it comes I bring it upstairs.	GHOET-heerĕn. als-sĕ-KOMT zal-ik-sĕ-DAAdĕlik naar- -BOOvĕn-laatĕn-brengĕn.	Goed, heeren. Als ze komt, zal ik ze dadelijk naar boven laten brengen.

2. Hints on Dutch Spelling

The conventional Dutch spelling has been given in the Basic Sentences and the Listening In thus far mainly for the benefit of the Guide; you, the students, have been advised to pay no attention to it. Now is the time for you to start learning it. First notice the following points about it:

1. The conventional spelling does not show the stress. Only rarely does it show the weakening of vowels in unstressed forms, though sometimes it does: *jij* for *JEI*, and frequently *je* for *jĕ*. It does not show the changes of voiced and unvoiced mutes, but writes, for example, *BROOT* as *brood*, with a *d*.

2. It writes final *-en* where the pronunciation may be sometimes *-ĕn*, sometimes ĕ-.

3. Conventional Dutch spelling uses *ij* in most words for the sound *ei*, though you will find *ei* too.

4. It writes *g* for the sound marked by *gh* in the Aid to Listening. But it uses the letter *g* also for the sound of *zj*: *baaGHAAzjĕ* is spelled *bagage*. In words from French or English the letter *g* is sometimes pronounced as *g*: the word spelled *garage* is pronounced both *gaaRAAzjĕ* and *ghaaRAAzjĕ*.

5. It often writes simple vowel letters for long vowels. In conventional Dutch spelling, a simple vowel letter means a long vowel whenever the vowel is stressed and is followed by only one consonant letter plus another vowel letter: *laten* in *LAAtĕn*, *geven* is *GHEEvĕn*, *komen* is *KOOmĕn*.

These points will not take care of everything. The Aid to Listening will help out when the conventional spelling does not make the pronunciation clear.

After going through the Basic Sentences several more

times in the usual way, with group repetition and individual repetition, go through it once or twice following the third column with your eyes instead of the second column. You can also use the records and go through the Basic Sentences and the Listening In in the first five Units doing the same thing. This will pretty well fix in your minds how the ordinary writing system works. However, continue to use the Aids to Listening rather than the conventional spelling the *first time through* each group of Basic Sentences or Listening In conversations, until you have finished Part Two (Unit 12).

B. WORD STUDY

1. Word Study

Point 1. De verdieping. All over Europe, the ground floor is not counted. In the Netherlands (or, for that matter, in England), the 'second' floor means what we in the USA call the *third* floor: *de derde verdieping* (*dĕ-DERdĕ vĕrDIEping*) 'the fourth floor (USA); the third storey (England)'.

Point 2. Laten zien. The verb *laten* (*LAAtĕn*) means 'to let, allow, permit, cause, have', and so on; it is used when someone lets or causes someone else to do something, and when one lets or causes something to be done:

Laat de man binnen komen. (laat-dĕ-MAN BINNĕn-koomĕn.) '*Let the man come in.*'

Ik laat mijn auto repareeren. (ik-laat-mĕn--OOtoo reepaaREErĕn.) '*I'm having my auto repaired.*'

The combination *laten zien* (*laatĕn-ZIEN*) 'to let see' is used for 'to show':

Laat me de kamer zien. (laat-mĕ-dĕ-KAAmĕr--zien.) '*Let me see the room.*'—'*Show me the room.*'

The phrase 'let us' (do so and so) is *laat ons* (*LAAT--ons*) or *laten we* (*LAAtĕn-wĕ*):

Laat ons naar de bioscoop gaan. (laat-ons-naar--dĕ-biejĕSKOOP-ghaan.) *or* Laten we naar de bioscoop gaan. (laatĕn-wĕ-naar-dĕ-biejĕ--SKOOP-ghaan.) '*Let's go to the movie.*'

Point 3. Mogen. The verb *mogen* has irregular forms: *ik mag* (*ik-MACH*), *hij mag* (*hei-MACH*), *U moogt* (uu-MOOCHT). It means something like 'be allowed, may':

> Wij mogen vandaag niet uitgaan. (wĕ-MOOghĕn van-DAACH niet-UIT-ghaan.) *'We aren't allowed to go out today.'*
>
> Mag ik eeǹ lucifer? (mach-ik-ĕn-LUUsiefĕr?) *'May I (have) a match?'*
>
> Hij mag vanavond niet naar de bioscoop. (hei-

-MACH van-AAvĕnt NIET naar-dĕ-biejĕ--SKOOP.) *'He isn't permitted to go to the movie tonight.'*

> Dat moogt u niet doen. (dat-MOOCHT-uu nie-DOEN.) *'You aren't allowed to do that.'*

You have now met all the Dutch verbs that are any way peculiar in the present-tense forms. There are seven of them. They are repeated here, the forms which do not fit the regular pattern are printed in italics:

Form 1

(to ——)	zijn	hebben	komen	zullen	kunnen	mogen	willen
(we ——)							
(they ——)							
(the men ——)							

Form 2a

(command)	*wees*	heb	*kom*

Form 2b

(I ——)	*ben*	heb	*kom*	zal	kan	*mag*	wil

(he ——)	is	heeft	komt	zal	kan	mag	wil
(she ——)							
(it ——)							
(the man ——)							

Form 3b

(you ——)	bent	hebt	komt	zult	kunt	moogt	wilt, *wil*

Point 4. Numbers. In Unit 1 you learned the numbers from one to twelve. The other numbers are based on these, but there are quite a few irregularities. The -teens and -ty's are based on the units, as in English. Note the differences, however:

een : elf : tien *'one : eleven : ten'*
twee : twaalf : twintig (TWINtich) *'two : twelve : twenty'*
drie : dertien : dertig (DERtich) *'three : thirteen : thirty'*
vier : veertien : veertig (FEERtich) *'four : fourteen : forty'*
vijf (VEIF) : vijftien : vijftig (FEIFtich) *'five : fifteen : fifty'*
zes : zestien : zestig (SEStich) *'six : sixteen : sixty'*

zeven (ZEEvěn) : zeventien : zeventig (SEEvěntich) *'seven : seventeen : seventy'*
acht : achttien (ACHtien) : tachtig (TACHtich) *'eight : eighteen : eighty'*
negen (NEEghěn) : negentien : negentig *'nine : nineteen : ninety'*

When one's are added to ty's, one says 'one and twenty' and so on. The word 'and' is here ěn, sometimes shortened to ě:

een en twintig (een-ěn-TWINtich) *'twenty-one'*
twee en twintig (twee-ěn-TWINtich) *'twenty-two'*
drie en dertig (drie-ěn-DERtich) *'thirty-three'*
vier en zestig (vier-ěn-SEStich) *'sixty-four'*
acht en tachtig (acht-ěn-TACHtich) *'eighty-eight'*

Before ěn (ě) 'and', the numbers *VEIF* and *ZES* often become *VEIV* and *ZEZ:*

vijf en twintig (veiv-ĕn-TWINtich) *'twenty-five'*
zes en dertig (zez-ĕn-DERtich, zes-ĕn-DERtich)
'thirty-six'

Before *ĕn* (*ĕ*), the numbers *ZEEvĕn* and *NEEghĕn* do *not* drop the final *n*:

zeven en twintig (zeevĕn-ĕn-TWINtich) *'twenty-seven'*

negen en tachtig (neeghĕn-ĕn-TACHtich) *'eighty-nine'*

After ĕn (*ĕ*), the numbers *FEERtich, FEIFtich,* usually replace the sound *f-* by *v-*:

een en veertig (een-ĕn-VEERtich) *'forty-one'*
vijf en vijftig (veiv-ĕn-VEIFtich) *'fifty-five'*

The remaining numbers are as follows:

honderd (HONdĕrt) *'hundred, one hundred'*
twee honderd (TWEE HONdĕrt) *'two hundred'*
duizend (DUIzĕnt) *'thousand, one thousand'*
twee duizend (TWEE DUIzĕnt) *'two thousand'*
een millioen (EEN milJOEN) *'one million'*
nul (NUL) *'zero'*

Note that 'one' is omitted before 'hundred' and 'thousand':

duizend negenhonderd drie en veertig; negentienhonderd drie en veertig. (DUIzĕnt NEEghĕn-hondĕrt drie-ĕn-VEERtich; NEEghĕntien-hondĕrt drie-ĕn-VEERtich) '1943'

2. Review of Basic Sentences with English Covered

C. What Would You Say?

1. What Would You Say?

1. *You want to take a hot bath.   You tell your landlady:*
  a. dĕ-vĕrWARming-werkt-niet-ghoet.
  b. ik-WOU-ghraach ĕn-WARM-BAT-neemĕn.
  c. ĕt-is-niet-GHOET-voor-uu zoo-WEInich tĕ--BAAdĕn.

De verwarming werkt niet goed.
Ik wou graag een warm bad nemen.
Het is niet goed voor u·zoo weinig te baden.

2. *You want to know if your baggage has arrived.   You ask:*

   a. WEET-uu of-měn-baaGHAAzjě al-HIER-is?   Weet u of mijn bagage al hier is?

   b. uu-moet-měn-baaGHAAzjě DAAdělik naar-   U moet mijn bagage dadelijk naar boven brengen.
      -BOOvěn-brengěn.

   c. měn-baaGHAAzjě komt-met-dě-TREIN van-   Mijn baga·e komt met de trein van vijf uur.
      -VEIV-uur.

3. *You want your breakfast brought at seven o'clock.   You say:*

   a. breng-měn-ont-BEIT als-tuu-BLIEFT om-   Breng mijn ontbijt alstublieft om zeven uur·
      -ZEEvěn-UUR.

   b. om-ZEEvěn-UUR wil-ik-NOOJT EEtěn.   Om zeven uur wil ik nooit eten.

   c. bei-ět-ont-BEIT drink-ik-NOOJT KOFFie.   Bij het ontbijt drink ik nooit koffie.

4. *Someone asks how long you have been living in your present location.   You answer:*

   a. ik-WOON-hier-al TWEE WEEkěn.   .Ik woon hier al twee weken.

   b. DEEzě-KAaměr is-ghoetKOOP.   Deze kamer is goedkoop.

   c. ik-moet-dě-HUUR ALteit voorUIT-bětaalěn.   Ik moet de huur altijd vooruitbetalen.

5. *You and your friend look at a room and you think it isn't clean.   You say to him:*

   a. dě-verWARming WERKT-hier niet-GHOET.   De verwarming werkt hier niet goed.

   b. ět-is-hier-tě-DUUR-voor-ons.   Het is hier te duur voor ons.

   c. ik-vint-dě-KAaměr niet-SCHOON.   Ik vind de kamer niet schoon.

6. *It's been raining for two days already.   You say:*

   a. ět-REEghěnt-hier maar-ZELděn.   Het regent hier maar zelden.

   b. ět-REEghěnt-al TWEE DAAghěn.   Het regent al twee dagen.

   c. ět-REEghěnt VEEL in-ět-NAAjaar.   Het regent veel in het najaar.

7. *Your car is out of order.   You say:*

   a. zoo-ěn-OOtoo is-NIET-ghoetKOOP.   Zoo'n auto is niet goedkoop.

b. dĕ-niewĕ-OOtoo is-in-dĕ-ghaaRAAzjĕ.   De nieuwe auto is in de garage.

c. ik-moet-mĕn-OOtoo laatĕn-reepaaREErĕn.   Ik moet mijn auto laten repareeren.

8. *Your room is number 487.   You tell your friend:*

    a. mĕn-KAAmĕr-is-nummĕr VIER-hondĕrt ACHT-   Mijn kamer is nummer vierhonderd acht en zeventig.
       -ĕn-SEEvĕntich.

    b. mĕn-KAAmĕr-is-nummĕr VIER-hondĕrt SEEvĕn-   Mijn kamer is nummer vierhonderd zeven en tachtig.
       -ĕn-TACHtich.

    c. mĕn-KAAmĕr-is-nummĕr VIER-hondĕrt SEEvĕn-   Mijn kamer is nummer vierhonderd zeven en zestig.
       -ĕn-SEStich.

2. What Did You Say?

D. Listening In

Remember that the first time you listen to these conversations and follow in the book you should follow the Aids to Listening spelling, on the left, rather than the conventional spelling on the right.   In later times though you can concentrate on the conventional spelling.

1. *The Dekkers have trouble with their heating system.*

Mevrouw Dekker:	wat-IS-ĕt-hier KOUT!	Wat is het hier koud!
Dekker:	JAA, IK-heb-ĕt OOK-kout.	Ja, ik heb het ook koud.
Mevrouw Dekker:	OCH, naaTUURlik is-ĕt-KOUT.	Och, natuurlijk is het koud.
	dĕ-vĕrWARming-werkt-niet.	De verwarming werkt niet.
	wei-moetĕn-haar-DAAdĕlik laatĕ- -reepaaREErĕn.	Wij moeten haar dadelijk laten repareeren.

Dekker:	en-wei-MOEtĕn voor-ĕn-DACH-of-twee in-ĕt--hooTEL-ghaan-woonĕn.	En wij moeten voor een dag of twee in het hotel gaan wonen.
Mevrouw Dekker:	maar-DAAR is-ĕt-soo-DUUR. DERtien-ghuldĕ per-DACH, als-wĕ TWEE KAAmĕrs-neemĕn.	Maar daar is het zoo duur. Dertien gulden per dag, als wij twee kamers nemen.
Dekker:	ghoetKOOP is-ĕt-seekĕr-NIET.	Goedkoop is het zeker niet.
	maar-voor-JOU en-voor-PIETJĕ-is-ĕt-HIER--in-huis tĕ-KOUT.	Maar voor jou en Pietje is het hier in huis te koud.
	KOM, maaRIE, LAAtĕn-wĕ naar-ĕt-hooTEL--ghaan.	Kom, Marie, laten we naar het hotel gaan.

2. *Mr. Carver gets a room in a hotel.*

Klerk:	ghoedĕn-DACH-mĕneer.	Goeden dag, mijnheer.
Carver:	ghoeden-DACH, mĕneer.	Goeden dag, mijnheer.
	hept-uu-ĕn-KAAmĕr-voor-mĕ?	Hebt u een kamer voor me?
Klerk:	voor-EEN pĕrSOON?	Voor een persoon?
Mr. Carver:	JAA-mĕneer; ik-ben-aLEEN.	Ja, mijnheer, ik ben alleen.
Klerk:	ik-KAN-uu ĕn-MOOjĕ KAAmĕr-gheevĕn, DRIE--trappĕn HOOCH.	Ik kan u een mooie kamer geven, drie trappen hoog.
Carver:	hoe-veel-KOST dĕ-KAAmĕr?	Hoeveel kost de kamer?
Klerk:	TWEE-ghuldĕn TACHtich per-DACH.	Twee gulden tachtig per dag.
Carver:	en-HOE-veel per-WEEK?	En hoeveel per week?
Klerk:	als-uu-dĕ-KAAmĕr bei-dĕ-WEEK-neemt, is-ĕt--ACHtien FEIFtich.	Als u de kamer bij de week neemt, is het achttien vijftig.
	dat-s-voor-dĕ-WEEK.	Dat's voor de week.

Carver:	wilt-uu-mĕ-dĕ-KAAmĕr laatĕ-ZIEN?	Wilt u mij de kamer laten zien?
Klerk:	JAA heel-GHRAACH.	Ja, heel graag.
	wilt-uu-EEvĕn naar-BOOvĕ-koomĕn?	Wilt u even naar boven komen
	NUU, uu-ZIET-wel-mĕneer, dĕ-KAAmĕr-is-HEEL-mooj en-hĕt-BET is-GHOET.	Nu, u ziet wel, mijnheer, de kamer is heel mooi en het bed is goed.
Carver:	GHOET, ik-neem-dĕ-KAAmĕr voor-ĕn-WEEK.	Goed, ik neem de kamer voor een week.
	WAAR is-dĕ-BAT-kaamĕr?	Waar is de badkamer?
	ik-zou-graach ĕn-warm-BAT willĕn-NEEmĕn.	Ik zou graag een warm bad willen nemen.
Klerk:	dĕ-BAT-kaamĕr is-hier-RECHS an-ĕt-EINT-van-dĕ-GHANG.	De badkamer is hier rechts aan het eind van de gang.
	hept-uu-baaGHAAzjĕ, mĕnEER?	Hebt u bagage, mijnheer?
	als-uu-GHEEN-baaghaazjĕ-hept moet-dĕ-HUUR vooruit bĕTAALT-wordĕ.	Als u geen bagage hebt, moet de huur vooruit betaald worden.
Carver:	mein-baaGHAAzjĕ is-noch-an-ĕt-staaSJON.	Mijn bagage is nog aan het station.
	KUNT-uu-zĕ-voor-mĕ naar-ĕt-hooTEL-laatĕ-brengĕn?	Kunt u ze voor me naar het hotel laten brengen?
Klerk:	jaa-ZEEkĕr, mĕneER.	Ja, zeker, mijnheer.
	uu-baaGHAAzjĕ kom-DAAdĕlik.	Uw bagage komt dadelijk.
	HIER is-uu-SLEUtĕl, mĕNEER, uu-KAAmĕr-sleutĕl.	Hier is uw sleutel, mijnheer, uw kamersleutel.
	uuw-KAAmĕr is-nummĕr-DRIE-hondĕrt VIER en-VEIFtich.	Uw kamer is nummer driehonderd vier en vijftig.

3. Mr. Kuypers tries to locate Mr. Dekker, and comes to the wrong home.

Juffrouw:	ghoedĕn-DACH-mĕneer, wat wilt-uu-HEBBĕn?
	Goeden dag, mijnheer. Wat wilt u hebben?
Kuypers:	ghoeden-DACH-mĕvrou. woont-mĕneer-DEKKĕr HIER?
	Goeden dag, mevrouw. Woont Mijnheer Dekker hier?
Juffrouw:	Nee-mĕneer. DIE woont-hier-NIET.
	Neen, mijnheer. Die woont hier niet.
Kuypers:	nee-mĕ-niet-KWAAlijk-mĕvrou. WEET-uu-waar-mĕneer-DEKKĕr-woont?
	Neem me niet kwalijk, mevrouw. Weet u waar Mijnheer Dekker woont?
Juffrouw:	NEE-mĕneer. ik-KEN gheen-mĕneer-DEKKĕr.
	Neen, mijnheer. Ik ken geen Mijnheer Dekker.
	maar-mein-MAN kent-ĕm-miSCHIEN.
	Maar mijn man kent hem misschien.
	HENDrik!
	Hendrik!
Man:	JAA, wat-IS-ĕr?
	Ja, wat is er?
Juffrouw:	ĕr-is-hier-ĕn-HEER die-GHRAACH-weetĕn-wou waar-mĕneer-DEKKĕr-woont.
	Er is hier een heer, die graag weten wou, waar Mijnheer Dekker woont.
Man:	ALfret DEKKĕr, mĕneer?
	Alfred Dekker, mijnheer?
Kuypers:	JAA-mĕneer.
	Ja, mijnheer.
Man:	DIE-woont in-ĕt-TWEEdĕ-huis hier-LINKS.
	Die woont in het tweede huis hier links.
	nummĕr-ACHtien, EEN-trap HOOCH.
	Nummer achttien, één trap hoog.
Kuypers:	dank-uu-WEL-mĕneer.
	Dank u wel, mijnheer.
Man:	niets-tĕ-DANkĕn-mĕneer.
	Niets te danken, mijnheer.
	DACH-mĕneer!
	Dag, mijnheer!

E. CONVERSATION

1. Review of Basic Sentences with Dutch Covered

2. Vocabulary and Word Study Check-up

3. Carrying on Conversation

More names: Middendorp (MIDDĕndorp); Stolp (STOLP); girl's first name: Elsje (ELsjĕ).

Conversation 1. A speaks to his daughter, B. Later Mrs. A joins the conversation.

A: asks B where the keys to her mother's room are.

B: says she doesn't know; she hasn't seen them.

A: says maybe they're upstairs. He asks B to bring them to him.

B: says very well, she'll go upstairs and bring them to him right away.

A: says thanks.

B: speaks to her mother through the door of Mrs. A's room and asks if she may come in, since her father would like to have the keys to Mrs. A's room.

Mrs. A: says yes. But she doesn't know where the keys are. She has the keys to the garage. She asks B why B doesn't go to Pete's room? Pete will surely have the keys.

B: says yes, but she's in a hurry, since she has to go to the station, since the Stolps are coming at eleven.

Mrs. A: says very well, she herself will take the keys to Father.

B: tells her father that her mother will bring him the keys. She says she has to go to the station to bring the Stolps here.

A: says OK, thanks.

Conversation 2. A (same as the above) meets Mrs. Stolp and her husband.

A: greets Mrs. Stolp and asks if he can show her to her rooms, which are one flight up.

Mrs. Stolp: says all right; they're probably late, since the train was late.

A: says here's your room, and there is the bathroom.

Mrs. Stolp: says oh, this is a lovely room, and everything *so* clean and light! She asks if the heating works well.

Mrs. A: says yes, very well. Now she'll show Mrs. Stolp the bathroom, which is at the end of the hall.

Mr. Stolp: says he'd like to take a hot bath. He asks for the numbers of the rooms.

Mr. A: says they are eight and seven. He asks if the Stolps' baggage has arrived yet.

Mr. Stolp: says yes. He asks if the rent is to be paid in advance.

Mr. A: Says no, and that the price, twenty guilders per week, includes breakfast. He is sure that the Stolps will take the rooms.

Mrs. Stolp: says she thinks so, and that the price is very cheap.

FINDER LIST

The new words are listed here in the conventional Dutch spelling; the pronunciation is given in parentheses.

aan (AAN, unstressed an) 'at, on'
 aan het eind (an-ĕt-EINT) 'at the end'
achttien (ACHtien) 'eighteen'
alles (ALLĕs) 'everything'
ander (ANdĕr) 'other'
 de andere kamer (dĕ-andĕrĕ-KAAmĕr) 'the other room'

het-bad (ĕt-BAT) 'the bath'
 de badkamer (dĕ-BAT-kaamĕr) 'the bathroom'
de bagage (dĕ-baGHAAzjĕ, dĕ-baaGHAAzjĕ) 'the baggage'
het bed (ĕt-BET) 'the bed'
 begrepen see inbegrepen

betalen (bĕTAAlĕn) 'to pay'
 betaald (bĕTAALT) 'paid'
 Het wordt betaald (ĕt-wort-bĕTAALT) 'It gets paid'
binnen (BINNĕn) 'inside'
 Kom binnen (kom-BINNĕn) 'Come in'
boven (BOOvĕn) 'up above, upstairs'
 Hij is boven (hei-iz-BOOvĕn) 'He's upstairs'
 Hij gaat naar boven (hei-ghaat-naar-BOOvĕn) 'He goes upstairs'
brengen (BRENGĕn) 'to bring'

dadelijk (DAAdĕlik) 'right away'
denken (DENkĕn) 'to think'

Ik denk van ja (ik-denk-van-JAA) 'I think so.'
dertien (DERtien) 'thirteen'
dertig (DERtich) 'thirty'
duizend (DUIzĕnt) 'thousand, one thousand'
duur (DUUR) 'dear'

het-eind (ĕt-EINT, ĕt-ENT) 'the end'
even (EEvĕn) 'just, do please'

de-gang (dĕ-GHANG) 'the hallway'
geven (GHEEvĕn) 'to give'
goedkoop (ghoet-KOOP) 'cheap'

honderd (HONdĕrt) 'hundred, one hundred'
hoog (HOOCH) 'high'
het huis (ĕt-HUIS) 'the house'
bij ons in huis (bei-ons-in-HUIS) 'at our house'
de huur (dĕ-HUUR) 'the rent'
te huur (tĕ-HUUR) 'for rent'

inbegrepen (IN-bĕghreepĕn) 'included'

de kamer (dĕ-KAAmĕr) 'the room'
kosten (KOStĕn) 'to cost'

laten (LAAtĕn) 'to let, to allow'
Laat me dat zien (laat-mĕ-dat-ZIEN) 'Show me that'
het licht (ĕt-LICHT) 'the light'

millioen (milJOEN) 'million'
mogen (MOOghĕn) 'to be permitted'
Mag ik? (MACH-ik?) 'May I?'
Hij mag niet (hei-MACH-niet) 'He is not permitted to'

negentien (NEEghĕntien) 'nineteen'
negentig (NEEghĕntich) 'ninety'
nul (NUL) 'zero'
het nummer (ĕt-NUMMĕr) 'the number'
het ontbijt (ĕt-ont-BEIT) 'the breakfast'

per (per, pĕr) 'per'
per dag (per-DACH, pĕr-DACH) 'per day'
de persoon (dĕ-perSOON, dĕ-pĕrSOON) 'the person'

schoon (SCHOON) 'clean'
de sleutel (dĕ-SLEUtĕl) 'the key'

tachtig (TACHtich) 'eighty'
de trap (dĕ-TRAP) 'the stair, the flight of stairs'
tweede (TWEEdĕ) 'second'
twintig (TWINtich) 'twenty'

veertien (VEERtien) 'fourteen'
veertig (FEERtich) 'forty'
de verdieping (dĕ-vĕrDIEping) 'the floor (above the ground floor)'

de verwarming (dĕ-vĕrWARming) 'the heating'
    vijftien (VEIFtien) 'fifteen'
    vijftig (FEIFtich) 'fifty'
    vinden (VINdĕn) 'to find'
  vooruit (voorRUIT) 'ahead, in advance'
    vooruitbetalen (voorRUIT-bĕtaalĕn) 'to pay in advance'

worden (WORdĕn) 'to get'
  Het zal betaald worden (ĕt-zal-bĕTAALT-wordĕn) 'It will be paid'

zestien (ZEStien) 'sixteen'
zestig (SEStich) 'sixty'
zeventien (ZEEvĕntien) 'seventeen'
zeventig (SEEvĕntich) 'seventy'

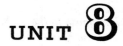
BARBER AND LAUNDRY

A. Basic Sentences

Mr. Enders and Mr. Carver meet on the street and go to the barber together.

ENGLISH EQUIVALENTS	AIDS TO LISTENING	CONVENTIONAL SPELLING

Mr. Enders

| *How d'do, Mr. Carver.* | dach-mĕneer-KAARvĕr. | Dag, Mijnheer Carver. |
| *Fine day today.* | mooj-WEER-van-daach. | Mooi weer vandaag. |

Mr. Carver

| *How are you making out?* | hoe-maakt-UU-ĕt? | Hoe maakt u het? |

Mr. Enders

| *Very well, thanks.* | heel-GHOET, dank-uu-WEL. | Heel goed, dank u wel. |
| *Where are you bound for?* | waar-ghaat-UU-naar-toe? | Waar gaat u naartoe? |

Mr. Carver

I'm going to the barber's.	IK ghaa-naar-dĕ-KAPPĕr.	Ik ga naar de kapper.
the hair	hĕt-HAAR	het haar
to cut	KNIPPĕm	knippen
I have to get a hair cut.	ik-moet-mĕn-HAAR laatĕn-KNIPPĕn.	Ik moet mijn haar laten knippen.

Mr. Enders

along	MEE	mee
Then can I go along with you?	mach-IK-dan met-uu-MEE?	Mag ik dan met u mee?
You see, I have to go to the barber's too.	IK moet-immĕrs-OOK naar-dĕ-KAPPĕr.	Ik moet immers ook naar de kapper.
to shave	SCHEErĕn	scheren
I have to get a shave.	ik-moet-mĕ-laatĕn-SCHEErĕn.	Ik moet me laten scheren.

Mr. Carver

together	SAAmĕn	samen
Fine; then we'll go together.	GHOET; dan-GHAAN-wĕ-ĕr SAAmĕn naar-TOE.	Goed; dan gaan we er samen naar-toe.

Barber

Good morning, gentlemen.	ghoedĕ-MORghĕn-heerĕn.	Goden morgen, heeren.
to sit	ZITTĕn	zitten

Just be seated, please.	ghaat-uu-eevĕ-ZITTĕn als-t-uu--BLIEFT.	Gaat u even zitten, alstublieft.
the turn	dĕ-BEURT	de beurt
Your turn will come right away.	uu-komt-DAAdĕlik an-dĕ-BEURT.	U komt dadelijk aan de beurt.

Mr. Enders

I can't shave myself.	ik-KAN-mĕ-nie-SCHEErĕn.	Ik kan me niet scheren.
to cut	SNEIdĕn	snijden
I always cut myself.	ik-SNEIT-mĕ-alteit.	Ik snijd me altijd.

Mr. Carver

the knife	hĕt-MES	het mes
the razor	hĕt-SCHEER-mes	het scheermes
sharp	SCHERP	scherp
enough	ghĕNOEGH	genoeg
Maybe your razor isn't good.	miSCHIEN is-uuw-SCHEER-mes--niet-ghoet.	Misschien is uw scheermes niet goed.
Or the blades aren't sharp enough.	ov-dĕ-SHEER-mesjĕs zein-niet--SCHERP-ghĕnoech.	Of de scheermesjes zijn niet scherp genoeg.
When I use a new blade, I can always get a good shave.	als-ik-ĕ-niew-SCHEER-mesjĕ--neem, kan-ik-mĕ-ALteit ghoet--SCHEErĕn.	Als ik een nieuw scheermesje neem, kan ik me altijd goed scheren.
I practically never cut myself.	ik-SNEIT-mĕ maar-ZELdĕn.	Ik snijd me maar zelden.

| first | EERST | eerst |
| Who comes first, gentlemen? | wie-komt-EERST, HEErĕn? | Wie komt eerst, heeren? |

Mr. Enders

You go first, Mr. Carver.	ghaat-uu-maar-EERST, mĕneer-KAARvĕr.	Gaat u maar eerst, Mijnheer Carver.
to last	DUUrĕn	duren
long	LANG	lang
then	DAN	dan
The hair cut will probably take longer than the shave.	HAAR-knippĕn zal-wel-LANGĕr-duurĕn dan-SCHEErĕn.	Haarknippen zal wel langer duren dan scheren.

Mr. Carver

| Haircut, please. | HAAR-knippĕn, als-t-uu-BLIEFT. | Haar knippen, alstublieft. |

Barber

| cut | ghĕKNIPT | geknipt |
| How do you want it cut, sir? | hoe-WILT-uu-ĕt-ghĕKNIPT heb-bĕn, mĕNEER? | Hoe wilt u het geknipt hebben, mijnheer? |

142   [8–A]

Mr. Carver

short	KORT	kort
behind	ACHtĕr	achter
the side	dĕ ZEI	de zij
at the side	op-ZEI	op zij
in front	VOOR	voor
Make it not too short in back and at the sides.	maak-ĕt-niet-tĕ-kort-van-ACHtĕr `en-op-SEI.	Maak het niet te kort van achteren en op zij.
And a little longer in front.	en-van-VOORĕn ĕn-beetjĕ-LANGĕr.	En van voren een beetje langer.

Second Barber

And you sir?	en-UU, mĕNEER?	En u, mijnheer?
the service	dĕ-DIENST	de dienst
What can I do for you?	wat-is-ĕr-van-UU-dienst?	Wat is er van uw dienst?

Mr. Enders

A shave, please.	WILT-uu-mĕ als-t-uu-blieft- -SCHEErĕn?	Wilt u me alstublieft scheren?

Mr. Carver

done or *ready*	KLAAR	klaar
Are you ready, Mr. Enders?	bent-uu-al-KLAAR, mĕneer- -ENdĕrs?	Bent u al klaar, Mijnheer Enders?

Mr. Enders

Yes, I'm ready.	JAA, ik-ben-KLAAR.	Ja, ik ben klaar.
the things	ĕt-GHOET	het goed
to wash	WASSĕn	wasschen
the laundry	dĕ-wassĕREI	de wasscherij
But I still have to take my things to the laundry.	maar-ik-moet-mein-GHOET noch--naar-dĕ-wassĕREI brengĕn.	Maar ik moet mijn goed nog naar de wasscherij brengen.

Mr. Carver

Is there a good laundry here?	is-hier-ĕn-ghoedĕ-wassĕREI?	Is hier een goede wasscherij?

Mr. Enders

bad	SLECHT	slecht
No, it's bad and expensive.	NEE, zĕ-is-SLECHT en-DUUR.	Neen, ze is slecht en duur.
sick	ZIEK	ziek
so	DUS	dus
I have a good laundress, but she's sick now.	ik-heb-ĕn-GHOEdĕ WAS-frou, maar-die-is-nuu-ZIEK.	Ik heb en goede waschvrouw, maar die is nu ziek.
And so I have to get my washing done at the laundry.	en-dus-MOET-ik mein-WAS-ghoet in-dĕ-wassĕREI-gheevĕn.	En dus moet ik mijn waschgoed in de wasscherij geven.

144   [8–A]

the tailor	dĕ-KLEER-maakĕr	de kleermaker
the suit of clothes	hĕt-PAK	het pak
to press	PERsĕn	persen
And I have to go to the tailors.	en-IK moet-naar-dĕ-KLEER--maakĕr.	En ik moet **naar** de kleermaker.
I have· a suit cleaned and pressed.	ik-moet-ĕn-PAK laatĕn-SCHOON--maakĕn en-PERsĕn.	Ik moet een pak laten schoonmaken en persen.

Mr. Enders

the café	hĕt-kaaFEE	het café
the glass	hĕt-GHLAS	het glas
the cup	dĕ-KOP	de kop
But let's go to a café first and have a cup of coffee or a glass of beer.	laatĕn-wĕ-EERST-eevĕn naar-ĕn--kaaFEE-ghaan en-ĕn-ghlas-BIER ov-ĕ-kop-KOFFie-drinkĕn.	Laten we-eerst even naar een **café** gaan en een **glas** bier of een **kop** koffie drinken.

Mr. Carver

Yes, let's.	JAA, heel-GHRAACH.	Ja, heel graag.

B. Word Study

1. Word Study

Point 1. Different Words in English and Dutch.
If we tried to translate word by word from one language to the other, we should often get nonsense. Notice the following Dutch ways of saying things:

Hoe maakt u het? (hoe-MAAKT-uu-ět?) 'How make you it?' for *'How are you getting along?'*

Waar gaat u naartoe? (waar-ghaat-uu-naar-TOE?) literally something like 'Where go you to thither?' for *'Where are you going to?'*

Ga zitten. 'Go sit.' for *'Sit down.'*

Hij komt aan de beurt. (hei-komt-an-dě-BEURT.) 'He comes to the turn.' for *'It's his turn.'*

Wat is er van uw dienst? (wat-is-ěr-van-uu- -DIENST?) 'What is there of your service?' for *'What can I do for you?'*

Where we say *cut* the Dutch use several different words. The most general word is *snijden* (*SNEIděn*), but for cutting hair they say *knippen*.

The expressions *het goed* (*ět-GHOET*) 'goods' is used of things in general, and especially of cloth (like 'goods' in English) and still more especially of cloth goods ('linen') to be washed. For this last meaning they also say *waschgoed* (*WAS-ghoet*) 'things for the wash'.

Point 2. Me; Myself. In English we distinguish: if someone else cuts a person, the person says 'He cuts *me*', but if the person does it himself he says 'I cut *myself*'. In Dutch this distinction is not made:

Hij snijdt me.	(hei-SNEIT-mě.)	*'He cuts me.'*
Hij scheert me.	(hei-SCHEERT-mě.)	*'He shaves me.'*
Hij wascht me.	(hei-WAST-mě.)	*'He washes me.'*
Ik snijd me.	(ik-SNEIT-mě.)	*'I cut myself.'*
Ik scheer me.	(ik-SCHEER-mě.)	*'I shave (myself).'*
Ik wasch me.	(ik-WAS-mě.)	*'I wash (myself).'*

However, there is a special word *zich* for 'himself, herself, itself, themselves' when someone is doing something to himself. So there is a distinction here:

Hij snijdt haar.	(hei-SNEIT-ĕr.)	*'He cuts her.'*
Hij scheert hem.	(hei-SCHEERT-ĕm.)	*'He shaves him.*
Zij wascht ze.	(zĕ-WAST-sĕ.)	*'She washes them.'*
Zij snijdt zich.	(zĕ-SNEIT-sich.)	*'She cuts herself.'*
Hij scheert zich.	(hei-SCHEERT-sich.)	*'He shaves (himself).'*
Zij wasschen zich.	(zĕ-WASSĕn-zich.)	*'They wash (themselves).'*

Point 3. The Haircut. Verbs (in Form 1) are used as *dat*-nouns; mostly they have the word *het* before them:

Het leven is kort.	(ĕt-LEEvĕn is-KORT.)	*'Life is short.'*
Het scheren kost vijftig cent.	(ĕt-SCHEErĕn kost-FEIFtich SENT.)	*'A shave costs fifty cents.'*
Het haarknippen kost één gulden veertig.	(ĕt-HAAR-knippĕn kost-EEN--ghuldĕn FEERtich.)	*'A haircut costs one guilder forty.'*

Point 4. Razor; Blade. Notice the use of the diminutive ending *-jĕ*:

het mes : messen	(ĕt-MES : MESSĕn)	*'the knife : knives'*
het mesje : mesjes	(ĕt-MESjĕ : MESjĕs)	*'the little knife : little knives'*
het scheermes : scheermessen	(ĕt-SCHEER-mes : SCHEER--messĕn)	*'the razor : razors'*
het scheermesje : scheermesjes	(ĕt-SCHEER-mesjĕ : SCHEER--mesjĕs)	*'the razor-blade : razor-blades'*

Point 5. Cup of Coffee. Notice that the Dutch say 'a cup coffee' without using any word like our 'of':

een kop koffie	(ĕn-kop-KOFFie)	*'a cup of coffee'*
een glas water	(ĕn-ghlas-WAAtĕr)	*'a glass of water'*
een flesch wijn	(ĕn-fles-WEIN)	*'a bottle of wine'*

Point 6. GHOET : GHOEjĕ. You have seen that when the sound *d* comes to stand at the end of a Dutch word it is replaced by *t*:

handen (HANdĕn)	*'hands'*
de hand (dĕ-HANT)	*'the hand'*

Between vowels the sound *d* is often replaced by the sound *j*. In careful speech the *d* is kept. In this way one gets *d*, *t*, and *j* in different forms of the same word:

Hij is goed.	(hei-is-GHOET)	*'He is good.'*
een goede man	(ĕn-ghoedĕ-MAN, ĕn-ghoejĕ-MAN)	*'a good man'*

If the diphthong *ou* precedes, the *d* is replaced by *w* instead of *j*:

't Is koud.	(t-is-KOUT)	*'It's cold.'*
een koude dag	(ĕn-koudĕ-DACH, ĕn-kouwĕ-DACH)	*'a cold day'*

In some words the *d* drops out altogether:

de koude, de kou	(dĕ-KOUdĕ, dĕ-KOU)	*'the cold'*

Point 7. Adjectives, the describing and modifying words that come before nouns, add the ending -*ĕ* when the noun is a *die*-noun, including all nouns in the plural:

een groote stad	(ĕn-ghrootĕ-STAT)	*'a big city'*
groote steden	(ghrootĕ-STEEdĕn)	*'big cities'*
groote huizen	(ghrootĕ-HUIzĕn)	*'big houses'*

When the noun is a *dat*-noun, the adjective takes -*ĕ* whenever the word *het, dat,* or *dit* precedes, but otherwise takes no ending:

het groote huis	(ĕt-ghrootĕ-HUIS)	*'the big house'*
dat groote huis	(dat-ghrootĕ-HUIS)	*'that big house'*
dit groote huis	(dit-ghrootĕ-HUIS)	*'this big house'*
een groot huis	(ĕn-ghroot-HUIS)	*'a big house'*
het mooie weer	(ĕt-moojĕ-WEER)	*'the fine weather'*
mooi weer	(mooj-WEER)	*'fine weather'*

There are many special combinations which are not covered by the two statements given above:

een groot man	(ĕn-ghroot-MAN)	*'a great man'*
een groote man	(ĕn-ghrootĕ-MAN)	*'a tall man, a big man'*

Sometimes, when the words are long, the -*ĕ* is left off some of the time:

een amerikaansch matroos	(ĕn-ameeriekaans-maTROOS)	*'an American sailor'*

or:

een amerikaansche matroos	(ĕn-ameeriekaansĕ-maTROOS)	. *'an American sailor'*

Some adjectives ending in -*ĕn* never add an -*ĕ*, no matter how they are used; in rapid speech the *n* of -*ĕn* may drop:

een stalen mes	(ĕn-staalĕn-MES)	*'a steel knife'*

The possessive *onze, ons* goes like other adjectives:

onze stad	(onzĕ-STAT)	*'our city'*
onze huizen	(onzĕ-HUIzĕn)	*'our houses'*
ons huis	(ons-HUIS)	*'our house'*

But the other possessives do not take the -ĕ:

haar man	(haar-MAN)	*'her husband'*
haar kinderen	(haar-KINdĕrĕn)	*'her children'*
haar huis	(haar-HUIS)	*'her house'*

This is true of *mijn* 'my', *zijn* 'his', *haar* 'her', *uw* 'your', *jouw, je* 'your', *hun* 'their'.

Other adjectives which do not take the ending -ĕ are *een* (ĕn) 'a, an', *geen* 'no', *veel* 'much, many', *weinig* 'little, few', and all the numbers *ĕĕn, twee, drie*, and so on.

If no noun follows, there are two uses of adjectives.

No ending is added in expressions like 'is good', 'gets cold':

De koffie is goed.	(dĕ-KOFFie is-GHOET.)	*'The coffee is good.'*
De koffie wordt koud.	(dĕ-KOFFie wort-KOUT.)	*'The coffee is getting cold.'*

On the other hand, in many expressions when an adjective is used without a noun, especially after *het, de*, the adjective takes the ending -ĕ or -ĕn:

Ons huis is grooter dan het hunne.	(ONS-huis is-GHROOtĕr dan-ĕt--HUNNĕ.)	*'Our house is bigger than theirs.'*
't Is bij vijven.	(t-is-bei-VEIvĕn.)	*'It's about five (o'clock).'*
't Is bij eenen.	(t-is-bei-EEnĕn.)	*'It's about one (o'clock).'*

2. Review of Basic Sentences with English Covered

C. What Would You Say?

1. What Would You Say?

1. *The barber asks what you want done. You want a haircut, so you say:*
   a. HAAR-knippĕn, als-t-uu-BLIEFT.   Haarknippen, alstublieft.

b. wilt-uu-měn-HAAR-wassěn?   Wilt u mijn haar wasschen?

c. wilt-uu-mě als-t-uu-blieft-SCHEErěn?   Wilt u me alstublieft scheren?

2. *The laundress comes to your door.*   *You point to your bag of dirty linen and say:*

     a. kunt-uu-měn-GHOET naar-BOOvěn-brengěn?   Kunt u mijn goed naar boven brengen?

     b. kunt-uu-dit-GHOET voor-mě-WASSěn?   Kunt u dit goed voor mij wasschen?

     c. kunt-uu-mě-WASSěn, jěFROU?   Kunt u mij wasschen, juffrouw?

3. *You want razor blades.*   *You say to the salesman:*

     a. ik-SOU-ghraach ěn-SCHEERmes-willěn-hebběn.   Ik zou graag een scheermes willen hebben.

     b. ik-SOU-ghraach SCHEERmesjěs-willěn-hebběn.   Ik zou graag scheermesjes willen hebben.

     c. ik-wil-GHEEN SCHEERmesjěs-hebběn.   Ik wil geen scheermesjes hebben.

4. *You want a cup of coffee.*   *You say to the waiter:*

     a. GHEEF-mě ěn-ghlas-WAAtěr als-t-uu-BLIEFT.   Geef me een glas water, alstublieft.

     b. GHEEF-mě ěn-ghlas-BIER als-t-uu-BLIEFT.   Geef me een glas bier, alstublieft.

     c. GHEEF-mě ěn-kop-KOFFie als-t-uu-BLIEFT.   Geef me een kop koffie, alstublieft.

5. *You want a suit pressed.*   *You tell the tailor:*

     a. hoe-veel-KOST zoo-ěn-PAK?   Hoeveel kost zoo'n pak?

     b. wil-uu-dit-PAK voor-mě-SCHOON-maakěn?   Wilt u dit pak voor me schoonmaken?

     c. wilt-uu-dit-PAK voor-mě-PERsěn?   Wilt u dit pak voor me persen?

6. *You want your breakfast brought at seven o'clock.*   *You say:*

     a. ik-drink-ALteit MELK bei-ět-ontBEIT.   Ik drink altijd melk bij het ontbijt.

     b. ZEEvěn-UUR is-tě-LAAT voor-ět-ontBEIT.   Zeven uur is te laat voor het ontbijt.

     c. breng-ět-ontBEIT om-ZEEvěn-UUR, als-t-uu-
       -BLIEFT.   Breng het ontbijt om zeven uur, alstublieft.

7. *You've lost your room key.*   *You say:*

     a. ik-WEET-niet waar-měn SLEUtěl-is.   Ik weet niet waar mijn sleutel is.

b. ĕt-sal-noch-LANG DUUrĕn.   Het zal nog lang duren.

c. waNEER kom-ik-an-dĕ-BEURT?   Wanneer kom ik aan de beurt?

8. *The barber asks you to sit down and wait.*   *You have only a certain amount of time, so you ask:*

a. is-ĕt-HAAR-knippĕn hier-DUUR?   Is het haarknippen hier duur?

b. hoe-LANG zal-ĕt-noch-DUUrĕn?   Hoe lang zal het nog duren?

c. mĕn-HAAR is-ERCH LANG.   Mijn haar is erg lang.

9. *Your friend comes to fetch you.*   *You have to shave and wash before you go out.*   *You say:*

a. EERST moet-ik-mĕ-noch-SCHEErĕn en-WASSĕn.   Eerst moet ik me nog scheren en wasschen.

b. EERST-ghaa-ik-noch ĕn-BAT-neemĕn.   Eerst ga ik nog een bad nemen.

c. VOOR-ik-naar-ĕt-kaaFEE-ghaa,   moet-ik-noch--mĕn-PAK-laatĕn-persĕn.   Voor ik naar het café ga, moet ik nog mijn pak laten persen.

2. What Did You Say?

D. Listening In

1. *Mr. Carver is at the tailors.*

de kleermaker: ghoedĕn-DACH-mĕneer.   wat-is-ĕr-van-uu--DIENST?   Goden dag, mijnheer. Wat is er van uw dienst?

Mr. Carver: kunt-uu-dit-PAK   foor-mĕ-reepaaREErĕn en--dan-PERsĕn?   Kunt u dit pak voor me repareeren en dan persen?

de kleermaker: jaa-ZEEkĕr-mĕneer.   Ja zeker, mijnheer.

laat-me-eens-ZIEN wat-ĕr-aan-tĕ DOEN-is.   Laat me eens zien wat er aan te doen is.

zal-ik-ĕt-OOK voor-uu-SCHOON-maakĕn?   Zal ik het ook voor u schoonmaken?

Mr. Carver:	NEE, ik-deNK dat-ět-noch-SCHOON ghě--NOECH-is.	Nee, ik denk dat het nog schoon genoeg is.
de kleermaker:	GHOET-měneer.	Goed, mijnheer.
	en-WANNeer wilt-uu-ět-HEBBěn?	En wanneer wilt u het hebben?
Mr. Carver:	kunt-uu-hět-om-DRIE-uur voor-mě-KLAAR--hebběn?	Kunt u het om drie uur voor me klaar hebben?
de kleermaker:	NEE-měneer.	Nee, mijnheer.
	om-DRIE-uur zal-ět-noch-NIET KLAAR-zein.	Om drie uur zal het nog niet klaar zijn.
	hět-zal-WEL ěn-beetjě-LANGěr-duurěn.	Het zal wel een beetje langer duren.
	maar-van-AAvěnt om-zes-UUR kan-ik-ět--ZEEkěr voor-uu-KLAAR-hebběn.	Maar vanavond om zes uur kan ik het zeker voor u klaar hebben.
Mr. Carver:	JAA, GHOET.	Ja, goed.
	maar-prěSIES om-ZES-uur?	Maar precies om zes uur?
de kleermaker:	JAA-měneer. om-ZEZ-uur zal-ět-ZEEkěr KLAAR-zein.	Ja, mijnheer. Om zes uur zal het zeker klaar zijn.
	als-ik-ět-SECH, dan-zal-ět-ook-ZEEkěr KLAAR--zein.	Als ik het zeg, dan zal het ook zeker klaar zijn.
Mr. Carver:	hoeveel-KOST-et?	Hoeveel kost het?
de kleermaker:	voor-hět-reepaaREErěn TWEE-ghulděn veiv--ěn-SEEvěntich.	Voor het repareeren twee gulden vijf en zeventig.
	en-voor-hět-PERsěn TWEE-ghulděn FEIF-tich.	En voor het persen twee gulden vijftig.
	dat-is-SAAměn VEIF-ghulděn veiv-ěn-TWIN--tich.	Dat is samen vijf gulden vijf en twintig.
Mr. Carver:	wilt-uu-hět-fooRUIT-bětaalt-hebběn?	Wilt u het vooruitbetaald hebben?
de kleermaker:	NEE-měneer. uu-kunt-ět-fan-AAvěnt bětAAlěn.	Nee, mijnheer. U kunt het vanavond betalen.

Mr. Carver:	GHOET.	Goed.
	ik-KOM-dus om-ZEZ-uur prĕSIES.　tot-ZIENS.	Ik kom dus om zes uur precies.　Tot ziens.
de kleermaker:	dank-uu-WEL-mĕneer.	Dank u wel, mijnheer.
	tot-fan-AAvĕnt, mĕnEER.	Tot vanavond, mijnheer.

2. *Charles Petersen wants to buy a new suit.*

Karel:	ik-moet-ĕ-niew-PAK-hebbĕn.	Ik moet een nieuw pak hebben.
	wat-DENK-jĕ, HERman?	Wat denk je, Herman?
	zal-ik-bei-dĕ-KLEER-maakĕr　ĕn-niew-PAK　laatĕn- -maakĕn?	Zal ik bij de kleermaker een nieuw pak laten maken?
Herman:	hoe-veel-KOST-dat NUU?	Hoeveel kost dat nu?
Karel:	voor-ĕn-PAK wil-hei-HONdĕrt-GHULdĕn-hebbĕn.	Voor een pak wil hij honderd gulden hebben.
Herman:	ALLĕs wort-nuu-DUURdĕr en-DUURdĕr.	Alles wordt nu duurder en duurder.
	HEP-jĕ-wel hondĕrt-GHULdĕn?	Heb je wel honderd gulden?
Karel:	NEEN-broer, die-HEB-ik immĕrs-NIET.	Neen, broer, die heb ik immers niet.
	ik-hep-aLEEN-maar FEERtich-ghuldĕn.	Ik heb alleen maar veertig gulden.
Herman:	dan-KUN-jĕ-immĕrs gheen-PAK-laatĕn-maakĕn.	Dan kun je immers geen pak laten maken.
	maar-kĕ-KUNT-wel naar-dĕ-KLEErĕ-winkĕl-ghaan.	Maar je kunt wel naar de kleerenwinkel gaan.
	DAAR is-ĕt-ghoetKOOpĕr.	Daar is het goedkooper.
Karel:	JAA, dat-ZAL-ik dan-ook-maar-DOEN.	Ja, dat zal ik dan ook maar doen.

3. *Mr. Bell asks Mr. van Dam about laundry.*

Bell: is-ĕr-ĕn-ghoedĕ-wassĕREI hier-in-dĕ-STAT?

van Dam: NEE. ĕr-is-ĕn-wassĕREI, maar-zĕ-is-DUUR en--SLECHT.

Bell: wat-kan-ik-DAN met-mĕn-WASchoet-DOEN?

van Dam: ik-KEN-hier ĕn-HEEL-ghoedĕ WASfrou.
als-zĕ-van-DAACH bei-mĕ-in-HUIS-komt,
zal-ik-haar-ZEGHĕn dat-zĕ-BEI-uu in-ĕt-hooTEL--moet-koomĕn.

Bell: dank-uu-WEL, mĕneer-van-DAM.
hoe-lang-zou-ĕt-DUUrĕn als-zĕ-hĕt-GHOET-wast?

van Dam: DAT kan-ik-niet-prĕsies-ZEGHĕn.
DIKwĕls-duurt-ĕt-ĕn-WEEK, maar-ZELdĕn LANGĕr.

is-DAT-miSCHIEN tĕ-LANG-voor-uu?

Bell: ZEEkĕr NIET.
als-ĕt-maar-ĕn-WEEK DUURT, is-ĕt-GHOET.

Is er een goede wasscherij hier in de stad?

Nee. Er is een wasscherij, maar ze is duur en slecht.

Wat kan ik dan met mijn waschgoed doen?

Ik ken hier een heel goede waschvrouw.
Als ze vandaag bij mij in huis komt,
zal ik haar zeggen dat ze bij u in het hotel moet komen.

Dank u wel, Mijnheer van Dam.
Hoe lang zou het duren als ze het goed wascht?

Dat kan ik niet precies zeggen.
Dikwijls duurt het een week, maar zelden langer.

Is dat misschien te lang voor u?

Zeker niet.
Als het maar een week duurt, is het goed.

E. Conversation

1. Review of Basic Sentences with Dutch Covered

2. Vocabulary and Word Study Check-up

3. Carrying on Conversation

Conversation 1. Mr. van der Poel (van-dĕr-POEL) (A) is talking with his son Jan, whom he calls Jantje (JANTjĕ):

A: tells his son to show him his hair. He says he thinks it is too long. Jan has to go to the barber. A wants to go too, because he needs a shave.

Jan: asks his father if he can't go there too.

A: says fine. But why doesn't Jan go first? A will be coming along right away.

Jan: says all right, father. He'll see A at the barber's.

Conversation 2. Jan speaks to the barber (C):

Jan: says good morning.

C: asks how Jan is (he already knows the boy). He asks if Jan wants a haircut.

Jan: says sure.

C: says fine day today. But for him it isn't warm enough yet.

Jan: says please to make his hair short in front.

C: asks about the sides.

Jan: says as always, not too long. He asks if the haircut will take much time. He tells the barber that his father will be coming soon for a shave.

C: says it won't take long; Jan's turn is right now. Jan will be done at 10 o'clock.

Conversation 3. Mr. de Ruiter (dĕ-RUItĕr) (A) speaks to B, his wife.

A: says he has a lot of stuff for the laundry. He addresses his wife as Bertha (BERtaa). He asks his wife if he should take the stuff to the laundry.

B: says yes please. Leentje (LEENtjĕ) is sick and she has enough to keep her busy at home.

A: says fine. He says he also has to go to the tailor to get his suit pressed and cleaned. But it isn't late yet, and he'd like a cup of coffee first.

B: says very well, here it is. (Later.) She says are you ready now?

A: says yes, he'll go right away.

Conversation 4. Mr. de Ruiter enters the laundry and speaks to the laundress (C):

A: says good morning.

C: asks him how he is. She says bad weather today.

A: says yes, very bad.

C: asks what she can do for A.

A: asks her if she will please wash these things for him. He asks when they will be ready.

C: says late tonight. She says she sees that A has a suit for the tailor too. She offers to take it to him. She asks if he wants it pressed and cleaned.

A: says yes, and thanks. It will give him time to go to the barber. As C knows, A can't shave himself. His razor isn't sharp enough and he always cuts himself.

C: asks him why he doesn't use some new blades.

FINDER LIST

The words in the Finder Lists from now on are given in conventional Dutch spelling. The pronunciation is given only when the conventional spelling fails to show it. When the pronunciation is not indicated, the conventional spelling is to be interpreted as follows:

The stress is on the first syllable: *knippen* is pronounced *KNIPPĕn*.

A single vowel letter in the first syllable, followed by a single consonant letter plus a vowel letter, means that the first vowel is long: *nemen* is pronounced *NEEmĕn*.

The combination *ij* is pronounced *ei*: *wijn* is pronounced *WEIN*.

Unstressed *e* is pronounced *ĕ*: *mesje* is pronounced *MESjĕ*.

The letter *g* means *gh*: *geven* is pronounced *GHEEvĕn*. But at the end of a word the letter *g* means *ch*: *dag* is pronounced *DACH*.

At the end of a word, *b* means *p*: *heb* is pronounced *HEP*.

At the end of a word, *d* means *t*: *hand* is pronounced *HANT*.

A word pronounced with an initial *k* may be a French word taken into Dutch with the French spelling, which would use a *c*. If you don't find such a word listed in the *k*'s, be sure to look in the *c*'s.

achter 'behind, in back'
 van achteren 'in back'

de beurt 'the turn'

 Hij komt aan de beurt. 'It's his turn.'
het café (kaFEE, kaaFEE) 'the café, the coffee house'

 dan 'than'
 grooter dan ik 'taller than I'
de dienst 'the service'
 Wat is er van Uw dienst? 'What can I do for you?'
 duren 'to last, to take time'
 Het zal niet lang duren. 'It won't take long.'
 dus 'thus, so'

eerst 'first'
geknipt (ghĕKNIPT) see knippen
genoeg (ghĕNOECH) 'enough'
het glas 'the glass'
het goed 'the goods, the things'

het haar 'the hair'
 het haarknippen 'the haircut'
 klaar 'ready, done'
de kleermaker 'the tailor'

knippen 'to cut' (hair)
 geknipt (ghĕKNIPT) 'cut'
 Hij heeft mijn haar geknipt. 'He has cut my hair.'
de kop 'the cup'
kort 'short'

lang 'long'

mee 'along'
 Gaat U mee? 'Are you going along?'
het mes 'the knife'

 het mesje 'the little knife'
het pak 'the suit of clothes'
persen 'to press'

samen 'together'
scheren 'to shave'
 het scheermes (SCHEER-mes) 'the razor'
 het scheermesje (SCHEER-mesjĕ) 'the razor blade'
scherp 'sharp'
slecht 'bad'
snijden 'to cut'

voor 'in front, ahead, before'
 van voren 'in front'

wasschen (WASSĕn) 'to wash'
de wasscherij (wassĕREI) 'the laundry'
het waschgoed (WAS-ghoet) 'the things for
washing'
de waschvrouw (WAS-frou) 'the laundress'

ziek 'sick'
de zij, de zijde 'the side'
op zij 'at the side'
zitten 'to sit'
Ze gaat zitten.   'She sits down.'

EATING

A. Basic Sentences

Mr. de Jong and Mr. Carver go to dinner together.

ENGLISH EQUIVALENTS	AIDS TO LISTENING	CONVENTIONAL SPELLING
	de Jong	
afternoon	dĕ-MIDDach	de middag
eaten	ghĕGHEEtĕn	gegeten
Have you had your dinner yet?	HEPT-uu-al MIDDach- -ghĕgheetĕn?	Hebt u al middag gegeten?
	Carver	
the hunger	dĕ-HONGĕr	de honger
No, not yet; and I'm hungry too.	NEE, noch-NIET; en-ik-heb- -OOK-al HONGĕr.	Nee, nog niet; en ik heb ook al honger.
What time is it?	hoe-LAAT-is-ĕt?	Hoe laat is het?

drunk	ghĕDRONkĕn	gedronken
It's already seven o'clock, and I ate lunch at twelve.	hĕt-is-al-ZEEvĕn UUR, en-ik-hep- -om-TWAALF-uur KOFFie- -ghĕdronkĕn.	Het is al zeven uur, en ik heb om twaalf uur koffie gedronken.
the time	dĕ-TEIT	de tijd
I think it's time to eat.	ik-DENK dat-ĕt-TEIT-is om-tĕ- -EEtĕn.	Ik denk dat het tijd is om te eten.

Carver

Shall we eat here in the hotel, then?	zullĕn-wĕ-dan-HIER in-ĕt- -hooTEL-eetĕn?	Zullen we dan hier in het hotel eten?
It's a litt e expensive, but the food is always good.	ĕt-is-ĕn-beetjĕ-DUUR, maar-ĕt- -EEtĕn is-alteit-GHOET.	Het is een beetje duur, maar het eten is altijd goed.

de Jong

Yes, let's eat here. (they enter the restaurant)	JAA, laatĕn-wĕ-HIER EEtĕn.	Ja, laten we hier eten.

Waiter

Two (persons)?	TWEE pĕrSOOnĕ?	Twee personen?
the table	dĕ-TAAfĕl	de tafel
Here's a good table for two (persons).	hier-is-ĕn-GHOEdĕ-taafĕl voor- -twee-pĕrSOOnĕn.	Hier is een goede tafel voor twee personen.

to use	ghĕBRUIkĕn	gebruiken
What'll you have, gentlemen?	wat-wilt-uu-ghĕBRUIkĕn, HEErĕn?	Wat wilt u gebruiken, heeren?
the plate	hĕt-BORT	het bord
the soup	dĕ-SOEP	de soep
Do you want to start with (a plate of) soup?	wilt-uu-bĕGHINNĕn met-ĕn-bort-SOEP?	Wilt u beginnen met en bord soep?

Carver

Yes, let's have some soup.	JAA, LAAtĕn-wĕ wat-SOEP-neemĕn.	Ja, laten we wat soep nemen.
the fish	dĕ-VIS	de visch
What sort of fish have you today?	wat-voor-VIS HEPT-uu van-DAACH?	Wat voor visch hebt u vandaag?

Waiter

We haven't any fish today.	wĕ-HEBBĕn-van-daach GHEEN VIS.	Wij hebben vandaag geen visch.

Carver

What kind of meat have you?	wat-voor-VLEES-hept-uu?	Wat voor vleesch hebt u?

162   [9–A]

the head of cattle	hĕt-RUNT	het rund
the pig	hĕt-VARkĕn	het varken
the steak	dĕ-BIEF-stuk	de biefstuk
roast	ghĕBRAAdĕn	gebraden
the chicken	dĕ-KIP	de kip
We have beef, pork, steak, and roast chicken.	wĕ-hebbĕn-RUNT-vlees, VARkĕns--vlees, BIEF-stuk, en-ghĕbraadĕn--KIP.	Wij hebben rundvleesch, varkens-vleesch, biefstuk, en gebraden kip.

de Jong

Give me roast chicken.	GHEEF-mĕ ghĕbraadĕn-KIP.	Geef me gebraden kip.

Waiter

And potatoes with the chicken?	en-AARappĕlĕn bei-dĕ-KIP?	En aardappelen bij de kip?

de Jong

Yes, please.	JAA, als-t-uu-BLIEFT.	Ja, als 't u blieft.
green	GHROEN	groen
the vegetable	dĕ-GHROENtĕ	de groente
What kind of vegetables is there this evening?	wat-voor-GHROENTĕ IS-ĕr-van--aavĕnt?	Wat voor groente is er vanavond?

Waiter

the pea	dĕ-ERT	de erwt
the carrot	dĕ-WORtĕl	de wortel
the bean	dĕ-BOON	de boon
the lettuce or (*the*) *salad*	dĕ-SLAA	de sla
There are peas, carrots, beans, and salad.	ĕr-zein-ERTjĕs, WORtĕltjĕs, BOONtjĕs, en-SLAA.	Er zijn erwtjes, worteltjes, boontjes, en sla.

de Jong

to hold	HOUdĕn	houden
I don't like beans.	ik-HOUT-niet-van-boonĕn.	Ik houd niet van boonen.
Bring me peas with the chicken, and salad.	breng-mĕ-ERTjĕs bei-dĕ-KIP, en-SLAA.	Breng me erwtjes bij de kip, en sla.

Waiter

And you, sir?	en-UU-mĕneer?	En u, mijnheer

Carver

the same	hĕt-ZELVdĕ	hetzelfde
I'll take the same.	IK neem-ĕt-ZELVdĕ.	Ik neem hetzelfde.

de Jong

the salt	hĕt-ZOUT	het zout
the butter	dĕ-BOOtĕr	de boter

(Will you) please pass (me) the salt and the butter, Mr. Carver.	WILT-uu-mě-eevěn ět-ZOUT en-dě-BOOtěr-aan-gheevěn, měneer-KAARvěr?	Wilt u me even het zout en de boter aangeven, Mijnheer Carver?

the waiter	dě-KELLněr	de kellner
Waiter!	KELLněr!	Kellner!

Waiter

Be right with you, sir.	kom-BEI-uu, měNEER.	Kom bij u, mijnheer.

Carver

the fork	dě-VORK	de vork
This fork isn't clean.	deezě-VORK is-niet-SCHOON.	Deze vork is niet schoon.
Bring me another, please.	breng-mě-ěn-ANděrě, als-t-uu--BLIEFT.	Breng me een andere, als 't u blieft.

de Jong

the pair	hět-PAAR	het paar
the spoon	dě-LEEpěl	de lepel
needed	NOOdich	noodig
And we need a couple of spoons, too.	en-wě-hebběn-OOK-noch ěn-paar--LEEpěls-noodich.	En wij hebben ook nog een paar lepels noodig.

the dessert	hĕt-deSERT	het dessert
the ice or ice cream	hĕt-EIS	het ijs
the tart	dĕ-TAART	de taart
the pudding	dĕ-PUDDing	de pudding
For dessert we have ice cream, tart, pudding, and apples.	voor-deSERT hebbĕn-wĕ-EIS, TAART, PUDDing, en-APPĕlĕn.	Voor dessert hebben we ijs, taart, pudding, en appelen.

de Jong

| Shall we have ice cream? | zullĕn-wĕ-EIS-neemĕn? | Zullen we ijs nemen? |

Carver

| All right. | GHOET. | Goed. |
| I like ice cream. | ik-HOUT-van-eis. | Ik houd van ijs. |

de Jong

| And two cups of coffee. | en-TWEE KOFFie. | En twee koffie. |

Waiter

| Here's the coffee, gentlemen. | HIER iz-dĕ-KOFFie, HEErĕn. | Hier is de koffie, heeren. |
| careful | voorZICHtich | voorzichtig |

Be careful, please.	wees-voorZICHtich, als-t-uu--BLIEFT.	Wees voorzichtig, als 't u blieft.
It's still very hot.	zě-is-noch-ERCH HEET.	Ze is nog erg heet.
the sugar	dě-SUIkěr	de suiker
the cream	dě-ROOM	de room
Here's the sugar and cream.	HIER iz-dě-SUIkěr en-dě-ROOM.	Hier is de suiker en de room.

de Jong

the bill or *the check*	dě-REEkěning	de rekening
Waiter! The check, please.	KELLněr, dě-REEkěning, als-t-uu--BLIEFT.	Kellner, de rekening, als 't u blieft.

Waiter

Here's the bill, sir.	hier-is dě-REEkěning, měNEER.	Hier is de rekening, **mijnheer.**

de Jong

Here's ten guilder.	HIER-zein TIEN GHULděn.	Hier zijn tien gulden.
to get	KREIghěn	krijgen
back	těRUCH	terug
I have some change coming.	ik-KREICH-noch wat-těRUCH.	Ik krijg nog wat terug.
the money	hět-GHELT	het geld
the small change	hět-KLEIN-ghelt	het kleingeld
Bring me back some small change.	BRENG-mě wat-KLEIN-ghelt--těruch.	Breng me wat kleingeld terug.

Please tell me how much the bill is.	ZECH-mĕ als-t-uu-BLIEFT HOE-veel dĕ-REEkĕning-is.	Zeg me, als 't u blieft, hoeveel **de** rekening is.
I want to pay for my share.	ik-wil-voor-MEIN-deel bĕTAAlĕn.	Ik wil voor mijn deel betalen.

No, you can't pay anything.	NEE, UU-moocht niets- -bĕTAAlĕn.	Neen, u moogt niets betalen.
the guest	dĕ-GHAST	de gast
This evening you're my guest.	van-AAvĕnt bent-uu-MEIN-ghast.	Vanavond bent u mijn gast.

Here's your money, sir.	hier-is-uuw-GHELT, mĕNEER.	Hier is uw geld, mijnheer.

Good.	GHOET.	Goed.
the tip	dĕ-FOOJ	de fooi
Oh yes, the tip!	oo-JAA, dĕ-FOOJ-noch!	O ja, de fooi nog!
Waiter, that's for you.	KELLnĕr, dat-is-voor-UU.	Kellner, dat is voor u.

Thank you, sir	dank-uu-WEL, mĕNEER.	Dank u wel, mijnheer.

168   [9–A]

B. Word Study

1. Word Study

Point 1. Ways of Saying Things. 1. Meals. The Dutch eat the big meal of the day either between twelve and two o'clock in the afternoon or else between six and eight in the evening, but they call it *het middag--eten* (*ĕt-MIDDach-eetĕn*) 'the afternoon eating', using the word *de middag* 'the afternoon'. A light meal at noon is called *koffie drinken* 'coffee drinking' or *boterham eten* (*BOOtĕram-eetĕn*) 'sandwich eating', or else by the English name *de lunch* (*LUNSJ*). A light meal in the evening is called *het avondeten* (*ĕt-AAvĕnt-eetĕn*) 'the evening eating'.

2. Vegetables. The word *groente* (*GHROENtĕ*) literally means something like 'green stuff' or 'greens'. It is used both for one 'vegetable' and for the plural 'vegetables'. Peas, beans, and carrots are very often named in the diminutive form—*dat*-nouns ending in -*jĕ* or -*tjĕ* and making the plural in -*s*. The word *sla* means both 'lettuce' and 'salad'.

3. Notice the following other ways of saying things which differ very much from English:

Ik heb honger.	(ik-hep-HONGĕr.)	'I have hunger.' for *'I'm hungry.'*
Wat wilt u gebruiken?	(wat-wilt-uu-ghĕBRUIkĕn?)	'What will you use?' for *'What will you have?'*
Wat voor vleesch?	(wat-voor-VLEES?)	'What for meat?' for *'What sort of meat?'*
Ik houd van dat meisje.	(ik-HOUT van-dat-MEIsjĕ.)	'I hold from that girl.' for *'I like that girl.'*
Geef me de boter aan.	(gheef-mĕ-dĕ-BOOTĕr-aan.)	'Give me the butter on.' for *'Pass me the butter.'*
Ik heb een mes noodig.	(ik-hep-ĕn-MES-noodich.)	'I have a knife needed.' for *'I need a knife.'*
Aannemen!	(AAN-neemĕn!)	'On take!' for *'Check, please!'*

In Dutch 'to take on' means 'to accept.':

Hij wil het geld niet aannemen. (hei-wil-ĕt-GHELT niet-AAN-neemĕn.) *'He won't accept the money.'*

Point 2. Plurals. Two of the new nouns of this Unit have irregular plural forms:

het rund : runderen (ĕt-RUNT : RUNdĕrĕn) *'the head of cattle (cow or bull or calf)* : *cattle'*
de wortel : wortelen (dĕ-WORtĕl : WORtĕlĕn) *'the root, the carrot* : *carrots'*

The plural *wortelen* is not much used; mostly one says *worteltjes*. In the meaning 'roots' the plural is regular: *wortels (WORtĕls)*.

Point 3. The Same and Another. The word for 'same' is really *ZELVdĕ*, but it always has *dĕ* or *ĕt* before it:

dezelfde man (dĕ-zelvdĕ-MAN) *'the same man'*
hetzelfde huis (ĕt-zelvdĕ-HUIS) *'the same house'*
deze fde huizen (dĕ-zelvdĕ-HUIzĕn) *'the same houses'*

Your fork is dirty and you want another *in place of it*; you say:

Deze vork is niet schoon; geef me   (deezĕ-VORK is-niet-SCHOON;   *'This fork isn't clean; give me an-*
een andere, als 't u blieft.   gheef-mĕ-ĕn-ANdĕrĕ, als-t-uu-   *other one (in place of it), please.'*
   -BLIEFT.)

But if you have one fork, and need two—another one *added to* the one you have—you say:

Geef me nog een vork, als 't u   (gheef-mĕ-NOCH-ĕn-vork, als-t-   *'Give me another fork, please (besides*
blieft.   -uu-BLIEFT.)   *the one I have).'*

This is the difference between *ander* and *nog een*.

Point 4. Time to Eat. The form of a verb that we have in expressions like *to eat, to go, to be* is called the *infinitive*. The Dutch for this is Form *1* of the verb (ending *-ĕn* or *-n*: *eten, gaan, zijn*) (EEtĕn, GHAAN, ZEIN). In Dutch the infinitives are used chiefly in three ways:

1. plain
Hij zal komen.   (hei-zal-KOOmĕn.)   *'He will come.'*

2. with *te*

Hij hoopt te komen.   (hei-hoopt-tĕ-KOOmĕn.)   *'He hopes to come.'*

3. with *om te*

Het is tijd om te eten.   (ĕt-is-TEIT om-tĕ-EEtĕn.)   *'It's time to eat.'*

This last one is so different from English that it is likely to fool us; watch carefully for sentences that contain it.

The infinitive is also used to form *dat*-nouns, often with another word tacked on at the beginning, as was explained in Unit VIII:

4. as a *dat*-noun

het eten   (ĕt-EEtĕn)   *'the food, the meal'*

het middageten   (ĕt-MIDDach-eetĕn)   *'the dinner'*

Point 5. Dutch Word Order. You have probably noticed the strange order of words in Dutch. If you go at a foreign language in the right way, you will at first say only the sentences which you have actually learned. But after a while you will want to say new things, and then you will often go wrong. A few hints about the order of words will help you avoid errors.

Verb second. In a Dutch statement (not a question or an order) the verb comes second. Before the verb there is only one word or one phrase. The trouble is to know what counts as 'one phrase'. For instance, 'in this house' counts as one phrase:

In dit huis wil ik niet wonen.   (in-dit-HUIS wil-ik-NIET   *'In this house I don't want to live.'*
                         WOOnĕn.)

And here *wil* is the verb and comes second. But 'here I' does not count as one phrase; either word may come first, but the verb will always come second:

Hier ben ik.   (hier-BEN-ik.)   *'Here I am.'*

Ik ben hier.   (ik-ben-HIER.)   *'I am here.'*

Other examples:

Nu moet ik gaan.	(nuu-moet-ik-GHAAN.)	*'Now I must go.'*
Dan moeten we wel gaan.	(dan-MOEtĕ-wĕ wel-GHAAN.)	*'Then we must go, I guess.'*

The Dutch often begin a sentence with some emphatic word or phrase:

Dit slechte bier kan ik niet drinken.	(DIT-slechtĕ-bier kan-ik-NIET DRINkĕn.)	*'I can't drink this bad beer.'*

Infinitive last. The infinitive differs from the other verb forms which you have studied; it comes last or nearly last in the sentence:

Hij zou vandaag komen.	(hei-zou-van-DAACH-koomĕn.)	*'He was to come today.'*

Here the infinitive *komen* is last. Other examples:

Hij hoopt morgen te komen.	(hei-HOOPT MORghĕn-tĕ-koomĕn.)	*'He hopes to come tomorrow.'*
Ik ben blij u terug te zien.	(ik-ben-BLEI uu-tĕRUCH-tĕ-zien.)	*'I'm glad to see you back.'*
Het is tijd om naar bed te gaan.	(ĕt-is-TEIT om-naar-BET-tĕ--ghaan.)	*'It's time to go to bed.'*

Sometimes there are two infinitives:

Ik zou graag een biefstuk en aar--dappelen willen hebben.	(ik-zou-GHRAACH ĕn-BIEF-stuk en-AARdappĕlĕn-willen-hebbĕn.)	*'I should like to have a steak and potatoes.'*

Literally, 'I should (*zou*) want (*willen*) to have (*hebben*)'; the two infinitives come last.

End-Words. Some Dutch words almost always come at the end of the sentence or near it; they may be called *end-words*. Here are a few:

1. *op* 'up'

Zoek hun eens op.	(zoek-hun-ĕs-OP.)	'*Look them up (pay them a call) sometime.*'

Notice that *op* comes last.

Ik sta iedere morgen om zeven uur op.	(ik-STAA iedĕrĕ-MORghĕn om--ZEEvĕn-uur OP.)	'*I get up at seven o'clock every morning.*
Zij maakt de bedden op.	(zĕ-maak-tĕ-BEDDĕn-op.)	'*She is making the beds.*'

2. *uit* 'out'

Ik ga vandaag niet uit.	(ik-GHAA-van-daach niet-UIT.)	'*I'm not going out today.*'

3. *mee* 'along'

Zij gaat dikwijls met ons mee.	(zĕ-ghaat-DIKwĕls met-ons-MEE.)	'*She often goes along with us.*'

4. *vooruit* 'ahead'

Wij betalen de huur altijd vooruit.	(wĕ-betaalĕn-dĕ-HUUR alteit--vooRUIT.)	'*We always pay the rent in advance.*'

5. *aan* 'on'

Geef me even de suiker aan.	(GHEEF-mĕ-eevĕn dĕ-SUIkĕr--aan.)	'*Pass me the sugar, please.*'

Literally, 'Give me just the sugar on.'

Dat geld neem ik niet aan.   (DAT-ghelt neem-ik-niet-AAN.)   *'I don't (won't) accept that money.'*

Literally, 'That money take I not on.'

6. *terug* 'back'

Geef hem zijn geld terug.   (gheev-ĕm-zĕn-GHELT-tĕruch.)   *'Give him back his money.'*
Hij komt morgen terug.   (hei-komt-MORghĕn tĕRUCH.)   *'He's coming back tomorrow.'*

Clause verbs last. A clause is a sentence which forms part of a longer sentence. The verb in a clause comes last:

Ik ben blij dat u het *weet*.   (ik-ben-BLEI dat-uu-ĕt-*WEET*.)   *'I'm glad that you know it.'*

Here the clause is 'that you know it'. The words 'you know it' (Dutch *U weet het*) form a sentence, but by the use of the word 'that' they are made part of a longer sentence. In Dutch this makes the verb (*weet*) come last. Other examples:

Ik heb een nicht die met een   (ik-heb-ĕn-NICHT die-met-ĕn-   *'I have a niece who is married to an*
Amerikaan getrouwd *is*.   -ameerieKAAN ghĕTROUT-*is*.)   *American.*

Here the verb of the clause (*is*) comes last. Compare the statement, where the verb comes second:

Mijn nicht *is* met een Amerikaan   (mĕn-NICHT *is*-met-ĕn-   *'My niece is married to an Ameri-*
getrouwd.   -ameerieKAAN-ghĕtrout.)   *can.'*
Van welk station *gaat* mijn trein?   (van-welk-staaSJON *ghaat*-mĕn-   *'From what station does my train go?'*
      -TREIN?   (ordinary question, with verb second.)

Ik weet niet van welk station mijn trein *gaat*.	(ik-WEET-niet van-welk--staaSJON mĕn-TREIN-*ghaat*.	'*I don't know from what station my train goes.*' (clause in a longer sentence, with verb last)
Is dit onze trein?	(*iz*-DIT onzĕ-TREIN?)	'*Is this our train?*' (question with verb first)
Ik weet niet of dit onze trein *is*.	(ik-WEET-niet of-DIT onzĕ--TREIN-*is*.)	'*I don't know whether this is our train.*' (clause in longer sentence, with verb last)
Hij *komt* vanavond.	(hei-*komt*-van-AAvĕnt.)	'*He'll come tonight.*' (statement, verb second)
Als hij vanavond *komt*, geef ik hem zijn geld.	(als-ie-van-AAvĕnt-*komt*, gheef-ik--ĕm-zĕn-GHELT.)	'*If (or when) he comes tonight, I'll give him his money.*' (clause with verb last)

Notice also, in this last example, that the verb of the whole sentence (*geef*) is second in the whole sentence, since the clause at the beginning (*Als hij vanavond komt*) is one of the things that counts as 'one phrase'.

However, after a long clause at the beginning of a sentence, the Dutch often sum it up with such a word as 'then' before the verb of the sentence:

Als hij vanavond nog komt, dan geef ik hem zijn geld.	(als-ie-van-AAvĕnt-noch-KOMT, dan-GHEEV-ik-ĕm zĕn-GHELT.)	'*If he still comes tonight, then I'll give him his money.*'

Combinations. You have seen three things that come last: infinitives, end-words, and verbs of a clause. If two or more of these come together, various sequences are used. However, an end-word always comes before the verb or infinitive to which it belongs. If the end-word comes immediately before its verb or infinitive, the two are usually written in conventional Dutch orthography as one word, but the Dutch are not consistent in this.

Examples of combinations:

Hij zegt dat hij het niet *betalen kan*.	(hei-ZECHT dat-ie-ĕt-niet- -bĕTAAlĕn-kan.)	'*He says that he can't pay it.*'
Hij zegt dat hij het niet *kan betalen*.	(hei-ZECHT dat-ie-ĕt-NIET *kan*- -bĕTAAlĕn.)	(same meaning)
Dat geld kan ik niet *aannemen*.	(DAT-ghelt kan-ik-NIET *AAN*- -neemĕn.)	'*I can't accept that money.*'
U moet hem zijn geld *teruggeven*.	(uu-moet-ĕm-zĕn-GHELT *tĕRUCH*-gheevĕn.)	'*You must give him back his money.*'
Hij zal morgen *terugkomen*.	(hei-zal-MORghĕn *tĕRUCH*- -koomĕn.)	'*He'll come back tomorrow.*'
Hij hoopt morgen *terug te komen*.	(hei-hoopt-MORghĕn *tĕRUCH-tĕ*- -koomĕn.)	'*He hopes to come back tomorrow.*'
Ik zeg dat ik dat geld niet *aanneem*.	(ik-ZECH dat-ik-DAT-ghelt niet- -*AAN*-neem.)	'*I say that I don't accept that money.*'
Ik denk dat ik dat geld niet *aannemen kan*.	(ik-DENK dat-ik-DAT-ghelt niet- -*AAN*-neemĕn-kan.)	'*I think that I can't accept that money.*'
Hij zegt dat hij morgen misschien nog niet *terugkomen kan*.	(hei-ZECHT dat-ie-MORghĕn mischien-noch-NIET *tĕRUCH*- -koomĕn-kan.)	'*He says that he probably can't come back yet tomorrow.*'
Hij zegt dat hij morgen misschien nog niet *terug kan komen*.	(hei-ZECHT dat-ie-MORghĕn mischien-noch-NIET *tĕRUCH*- -kan-koomĕn.)	(same meaning)
Hij zegt dat hij morgen misschien nog niet *kan terugkomen*.	(hei-ZECHT dat-ie-MORghĕn mischien-noch-NIET *kan*- -tĕRUCH-koomĕn.)	(same meaning)

2. Review of Basic Sentences with English Covered.

C. What Would You Say?

1. What Would You Say?

1. *You think it's time to go to bed.   You say:*
    a. ět-is-TEIT om-naar-BET-tě-ghaan.
    b. ět-is-TEIT om-ět-BET op-tě-maakěn.
    c. ik-hep-gheen-TEIT.

Het is tijd om naar bed te gaan.
Het is tijd om het bed op te maken.
Ik heb geen tijd.

2. *You find a hair in your soup.   You tell the waiter:*
    a. ěr-is-ěn-HAAR-in-deezě-soep.
    b. měn-HAAR is-noch-niet-LANG-ghěnoech om-tě-
       -laatěn-KNIPPěn.
    c. ěr-zein-niet-ghěnoegh-HAARěn in-deezě-SOEP.

Er is een haar in deze soep.
Mijn haar is nog niet lang genoeg om te laten knippen.
Er zijn niet genoeg haren in deze soep.

3. *You want a fresh plate of soup instead of this one.   You say:*
    a. breNG-mě noch-ěn-bort-SOEP.
    b. breng-mě-ěn-ANděr bort-SOEP.
    c. DOE-noch ěn-PAAR HAARěn-in-dě-soep.

Breng me nog een bord soep.
Breng me een ander bord soep.
Doe nog een paar haren in de soep.

4. *Your bill is seven guilders and twenty cents, and you have given the clerk a ten guilder bill, and nothing happens.*
You wait a while and then you say:
    a. GHEEF-mě-wat KLEIN-ghelt.
    b. ik-sal-uu-noch-ěn-FOOJ-gheevěn.
    c. ik-KREICH-noch TWEE-ghulděn-TACHtich
      těRUCH.

Geef me wat kleingeld.
Ik zal u nog een fooi geven.
Ik krijg nog twee gulden tachtig terug.

5. *Your bill is exactly seven guilders and you give the waiter a ten guilder bill, and you want some of the change to be in small coin. You say:*

a. BRENG-mě-wat KLEIN-ghelt. Breng me wat kleingeld.

b. ik-sal-uu-noch-ěn-FOOJ-gheevěn. Ik zal u nog een fooi geven.

c. ik-KREICH-noch wat-GHELT těRUCH. Ik krijg nog wat geld terug.

6. *The waiter offers you carrots. You don't like carrots, and you say:*

a. ik-HOUT-niet van-ERTjěs. Ik houd niet van erwtjes.

b. ik-EET noojt-GHROENtě. Ik eet nooit groente.

c. ik-HOUT-niet van-WORtěltjěs. Ik houd niet van worteltjes.

7. *You want cream for your coffee. You say:*

a. ROOM is-tě-DUUR-voor-meě. Room is te duur voor me.

b. die-ROOM-is niet-GHOET. Die room is niet goed.

c. ik-neem-ROOM bei-dě-KOFFie. Ik neem room bij de koffie.

8. *You want to know how much you owe. You ask:*

a. zal-ik-dě-REEkěning van-DAAGH-běTAALěn? Zal ik de rekening vandaag betalen?

b. wilt-uu-mě-wat-GHELT-gheevěn? Wilt u me wat geld geven?

c. hoe-veel-KREICHT-uu-van-mě? Hoeveel krijgt u van me?

2. What Did You Say?

D. Listening In

1. *Mr. Carver has taken Miss Annie Jansen to dine.*

Carver: ZULLěn-wě met-ěn-bort-SOEP-běghinněn? Zullen we met een bord soep beginnen?

Annie: JAA als-jě-BLIEF. Ja, als je blieft.

als-ět-zoo-KOUT-is, HOUT-ik van-heetě-SOEP. Als het zoo koud is, houd ik van heete soep.

Carver: neemĕn-wĕ-dan OOK ĕn-ghĕbraajĕ-KIP met-AAR-
-dappĕlĕn en-SLAA?

Annie: as-jĕ-BLIEF.
ik-hout-ERCH van-ghĕbraadĕ-KIP en-van-SLAA,
maar-ik-eet-NOOJT AARdappĕlĕ.

Carver: GHOET, dan-NEEmĕ-wĕ-dus GHEEN-aardappĕlĕ.
wat-voor-GHROENtĕ wou-jĕ-GHRAACH bei-dĕ-KIP-
-hebbĕn?

Annie: als-ĕr-SLAA bei-dĕ-KIP-is, HEB-ik GHEEN-andĕre-
-ghroentĕ NOOdich.

Carver: NEEN-annie, zoo-ĕn-SLAAtjĕ is-niet-ghĕNOECH.
hou-jĕ-niet-van-ERtjĕs?

Annie: NUU, GHOET-dan.
laatĕ-wĕ-ERtĕn bei-dĕ-KIP-neemĕn.

Carver: en-WAT-wil-jĕ voor-ĕt-deSERT-hebbĕ?

Annie: kunnĕ-wĕ-EIS-kreighĕn?
ik-HOUT-zoo-veel van-EIS, en-ik-KREICH-ĕt maar-
-ZELdĕn
VAAdĕr HOUT-niet-van-eis, en-dus-hebbĕ-wĕ-ĕt-
-NOOJT bei-ons-in-HUIS.

Carver: WAArom hout-jĕ-VAAdĕr-niet van-EIS?

Annie: als-ie-EIS-ghĕgheetĕn-heeft, heeft-ie-ĕt-ALteit zoo-
-KOUT, ZECHT-ie.

Carver: en-DAN ĕn-kopjĕ-KOFFie?

Nemen we dan ook een gebraden kip met
aardappelen en sla?

Als je blieft.
Ik houd erg van gebraden kip en van sla,
maar ik eet nooit aardappelen.

Goed, dan nemen we dus geen aardappelen.
Wat voor groente wou je graag bij de kip
hebben?

Als er sla bij de kip is, heb ik geen andere
groente noedig.

Neen, Annie, zoo'n slaatje is niet genoeg.
Houd je niet van erwtjes?

Nu, goed dan.
Laten we erwten bij de kip nemen.

En wat wil je voor het dessert hebben?

Kunnen we ijs krijgen?
Ik houd zoo veel van ijs, en ik krijg het maar
zelden.
Vader houdt niet van ijs, en dus hebben we
het nooit bij ons in huis,

Waarom houdt je vader niet van ijs?

Als hij ijs gegeten heeft, heeft hij het altijd
zoo koud, zegt hij.

En dan een kopje koffie?

Annie:	als-jĕ-BLIEF.	Als je blieft.
Carver:	neem-jĕ-SUIkĕr en-ROOM in-dĕ-KOFFie?	Neem je suiker en room in de koffie?
Annie:	GHEEN ROOM, dank-jĕ-WEL.	Geen room, dank je wel.
	aLEEN ĕn-beetjĕ-SUIkĕr.	Alleen een beetje suiker.
Carver:	ANNie,,MACH-ik-jĕ wat-ZEGHĕ?	Annie, mag ik je wat zeggen?
	jĕ-bent-MOOJ.	Je bent mooi.
Annie:	NEE, dat-MOET-jĕ niet-ZEGHĕn.	Nee, dat moet je niet zeggen.
Carver:	maar-jĕ-BENT-immĕrs MOOJ-en-ghoet, ANNie.	Maar jij bent immers mooi en goed, Annie.
Annie:	DAT zech-jĕ-ZEEkĕr an-ALLĕ-meisjĕs.	Dat zeg je zeker aan alle meisjes.

2. *Mr. Hettema doesn't like his soup.*

Hettema:	KELLnĕr! kom-ĕs-HIER als-t-uu-BLIEFT.	Kellner! Kom eens hier als 't u blieft.
Kellner:	ik-kom-DAAdĕlik BEI-uu-mĕneer.	Ik kom dadelijk bij u, mijnheer.
Hettema:	ĕr-is-ĕn-HAAR-in-mĕn-soep.	Er is een haar in mijn soep.
Kellner:	zal-ik-uu-ĕn-ANdĕr-bort-soep-brengĕn, mĕNEER?	Zal ik u een ander bord soep brengen, Mijnheer?
Hettema:	NEE, dank-uu-WEL! die-SOEP is-tĕ-ZOUT-voor-mĕ.	Neen, dank u wel! Die soep is te zout voor me.
	ik-kan-zĕ-NIET EEtĕn.	Ik kan ze niet eten.
	waarom-DOEN-zĕ zoo-veel-ZOUT-in-dĕ-soep?	Waarom doen ze zooveel zout in de soep?
	niet-tĕ-EEtĕ!	Niet te eten!
Kellner:	wìlt-uu-NOCH-wat-ghĕbruikĕ-mĕneer?	Wilt u nog wat gebruiken, mijnheer?
Hettema:	NEE, ik-ghaa-naar-ĕn-ANdĕr-rĕstorang.	Neen, ik ga naar een ander restaurant.
	in-DIT-rĕstorang EET-ik-niet.	In dit restaurant eet ik niet.

Kellner:	wilt-uu-dan-bĕTAAlĕn-mĕneer?	Wilt u dan betalen, mijnheer?
	ĕn-ghlas-BIER, da-s-VEIV-ĕn-twintich SENT,	Een glas bier, dat's vijf en twintig cent,
	en-dĕ-SOEP is-FEIFtich-sent.	en de soep is vijftig cent.
	SAAmĕn IZ-dat-dus FEIV-ĕn-seevĕntich SENT,	Samen is dat dus vijf en zeventig cent,
	mĕnEER.	Mijnheer.
Hettema:	WAT?!	Wat?!
	NEE, voor-dĕ-SOEP bĕTAAL-ik-niet.	Nee, voor de soep betaal ik niet.
Kellner:	wat-BLIEFT-uu-mĕneer?	Wat blieft u, mijnheer?
	voor-dĕ-SOEP—	Voor de soep—
Hettema:	ik-SEGH dat-ik-voor-dĕ-SOEP NIET bĕTAAlĕ-wil.	Ik zeg dat ik voor de soep niet betalen wil.
	ik-HEP-zĕ-immĕrs niet-ghĕGHEETĕ.	Ik heb ze immers niet gegeten.
Waiter:	JAA-mĕneer. nee-mĕ-NIET KWAAlik.	Ja, mijnheer. Neem me niet kwalijk.
	dus-KREIGH-ik aLEEN-maar VEIV-ĕn-twintich	Dus krijg ik alleen maar vijf en twintig cent
	SENT-van-uu, voor-ĕt-BIER.	van u, voor het bier.
Hettema:	JAA, en-ĕt-BIER is-OOK-slecht.	Ja, en het bier is ook slecht.
	ĕt-is-niet-tĕ-DRINkĕ.	Het is niet te drinken.
	HIER zein-dĕ-veiv-ĕn-twintich-SENT,	Hier zijn de vijf en twintig cent,
	en-HIER zein-noch-TIEN-sent voor-dĕ-FOOJ.	en hier zijn nog tien cent voor de fooi.
	ghoedĕn-DACH!	Goeden dag!

E. Conversation

1. Review of Basic Sentences with Dutch Covered

2. Vocabulary and Word Study Check-up

3. Carrying on Conversation

Conversation 1. Perk (PERK) and Ruys (RUIS) are talking.

P: says he had a very good lunch at Heck's (HEKS) café today.

R: says yes? What did P have.

P: says Oh, some vegetable soup; they had no steak so he took roast chicken with potatoes and carrots and salad.

R: asks P if he had dessert too.

P: says yes. P doesn't like their ice cream, but their coffee is very good.

R: says he thinks he'll go there for dinner with his wife this evening.

Conversation 2. Ruys and his wife go into Heck's café.

R: says hello to the waiter, and asks for a table for two.

W: says yes sir. He asks if they want to start with a cocktail (KOK-teel).

R: says yes, and asks for a Manhattan (use English word); he asks for one for him and one for his wife.

Mrs. R: says no, she isn't going to drink today, thanks.

R: says all right then, and tells the waiter only one Manhattan.

W: says yes sir. He asks if they want to start with soup.

R: says no thanks. But he's hungry. He asks for beef with peas and beans and for his wife. . . .

Mrs. R: asks the waiter if they have any fish.

W: says no, but they have very good pork today.

Mrs. R: asks for pork with potatoes and salad.

W: says yes ma'am. (Later) He asks if they want dessert and coffee now.

Mrs. R: says yes please. She asks for one coffee pudding and one tart and two coffees.

Conversation 3. Storm (STORM) and Jet (JET) 'his

wife Henrietta) are having coffee after their meal at home.

S: asks Jet please to give him a cup of coffee with cream and sugar.

J: says OK, but be careful, because it's still very hot.

S: says thanks, but says she hasn't given him a spoon yet. Then he says Oh, he'll use the same spoon she uses.

Conversation 4. van Buuren (van-BUUrĕn) invites his friend Bert (BERT) to go to the restaurant with him.

vB: asks B if he'll come along to the restaurant with him, as vB's guest.

B: says he will.

vB: (at the restaurant) asks B what he'll have.

B: says just some chicken.

vB: says all right, he'll have chicken too.

Waiter: says here's the chicken, gentlemen. He says he'll pass them the salt and butter right away.

vB: says they need a couple of forks too.

B: says he likes chicken, but he doesn't like peas with chicken.

W: (later) says here's the bill, sir. It's two guilder fifty.

vB: says here's the money and please bring him back some small change. He says here's the tip. To Bert he says that Bert can't pay for his dinner, he can't pay anything, he's vB's guest.

W: says thank you, sir. He says Oh, here's still fifty cents change that vB has coming to him.

FINDER LIST

aan (end-word) 'at, on'
 aangeven 'to hand, to pass'
 Geef me even het zout aan. 'Pass the salt, please.'
 aannemen 'to accept'
 Kellner, aannemen! 'Waiter! Check please!'
 Hij neemt het aan. 'He accepts it.'

de biefstuk 'the steak'
de boon 'the bean'
 boonen, boontjes 'beans'
het bord 'the plate'
 een bord socp 'a plate of soup'
de boter 'the butter'
de cocktail (KOK-teel) 'the cocktail'

het dessert (deSERT) 'the dessert'
  dezelfde, hetzelfde (dě-ZELVdě, ět-ZELVdě) 'the same'

de erwt (ERT) 'the pea'
  erwten, erwtjes (ERtěn, ERtjěs) 'peas'

de fooi (FOOJ) 'the tip' (gift to an attendant)

de gast 'the guest'
  gebraden (ghěBRAAděn) 'roast'
    ghěbraaděn-VARkěns-vlees 'roast pork'
  gebruiken (ghěBRUIkěn) 'to use'
    Wat willen de heeren gebruiken? 'What will the gentlemen have (to eat or drink)?'
  gedronken (ghěDRONkěn) 'drunk' ('to have *drunk*', *not* 'he is *drunk*')
  gegeten (ghěGHEEtěn) 'eaten'
    Ik heb geen soep gegeten. 'I haven't eaten any soup.'
het geld 'the money'
  groen 'green'
    de groente 'the vegetable; vegetables'

  hetzelfde see dezelfde
de honger 'the hunger'
  Ze hebben honger. 'They are hungry.'

houden 'to hold'
  Ik houd van biefstuk. 'I like steak.'

het ijs 'the ice, the ice cream'

de kellner 'the waiter'
de kip 'the chicken'
het kleingeld 'change money, small coin'
het koffiedrinken 'the lunch'
  krijgen 'to receive, to get'

de lepel 'the spoon'

de Manhattan (menHETTěn) 'the Manhattan (cocktail)'
de middag 'the afternoon'
  het middageten 'the dinner'

noodig 'needed, necessary'
  We hebben nog een bord noodig. 'We need one more plate.'

het paar 'the pair, the couple'
  en paar lepels 'a couple of spoons; a few spoons'
de pudding 'the pudding'

de rekening 'the reckoning, the bill'
de room 'the cream'

het rund 'the head of cattle (cow *or* bull *or* calf)'
    runderen 'cattle'
    het rundvleesch (RUNT-vlees) 'the beef'

de sla 'the lettuce; the salad'
de soep 'the soup'
de suiker 'the sugar'

de taart 'the tart, the cake'
de tafel 'the table'
    terug (těRUCH, TRUCH; end-word) 'back'
      Ik krijg nog wat terug.   'I still have something coming to me.'
      Hij komt terug. 'He's coming back.'

de tijd 'the time'
    Het is tijd om te eten.   'It's time to eat.'

het varken 'the pig'
    het varkensvleesch (VARkěns-vlees) 'the pork'
de visch (VIS) 'the fish'
   voorzichtig (voorZICHtich) 'careful'
de vork 'the fork'

de wortel 'the root; the carrot'
    wortels 'roots'
    wortelen, worteltjes 'carrots'

   zelfde see dezelfde
het zout 'the salt'

IN TOWN

A. Basic Sentences

Mr. Carver wants to go to the bank.

ENGLISH EQUIVALENTS	AIDS TO LISTENING	CONVENTIONAL SPELLING

Mrs. Dekker

Where are you going, Mr. Carver?	waar-heen-ghaat-uu, měneer--KAARvěr?	Waarheen gaat u, Mijnheer Carver?

Mr. Carver

the museum	hět-muuZEEjum	het museum
I'd like to go to the museum,	ik-wou-GHRAACH naar-ět-muu--ZEEjum,	Ik wou graag naar het museum,
but first I have to go to the bank.	maar-EERST moet-ik-naar-dě--BANK.	maar eerst moet ik naar de bank.

| the way | dĕ-WECH | de weg |
| Do you know the way? | weet-uu-dĕ-WECH? | Weet u de weg? |

Mr. Carver

flat	VLAK	vlak
near to	vlak-BEI	vlak bij
the main square	hĕt-PLEIN	het plein
No, ma'am. I only know that the bank is near the square.	NEE-mĕvrou. Ik-weet-aLEEN dat-dĕ-BANK VLAK-bei-ĕt--PLEIN-is.	Nee, mevrouw. Ik weet alleen dat de bank vlak bij het plein is.

Mrs. Dekker

the street car	dĕ-TREM	de tram
to stop	STOPPĕn	stoppen
close	DICHT	dicht
The street car stops close by the hotel.	dĕ-TREM stopt-DICHT bei-ĕt--hooTEL.	De tram stopt dicht bij het hotel.
the side	dĕ-KANT	de kant
the street	dĕ-STRAAT	de straat
You take it on the other side of the street.	uu-NEEMT-ĕm an-dĕ-ANdĕrĕ--kant van-dĕ-STRAAT.	U neemt hem aan de andere kant van de straat.
the door	dĕ-DEUR	de deur
out	UIT	uit

over	OOvĕr	over
to stick	STEEkĕn	steken
to cross	OOvĕr-steekĕn	oversteken
As you go out the door of the hotel, you only have to cross the street.	als-uu-dĕ-DEUR van-ĕt-hooTEL--uit-ghaat, hept-uu-aLEEN--maar dĕ-STRAAT-oovĕr-tĕ--steekĕn.	Als u de deur van het hotel uitgaat, hebt u alleen maar de straat over te steken.

Mr. Carver

the line	dĕ-LEIN	de lijn
What line do I take?	welkĕ-LEIN moet-ik-NEEmĕn?	Welke lijn moet ik nemen?

Mrs. Dekker

to ask	VRAAghĕn	vragen
the policeman	dĕ-aaGHENT	de agent
Take Line Three up to the square.	neem-lein-DRIE tot-ĕt-PLEIN.	Neem Lijn Drie tot het plein.
And there (you) ask a policeman where the bank is.	en-DAAR vraacht-uu-ĕn-aaGHENT waar-dĕ-BANK-is.	En daar vraagt u een agent waar de bank is.

Mr. Carver

Thank you, ma'am.	dank-uu-WEL-mĕvrou.	Dank u wel, mevrouw.
Can you tell me too how I can get from the bank to the museum?	kunt-uu-mĕ-ook-SEGHĕn hoe-ik--van-dĕ-BANK naar-ĕt-muu--ZEEjum kan-ghAAN?	Kunt u me ook zeggen hoe ik van de bank naar het museum kan gaan?

188 [10–A]

Oh, that's quite a stretch!	OO, dat-is-ĕn-HEEL EINT!	O, dat is een héél eind!
far	VER	ver
The museum is pretty far from the bank.	ĕt-muuZEEjum is-HEEL-ver van--dĕ-BANK.	Het museum is heel ver van de bank.
the care or the map	dĕ-KAART	de kaart
Have you a map of the city?	hept-uu-ĕn-KAART van-dĕ-STAT?	Hebt u een kaart van de stad?

No, ma'am.	NEE-mĕvrou.	Nee, mevrouw.

the bus	dĕ-BUS	de bus
You can take the bus on the square; Line B.	uu-KUNT op-ĕt-PLEIN dĕ-BUS-neemĕn; lein-BEE.	U kunt op het plein de bus nemen; lijn B.
the king	dĕ-KOOning	de koning
the avenue	dĕ-LAAN	de laan
the park	hĕt-PARK	het park
to step	STAPPĕn	stappen
to transfer	OOvĕr-stappĕn	overstappen
But then you still have to transfer in King Avenue, by the park.	maar-dan-MOET-uu-noch-in-dĕ--KOOnings-laan bei-ĕt-PARK OOvĕr-stappĕn.	Maar dan moet u nog in de Koningslaan bij het park overstappen.

to find	VINděn	vinden
I don't know if you can find the way alone.	ik-weet-NIET of-uu-dě-wech--aLEEN kunt-vindĕn.	Ik weet niet of u de weg alleen kunt vinden.

Mr. Carver

better	BEEtĕr	beter
the taxi	dě-TAKsie	de taxi
Then I suppose I'd better take a taxi?	kan-ik-DAN mischien-niet-BEETĕr ěn-TAKsie-neemĕn?	Kan ik dan misschien niet beter een taxi nemen?

Mrs. Dekker

That'll probably be too expensive.	DAT-sal-mischien-tě-DUUR-zein.	Dat zal misschien te duur zijn.
You see, it's a long way.	ět-is-imměrs-ěn-EINT WECH.	't Is immers een eind weg.
But here comes our friend, Annie Jansen.	maar-HIER-komt onzě-vrienDIN annie-JANsěn.	Maar hier komt onze vriendin Annie Jansen.

Miss Jansen

Hello, Mrs. Dekker; Hello, Mr. Carver.	ghoeděn-DACH, měvrou-DEKKěr. dach-KAARvěr.	Goeden dag, Mevrouw Dekker; dag Carver.

Mrs. Dekker

Hello, Annie. Where are you bound for?	DACH-annie. waar-GHAA-jě naar-TOE?	Dag, Annie. Waar ga je naartoe?

Miss Jansen

I have to go down town, to Visscher and Son's clothing store.	ik-moet-dĕ-STAT-in, naar-dĕ--KLEErĕn-winkĕl van-VISSĕr--en-zoon.	Ik moet de stad in, naar de kleeren-winkel van Visscher en Zoon.
That's near the bank.	dat-is-FLAK bei-dĕ-BANK.	Dat is vlak bij de bank.

Mrs. Dekker

the guide	dĕ-GHITS	de gids
There's a guide for you, Mr. Carver.	daar-is-ĕn-GHITS-voor-uu, mĕneer--KAARvĕr.	Daar is een gids voor u, Mijnheer Carver.

Mr. Carver

May I go with you Annie?	mach-ik-met-jĕ-MEE-ghaan, ANNie?	Mag ik met je meegaan, Annie?
You see, I don't know the way very well.	ik-ken-dĕ-WECH immĕrs-niet--GHOET.	Ik ken de weg immers niet goed.

Miss Jansen

to walk	LOOpĕn	loopen
to ride in a street car	TREMMĕn	trammen
Yes, if you're willing to walk.	JAA, als-jĕ-LOOpĕn-wilt.	Ja, als je loopen wilt.
I don't like the street cars.	ik-HOUT-niet van-TREMMĕn.	Ik houd niet van tremmen.
half	HALF	half
It's only a half hour's walk.	ĕt-IS-maar ĕn-HALV-uur LOOpĕn.	Het is maar een half uur loopen.

Mr. Carver

pleasant	PRETTich	prettig
to ride	REIdĕn	rijden
I like walking better than riding too.	IK vint-ĕt-OOK-prettighĕr tĕ--LOOpĕn dan-tĕ-REIdĕn.	Ik vind het ook prettiger te loopen dan te rijden.

Mrs. Dekker

'Bye, Annie. Good day, Mr. Carver.	dach-ANNie. ghoedĕ-DACH, mĕneer-KAARvĕr.	Dag, Annie. Goden dag, Mijnheer Carver.

Mr. Carver

Have you been in Amsterdam, Annie?	ben-jĕ-in-amstĕrDAM-ghĕweest, ANNie?	Ben je in Amsterdam geweest, Annie?

Miss Jansen

to hear	HOOrĕn	hooren
Yes; where did you hear that?	Jaa; waar-HEP-jĕ-dat-ghĕhoort?	Ja; waar heb je dat gehoord?

Mr. Carver

Your father told me.	jĕ-VAAdĕr heeft-ĕt-mĕ ghĕZECHT.	Je vader heeft het me gezegd.

Miss Jansen

When did you see my father?	WANNeer hep-jĕ-mĕn VAAdĕr--ghĕzien?	Wanneer heb je mijn vader gezien?

Mr. Carver

Wednesday *I went to see you Wednesday evening.*	WOENZ-dach woenz-dach-AAvĕnt heb-ik-jĕ-OP--ghĕzocht.	Woensdag Woensdagavond heb ik je op-gezocht.
was *My friend de Jong was along.*	WAS mein-vrient-dĕ-JONG was-ĕr-BEI.	was Mijn vriend de Jong was erbij.

Miss Jansen

nobody *at home* *And there was no one at home?*	NIEmant TUIS en-ĕr-was-NIEmant TUIS, WEL?	niemand thuis En er was niemand thuis, wel?

Mr. Carver

Yes, certainly. Your father was there, and your sister.	jaa-ZEEkĕr. jĕ-VAAdĕr-was-ĕr, en-jĕ-ZUStĕr.	Ja zeker. Je vader was er, en je zuster.

Miss Jansen

then *What did you do then?*	TOEN w..t-hep-jĕ-TOEN ghĕDAAN?	toen Wat heb je toen gedaan?

Mr. Carver

Your sister (Mary) and Mr. de Jong went to the movie.	jĕ-zustĕr-maaRIE en-mĕneer-dĕ--JONG-zein-naar-dĕ-biejĕSKOOP--ghĕghaan.	Je zuster Marie en Mijnheer de Jong zijn naar de bioscoop gegaan.
to talk	PRAAtĕn	praten
Your father and I sat and talked a while.	jĕ-VAAdĕr en-IK hebbĕn-ĕn--TEIT-lang zittĕn-PRAAtĕn.	Je vader en ik hebben een tijd lang zitten praten.
Then I went home.	TOEN ben-ik-naar-HUIS--ghĕghaan.	Toen ben ik naar huis gegaan.
Didn't they say anything about it?	hebbĕn-zĕ-ĕr-NIETS-van ghĕZECHT?	Hebben ze er niets van gezegd?

Miss Jansen

to forget	vĕrGHEEtĕn	vergeten
Father forgot it, of course.	VAAdĕr heeft-ĕt-naaTUURlik vĕrGHEEtĕn.	Vader heeft het natuurlijk vergeten.
Mary probably didn't want to tell me that she went to the movie with Mr. de Jong.	maaRIE heeft-mĕ-miSCHIEN NIET-willĕn-zeghĕn dat-zĕ-met--mĕneer-dĕ-JONG naar-dĕ--biejĕSKOOP-is-ghĕghaan.	Marie heeft me misschien niet willen zeggen dat zij met Mijnheer de Jong naar de bioscoop is gegaan.

Mr. Carver

I'm glad to see you back.	ik-ben-BLEI jĕ-tĕRUCH-tĕ-zien.	Ik ben blij je terug te zien.

the uncle	dĕ-OOM	de oom
the aunt	dĕ-TANtĕ	de tante
to visit	bĕZOEkĕn	bezoeken
Mother and I were visiting my uncle and aunt in Amsterdam.	moedĕr-en-IK hebbĕ-mĕn-OOM en-TANtĕ in-amstĕrDAM--bĕzocht.	Moeder en ik hebben mijn oom en tante in Amsterdam bezocht.
yesterday	GHIStĕrĕn	gisteren
We came back yesterday.	wĕ-zein-GHIStĕrĕn tĕ-RUCH--ghĕkoomĕn.	Wij zijn gisteren teruggekomen.

Mr. Carver

| the building | ĕt-ghĕBOU | het gebouw |
| What is this big building here? | wat-is-dit-ghrootĕ-ghĕBOU-hier? | Wat is dit groote gebouw hier? |

Miss Jansen

the city hall	hĕt-stat-HUIS	het stadhuis
the theatre	hĕt-teeJAAtĕr	het theater
That is the city hall.	DAT is-ĕt-stat-HUIS.	Dat is het stadhuis.
And that building there at the other side of the street is the theatre.	en-DAT-ghĕbou DAAR, an-dĕ--ANdĕrĕ-kant van-dĕ-STRAAT, is-ĕt-teeJAAtĕr.	En dat gebouw daar, aan de andere kant van de straat, is het theater.

B. Word Study

1. Word Study

Point 1. Ways of Saying Things.   1. The word *vlak* means 'flat':

Het land is hier vlak.	(ĕt-LANT is-hier-VLAK.)	*'The land is flat here.'*

The word *dicht* means 'close, dense, shut':

De boomen staan hier dicht bijeen.	(dĕ-BOOmĕn staan-hier-dicht-bei--EEN.)	*'The trees are dense here.'*
De deur is dicht.	(dĕ-DEUR iz-DICHT.)	*'The door is shut.'*
Doe de deur dicht.	(doe-dĕ-DEUR-dicht.)	*'Shut the door.'*

But where we say 'near', the Dutch say *vlak bij* or *dicht bij*:

Het is vlak bij.	(ĕt-is-vlak-BEI.)	*'It's near.'*
Het is dicht bij.	(ĕt-is-dicht-BEI.)	(same meaning)
Hij woont vlak bij het station.	(hei-woont-VLAK bei-ĕt--staaSJON.)	*'He lives near the station.'*
Hij woont dicht bij het station.	(hei-woont-DICHT bei-ĕt--staaSJON.)	(same meaning)

To make yourself understood, you would need to know only one of these expressions; to understand what other people say to you, you have to know both of them.

2. *Vinden* 'to find' is used in stating one's opinion of things. We sometimes say 'I find it pleasant' for 'I think it's nice'. In Dutch they very often say this:

Ik vind het prettig.	(ik-vind-ĕt-PRETTich.)	*'I think it's nice.'*
Ik vind het koud.	(ik-vind-ĕt-KOUT.)	*'I think it's cold.'*

The ordinary meaning of the verb is as in English:

Zij kan de sleutels niet vinden.	(zĕ-kan-dĕ-SLEUtĕls niet- -VINdĕn.)	*'She can't find the keys.'*

3. The Dutch say 'sit to talk', not 'sit and talk':

Zij zitten te praten.	(zĕ-zittĕn-tĕ-PRAAtĕn.)	*'They sit and talk.'*

Often they talk this way where in English one would not mention the sitting:

Hij zit weer te bluffen.	(hei-ZIT-weer tĕ-BLUFFĕn.)	*'He's (sitting and) boasting again.'*

When the word *zitten* is itself in the infinitive form, the word *te* is usually omitted:

Zij zullen de heele avond zitten praten.	(zĕ-zullĕn-dĕ-heelĕ-AAvĕnt zittĕn-PRAAtĕn.)	*'They'll be sitting and talking all evening.'*
Hij heeft weer zitten bluffen.	(hei-HEEFT-weer zittĕn- -BLUFFĕn.)	*'He's been at his boasting again.'*

4. When the Dutch tell how long (*hoe lang*) someone did something, they often add the word *lang*:

Ik ben er een tijdlang geweest.	(ik-ben-ĕr-ĕn-TEIT-lang- -ghĕweest.)	*'I was there a while.'*
Zij hebben een jaar lang hier gewoond.	(zĕ-hebbĕn-ĕn-JAAR-lang hier- -ghĕWOONT.)	*'They lived here a year.'*
Wij hebben uren lang moeten loopen.	(wĕ-hebbĕn-UUrĕn-lang moetĕn- -LOOpĕn.)	*'We had to walk for hours.'*

Point 2. End-Words. The Dutch often use end-words where we use prepositions (words like *in, from, to* before a noun):

Zij gaat de deur *uit*.	(zĕ-ghaat-dĕ-DEUR-*uit*.)	*'She's going out (of) the door.'*
Ik ga de stad *in*.	(ik-ghaa-dĕ-STAT-*in*.)	*'I'm going down town (into the city).'*
Steek de straat *over*.	(steek-dĕ-STRAAT-*oovĕr*.)	*'Go across the street.'*

Point 3. Days of the Week.

Zondag	(ZONdach)	*'Sunday'*
Maandag	(MAANdach)	*'Monday'*
Dinsdag	(DINZdach)	*'Tuesday'*
Woensdag	(WOENZdach)	*'Wednesday'*
Donderdag	(DONdĕrdach)	*'Thursday'*
Vrijdag	(VREIdach)	*'Friday'*
Zaterdag	(ZAAtĕrdach)	*'Saturday'*

All seven are *die*-nouns, like the word *dag*. The first parts of three of them make sense:

de zon	(dĕ-ZON)	*'the sun'*
de maan	(dĕ-MAAN)	*'the moon'*
de donder	(dĕ-DONdĕr)	*'the thunder'*

Also *Vrijdag* sounds like *vrij* 'free' or like *vrijen* 'to court, make love.'

Point 4. Plurals. The new nouns *de oom* and *de tram* make their plurals with -*s* (although they end in a consonant): *ooms* 'uncles'; *trams* (*TREMS*) 'streetcars'. The plural of *de weg* 'the way, the road', has a long vowel: *wegen* (*WEEghĕn*) 'ways, roads'.

Point 5. Of it. Observe the following:

Hij heeft *er* niets *van* gezegd.	(hei-heeft-ĕr-niets-*van*- -ghĕZECHT.	*'He has said nothing of it.'*

Where English uses *it* after a preposition (*of it*, *with it*, *for it*), the Dutch use the word *daar* (unstressed *er*) and an end-word. Other examples:

Dit mes is niet scherp; ik kan *er* niet *mee* snijden.	(dit-MES is-niet-SCHERP; ik-kan-*ĕr*-niet-*mee*-SNEIdĕn.)	*'This knife isn't sharp; I can't cut with it.'*
Wat denkt u *er van?*	(wat-DENKT-uu-*ĕr-van?*)	*'What do you think of it?'*

Point 6. De and Den. In some phrases where the word *dĕ* comes before a vowel, an *n* is occasionally added:

aan de andere kant, aan den andere kant	(an-dĕ-andĕrĕ-KANT, an-dĕn-andĕrĕ-KANT)	*'at the other side'*

However, this is done only in certain expressions. In conventional Dutch spelling some writers add many such *n*'s, without regard to the actual pronunciation, to *de* and to adjectives; they are not consistent about these quirks of writing.

Ik heb het gegeten.	(ik-heb-ĕt-ghĕGHEEtĕn.)	*'I've eaten it.'*

They will say this also where we would say 'I ate it', 'I was eating it', 'I've been eating it', 'I did eat it', and so on:

Ik *heb* het gegeten.	(ik-HEB-ĕt-ghĕgheetĕn.)	*'I did eat it.'*
Ik heb het *niet* gegeten.	(ik-heb-ĕt-NIET-ghĕgheetĕn.)	*'I didn't eat it.'*

The participle comes at the end of the sentence or near it. If there is an end-word, it comes before the

Point 7. The Perfect-Phrase. A form of a verb like *eaten* (in *I've eaten it*) is called a *participle*. The ordinary Dutch way of talking about past happenings is to use the verb *hebben* and a participle:

participle. In conventional spelling the two words are then usually written without a space between:

Hij heeft het opgegeten.	(hei-heeft-ĕt-OP-ghĕgheetĕn.)	*'He's eaten it all up.'*

The phrase consisting of *hebben* with a participle is called the *perfect* phrase.

Making the Participle. Most Dutch verbs make the participle by prefixing the unstressed syllable *ge-* (*ghĕ-*) and adding an ending *-t*. Before this *t* there are only unvoiced mutes (*p, k, f, s, ch*), and *d-t* or *t-t* give just one *-t*, as when the *-t* is added for form 3 (*U gaat*, but *U weet*).

Examples:

Ik heb God *gedankt*. 'I thanked God.'

Het heeft maar een half uur *geduurd* (ghĕDUURT) 'I took only half an hour.'

Hebt u het al *gehoord* (ghĕHOORT)? 'Have you (already) heard it?'

Ik heb haar nooit *gekend* (ghĕKENT). 'I never knew her.'

Hij heeft Jans haar *geknipt*. 'He's been cutting Jack's hair.'

Dat heeft me veel geld *gekost*. 'That cost me lots of money.'

Hij heeft het niet *gekund* (ghĕKUNT). 'He wasn't able (to do) it.'

Hij heeft nog maar een jaar *geleefd* (ghĕLEEFT). 'He only lived one year longer.'

Zij heeft de bedden nog niet op*gemaakt*. 'She hasn't made the beds yet.'

Hij heeft niet *gemoogd* (ghĕMOOCHT). 'He wasn't allowed to.'

De kleermaker heeft mijn pak op*geperst*. 'The tailor pressed my suit.'

Wij hebben veel *gepraat*. 'We talked a lot.'

Gisteren heeft het *geregend* (ghĕREEghĕnt). 'Yesterday it rained.'

Ik heb de auto *gerepareerd* (ghĕreepaaREERT). 'I've fixed the car.'

Het heeft van nacht *gesneeuwd* (ghĕSNEEWT). 'It snowed in the night.'

De bus heeft niet *gestopt*. 'The bus didn't stop.'

Hij heeft voor dokter *gestudeerd* (ghĕstuuDEERT). 'He studied to be a doctor.'

Hij heeft een Hollandsche getrouwd (ghĕTROUT). 'He married a Dutchwoman.'

Waarom hebt u het niet aan een agent *gevraagd* (ghĕVRAACHT)? 'Why didn't you ask a policeman?'

Wij hebben de heele dag *gewerkt*. 'We've been working all day.'

Hij heeft niet *gewild* (ghĕWILT). *'He didn't want to.'*

Mijn oom heeft tien jaar in America *gewoond* (ghĕWOONT). *'My uncle lived in America for ten years.'*

Wie heeft dat *gezegd* (ghĕZECHT)? *'Who said that?'*

However, if a verb begins with the unstressed syllable *be-, ge-, ont-,* or *ver-* (or one of a few others), the participle does not add *ge-*. For instance, the verbs *betalen, gebruiken*:

Hebt u *betaald* (bĕTAALT)? *'Have you paid?'*

Wat hebt u *gebruikt*, mijnheer? *'What have you had (eaten or drunk), sir?'*

Double Infinitive. If there is an infinitive in a sentence, the perfect phrase is made with an infinitive instead of a participle, so that there are two infinitives. The one which replaces the participle comes first. There are some exceptions to this, but you have not yet come across any of them.

Ik *hoor* hem de trap *opgaan*. *'I hear him going up the stairs.'*

Ik *heb* hem de trap *hooren opgaan*. *'I heard him going up the stairs.'*

Kunt u het *verstaan?* *'Can you understand it?'*

Hebt u het *kunnen verstaan?* *'Were you able to understand it?'*

Zij *mag* niet *uitgaan*. *'She mayn't go out.'*

Zij *heeft* niet *mogen uitgaan*. *'She wasn't allowed to go out.'*

Hij *wil* het niet *doen*. *'He doesn't want to do it.'*

Hij *heeft* het niet *willen doen*. *'He didn't want to do it.'*

Irregular Perfect Phrase. Some verbs make the perfect phrase with *zijn* instead of *hebben*. In English we occasionally do this, as when we say 'He *is* come' instead of 'He *has* come'. The verbs that do this are mostly such as mean moving from one place to another (come, go, walk, run, and so on)

In Utrecht (UUtrecht) *zijn* we *overgestapt* op een andere trein. *"In Utrecht we changed to a different train.'*

Irregular Participles. About 150 of the commonest verbs form their participle in irregular ways.

a. Some take the ending *-ĕn* or *-n* (after vowels) instead of *-t*:

Zij *heeft* het vleesch *gebraden*. *'She has roasted the meat.'*

Wij *zijn* de stad in*gegaan*. '*We went down town.*'

Ik *heb* de kellner een fooi *gegeven*. '*I gave the waiter a tip.*'

Hoe *heeft* hij *geheeten*? '*What was his name?*'

Hij *heeft* me uren lang op*gehouden*. '*He delayed me (held me up) for hours.*'

Hij *is* gisteren *gekomen*. '*He came yesterday.*'

Zij *hebben* er ons niet in*gelaten*. '*They didn't let us in.*'

We *zijn* de heelĕ weg *geloopen*. '*We walked all the way.*'

Ik *heb* er een uur lang *gestaan*. '*I stood there an hour.*'

Ik *heb* me nog niet *gewasschen* (ghĕWASSĕn). '*I haven't washed (myself) yet.*'

Dat *heb* ik nooit *geweten*. '*I never knew that.*'

Maandag morgen *is* het kind ziek *geworden*. '*Monday morning the child got sick.*'

Ik *heb* het al *gezien*. '*I've already seen it.*'

Notice in the next few that before *ver-* and so on no *ge-* is added:

Ik *heb vergeten* de sleutel te nemen. '*I forgot to take the key.*'

U *hebt* me niet goed *verstaan*. '*You haven't understood me right.*'

And with double infinitive:

Hij *komt* bij ons *eten*. '*He is coming to our house for a meal.*'

Hij *is* bij ons *komen eten*. '*He came to our house for a meal.*'

Wij *laten* de auto *repareeren*. '*We are having the car repaired.*'

Wij *hebben* de auto *laten repareeren*. '*We've had the car repaired.*'

Zij *moet* het *doen*. '*She must do it.*'

Zij *heeft* het *moeten doen*. '*She had to do it.*'

Ik *zie* ze *komen*. '*I see them coming.*'

Ik *heb* ze *zien komen*. '*I saw them coming.*'

Ik *heb* er een uur lang *staan wachten*. '*I stood waiting there for an hour.*'

b. Some change in other ways. The verbs that you have had so far that have irregular participles are as follows:

beginnen : *is* begonnen
bezoeken : bezocht

brengen : gebracht
denken : gedacht
doen : gedaan
drinken : gedronken
eten : gegeten
hebben : gehad
krijgen : gekregen
nemen : genomen
rijden : *is* gereden

scheren : geschoren
snijden : gesneden
spreken : gesproken
steken : *heeft* or *is* gestoken
vinden : gevonden
vliegen : *is* gevlogen
zijn : *is* geweest
zitten : gezeten
zoeken : gezocht

Examples:

Is de bioscoop al *begonnen?* 'Has the movie begun yet?'

Ik *heb* mijn oom *bezocht.* 'I've been visiting my uncle.'

Hebt u mijn bagage naar het station *gebracht?* 'Have you brought my baggage to the station?'

Ik *heb* aan u *gedacht.* 'I've been thinking of you.'

Heeft hij het nog niet *gedaan?* 'Hasn't he done it yet?'

Je hebt te veel *gedronken*, Piet. 'You've been drinking too much, Pete.'

Hebt u al *gegeten?* 'Have you had dinner (already)?'

Ik *heb* geen tijd *gehad.* 'I haven't had time.'

Hebt u het geld al *gekregen?* 'Have you (already) received the money?'

Zij *hebben* de kinderen allemaal mee*genomen*. 'They took all the children along.'

We *zijn* naar Den Haag *gereden.* 'We rode (or drove) to The Hague.'

Ik *heb* me *geschoren.* 'I've shaved.'

Ik *heb* me *gesneden.* 'I've cut myself.'

Ik *heb* hem nog niet *gesproken.* 'I haven' yet spoken to him.'

Zij *is* de straat over*gestoken*. 'She has crossed the street.'

Hebben ze hun bagage *gevonden?* 'Have they found their baggage?'

We *zijn* naar Brussel *gevlogen.* 'We flew to Brussels.'

Ze *is* nooit in Engeland *geweest.* 'She's never been in England.'

We *hebben* een uurtje in het café *gezeten.* 'We sat just a wee hour in the café.'

De heele morgen *heeft* ze haar sleutels *gezocht.* 'She looked for her keys all morning.'

And with double infinitive:

Ze *zitten* te *praten.* 'They are sitting and talking.'

Ze *hebben* de heele avond *zitten praten.* 'They've been sitting and talking all evening.'

2. Review of Basic Sentences with English Covered

C. WHAT WOULD YOU SAY?

1. What Would You Say?

Practice giving various answers to each of the following questions. Say both question and answer repeatedly out loud until you get to the point where you can answer without any hesitation:

1. WAT-hept-uu ghistĕr-AAvĕnt ghĕDAAN?
2. bent-uu-OOJT in-niew-JORK-ghĕweest?
3. bent-uu-OOJT in-HOLLant-ghĕweest?
4. WAT-hept-uu van-DAACH al-ghĕDAAN?
5. hoe is-ĕt-WEER van-DAACH?
6. WOONT-uu in-ĕn-STAT ov-op-ĕt-LANT?
7. HOE-veel-BROERS en-ZUStĕrs-hept-uu?
8. SPREEKT-uu HOLLants?
9. HOUT-uu-van-ghĕBRAAdĕn-KIP?

Wat hebt u gisteravond gedaan?
Bent u ooit in New York geweest?
Bent u ooit in Holland geweest?
Wat hebt u vandaag al gedaan?
Hoe is het weer vandaag?
Woont u in een stad of op het land?
Hoeveel broers en zusters hebt u?
Spreekt u Hollandsch?
Houdt u van gebraden kip?

10. is-hier-ĕn-ghoedĕ-wassĕREI waar-ik-mĕn-GHOET kan-laatĕn-WASSĕn?

Is hier een goede wasscherij waar ik mijn goed kan laten wasschen?

2. What Did You Say?

D. LISTENING IN

1. *Mr. Bell asks directions from a waiter.*

De kellner:	wat-wilt-uu-ghĕBRUIkĕn, heerĕn?
Bell:	BRENG-mĕ ĕn-kop-KOFFie, als-t-uu-BLIEFT.
Carver:	voor-MEI ĕn-ghlas-BIER.
Bell:	KELLnĕr, hoe-KOOmĕn-wĕ van-HIER naar-ĕt--muuZEEjum?
De kellner:	met-dĕ-TREM.
	die-STOPT-hier an-dĕ-ANdĕrĕ-kant van-dĕ--STRAAT.
	REIT tot-dĕ-KOOnings-laan.
	an-dĕ-KOOnings-laan moet-uu-OOvĕr-stappĕn op--lein-BEE.
	REIT-DAN tot-ĕt-eint-van-dĕ-lein.
	ghaa-dan-RECHS tot-uu-an-ĕn-KLEIN PARK--komt, en-dan-LINKS.
	an-dĕ-ANdĕrĕ-kant van-dit-PARK zult-uu-ĕn--GHROOT ghĕBOU-zien.

Wat wilt u gebruiken, heeren?
Breng me een koop koffie, alstublieft.
Voor mij een glas bier.
Kellner, hoe komen we van hier naar het museum?
Met de tram.
Die stopt hier aan de andere kant van de straat.
Rijd tot de Koningslaan.
Aan de Koningslaan moet u overstappen op Lijn B.
Rijd dan tot het eind van de lijn.
Ga dan rechts tot u aan een klein park komt, en dan links.
Aan de andere kant van dit park zult u een groot gebouw zien.

	DAT is-ĕt-muuZEEjum.	Dat is het museum.
Bell:	ik-weet-NIET of-ik-DAT-nuu allĕmaal-WEET.	Ik weet niet of ik dat nu allemaal weet.
De kellner:	ik-HEP-hier ĕn-KAART van-dĕ-STAT.	Ik heb hier een kaart van de stad.
	DIE zal-ik-uu-laatĕn-ZIEN.	Die zal ik u laten zien.
	DAN-zult-uu-ĕt-wel-BEEtĕr kunnĕn-VINdĕn.	Dan zult u het wel beter kunnen vinden.

2. *Mr. and Mrs. Dekker want to go out, but have lost their keys.*

Dekker:	KOM, maaRIE. ĕt-is-LAAT.	Kom, Marie. 't Is laat.
	wĕ-moetĕn-nuu-GHAAN. dĕ-TAKsie is-al--HIER.	We moeten nu gaan. De taxi is al hier.
Mevrouw Dekker:	ik-kan-mĕn-SLEUtĕls-niet-findĕn.	Ik kan mijn sleutels niet vinden.
	hep-JEI-zĕ-ghĕzien, ALfret?	Heb jij ze gezien, Alfred?
Dekker:	NEE, maRIEtjĕ. ik-hep-zĕ-NIET.	Neen, Marietje. Ik heb ze niet.
	kan-PIET zĕ-mischien-ghĕNOOmĕn-hebbĕn?	Kan Piet ze misschien genomen hebben?
	PIEtjĕ! hep-jĕ-misCHIEN moedĕrs-SLEUtĕls--ghĕnoomĕn?	Pietje! Heb je misschien moeders sleutels genomen?
Piet:	NEE-vaadĕr. ik-hep-zĕ-nieet-ghĕHAT.	Nee, vader. Ik heb ze niet gehad.
	zal-ik-zĕ-ZOEkĕn?	Zal ik ze zoeken?
Mevrouw Dekker:	ik-hep-zĕ-al-ĕn-HALV-uur-lang-ghĕZOCHT.	Ik heb ze al een half uur lang gezocht.
Piet:	hier-ZEIN-zĕ, MOEdĕr.	Hier zijn ze, moeder.
	ik-hep-zĕ-ghĕVONdĕn; HIER, op-hĕt--TAAfĕltjĕ bei-jĕ-BET.	Ik heb ze gevonden—hier, op het tafeltje bij je bed.

3. *Mr. Bell is trying to find a certain store.   Mr. Kuypers asks him about it.*

Kuypers:	hept-uu-dĕ-WINkĕl-ghĕVONdĕn?
Bell:	NEE, ik-hep-ĕm-NIET kunnĕn-VINdĕn.
Kuypers:	hept-uu-LANG-ghĕzocht?
Bell:	OO, ĕn-halv-UURtjĕ.
	op-ĕt-PLEIN, voor-ĕt-stat-HUIS, staat-immĕrs-
	-ALteit ĕn-aaGHENT.
Kuypers:	en-DIE hept-uu-ĕt-ghĕVRAACHT?
Bell:	JAA; ghĕVRAACHT heb-ik-ĕt-ĕm-WEL.
Kuypers:	NUU, en-WAT heeft-ie-ghĕZECHT?
Bell:	ik-heb-ĕm-NIET kunnĕn-vĕrSTAAN.
	ik-heb-ĕm-dus-ghĕVRAACHT wat-LANGsaamĕr tĕ-
	-SPREEkĕn.
	toen-HEEFT-ie-ĕt-ALLĕmaal NOCH-ĕs-ghĕzecht.
	maar-IK-heb-ĕm NOCH-niet-kunnĕn-vĕrStaan.
Kuypers:	en-TOEN?
Bell:	JAA, HOOR-ĕs, heeft-ie-ghĕZECHT.
	als-uu-gheen-HOLLants-vĕrstaat, kan-ik-uu-NIET-
	-seghĕn waar-die-WINkĕl-is.
	ghaa-maar-naar-HUIS, heeft-ie-ghĕZECHT, en-
	-VRAAGH-ĕt an-jĕ-MOEdĕr.

Hebt u de winkel gevonden?
Neen, ik heb hem niet kunnen vinden.
Hebt u lang gezocht?
O, een half uurtje.
Op het plein, voor het stadhuis, staat immers
altijd een agent.
En die hebt u het gevraagd?
Ja; gevraagd heb ik het hem wel.
Nu, en wat heeft hij gezegd?
Ik heb hem niet kunnen verstaan.
Ik heb hem dus gevraagd wat langzamer te
spreken.
Toen heeft hij het allemaal nog eens gezegd.
Maar ik heb hem nog niet kunnen verstaan.
En toen?
"Ja, hoor eens" heeft hij gezegd.
"Als u geen Hollandsch verstaat, kan ik u
niet zeggen waar die winkel is.
"Ga maar naar huis," heeft hij gezegd, "en
vraag het aan je moeder."

E. Conversation

1. Review of Basic Sentences with Dutch Covered

2. Vocabulary and Word Study Check-up

In this check-up be sure to do the following two things:

1. Have the Guide, or some member of the group, read off the sentences given as examples in Point 7 of the Word Study. The other members of the group should take turns translating into English. Each Dutch sentence can be rendered in English in several ways, and it does not matter at all whether the same wording is used as is found in the book, so long as it is clear that the meaning of the Dutch is understood.

2. Have some member of the group give each of the English sentences from the same section, and have the rest of the group take turns trying to give the Dutch. Each English sentence, of course, might be rendered in Dutch in several ways, but you have no way of knowing any except the one given in Point 7 of the Word Study; therefore don't be satisfied until you can say the Dutch sentence in exactly the same words as are given there.

3. Carrying on Conversation

You know enough Dutch now not to need the help of suggested outlined conversations that have been given previously at this point. When possible, prepare in pairs or threes before the actual class meeting, so that when your turn comes in the group meeting you can carry on and act out your conversation as fluently as possible.

FINDER LIST

After each verb is given the participle (P) if it is irregular; if the perfect phrase is made with *zijn*, the participle is given with the word *is* before it.

de agent (aaGHENT) 'the policeman'
> beter 'better'
>> U neemt beter de bus. 'You'd better take the bus.'
>> bezoeken P bezocht (běZOEkěn, běZOCHT) 'to visit'
> de bus 'the bus'

de deur 'the door'
> dicht 'dense, close, shut'
>> De deur is dicht. 'The door is shut.'
>> dicht bij ons huis 'near our house'
> de Dinsdag 'the Tuesday'
> de Donderdag 'the Thursday'

het gebouw (ghěBOU) 'the building'
de gids (GHITS) 'the guide'
> gister, gisteren 'yesterday'

> half 'half'
> hooren 'to hear'

de kaart 'the card, the map'
de kant 'the side'
de koning 'the king'

de laan 'the avenue'
> de Koningslaan 'King Avenue'

de lijn 'the line'
> loopen P is geloopen 'to walk'

de Maandag 'the Monday'
het museum (muuZEEjum) 'the museum'

> niemand 'nobody'

de oom 'the uncle'
> ooms 'uncles'
> over (end-word) 'over'
>> overstappen 'to transfer, to change cars'
>> oversteken 'to cross' (a street)
>> Wij moeten hier de straat oversteken. 'We have to cross the street here.'

het park 'the park'
het plein 'the principal square' (of a town)
> praten 'to talk, to chat'
> prettig 'pleasant'

> rijden P is gereden 'to ride'

> staan P gestaan 'to stand'
het stadhuis (stat-HUIS) 'the city hall'
> stappen P is gestapt 'to step'
> steken P gestoken 'to stick'
>> oversteken 'to cross' (a street)

stoppen 'to stop'
de straat 'the street'

de tante 'the aunt'
de taxi (TAKsie, TEKsie) 'the taxi'
het theater (teeJAAtĕr) 'the theater'
   thuis (TUIS) 'at home'
   toen 'then'
de tram (TREM) 'the streetcar'
    trams (TREMS) 'streetcars'
    trammen (TREMMĕn) 'to ride on streetcars'

   uit (end-word) 'out'
    uitgaan 'to go out'

   ver 'far'
   vergeten P vergeten (vĕrGHEEtĕn) 'to forget'

vinden P gevonden 'to find'
   Hoe vindt U de soep? 'How do you like the soup?'
vlak 'flat'
   vlak bij 'near'
vragen 'to ask'
de Vrijdag 'the Friday'

was 'was'
de weg 'the way, the road'
   wegen 'ways, roads'
de Woensdag 'the Wednesday'

de Zaterdag 'the Saturday'
de Zondag 'the Sunday'

SHOPPING

A. BASIC SENTENCES

Mr. Bell goes shopping for clothes.

ENGLISH EQUIVALENTS	AIDS TO LISTENING	CONVENTIONAL SPELLING

Mr. Bell

old	OUT	oud
My clothes are very old	mein-KLEErĕ zein-ERCH OUT.	Mijn kleeren zijn erg oud.
more	MEER	meer
to wear or to carry	DRAAghĕn	dragen
I can't wear them any more.	ik-kan-zĕ-NIET-meer DRAAghĕn.	Ik kan ze niet meer dragen.
to buy	KOOpĕn	koopen
I guess I'll have to buy new ones.	ik-zal-wel-NIEwĕ-moete-koopĕn.	Ik zal wel nieuwe moeten koopen.

Mr. Olpers

What do you need?	wat-hept-uu-NOOdich?	Wat hebt u noodig?

[11–A]   **211**

the shirt	hĕt-HEMT	het hemd
under	ONdĕr	onder
the sock	dĕ-SOK	de sok
the shoe	dĕ-SCHOEN	de schoen
the hand	dĕ-HANT	de hand
the glove	dĕ-HANT-schoen	de handschoen
the necktie	dĕ-DAS	de das
the hat	dĕ-HOET	de hoed

Everything; a new suit, shirts, underwear, socks, shoes, gloves, neckties, and a new hat . . . ALLĕs; ĕn-niew-PAK, HEMdĕn, ONDĕr-ghoet, SOKKĕn, SCHOEnĕ, HANT-schoenĕn, DASSĕn, en-ĕn-niewĕ-HOET . . . Alles; een nieuw pak, . hemden, ondergoed, sokken, schoenen, handschoenen, dassen en een nieuwe hoed . . .

Mr. Olpers

| *Are you going to get married?* | ghaat-uu-TROUwĕn? | Gaat u trouwen? |

Mr. Bell

No, not that.	NEE, dat-NIET.	Neen, dat niet.
to help	HELpĕn	helpen
But will you help me?	maar-wilt-uu-mĕ-HELpĕn?	Maar wilt u me helpen?

Mr. Olpers

| *Yes, (very) gladly.* | JAA, heel-GHRAACH. | Ja, heel graag. |
| *best* | BEST | best |

212   [11–A]

the department store	hĕt-WAArĕn-huis	het warenhuis
We'd better go to a department store.	wĕ-kunnĕn-hĕt-BEStĕ naar-ĕn--WAArĕ-huis-ghaan.	We kunnen het beste naar ᴇᴠ ɪ warenhuis gaan.
Do you know Vink and Sons' store?	kent-uu-ĕt-WAArĕ-huis van--VINK-en-zoonĕn?	Kent;u het warenhuis van Vin ᴇɴ Zonen?
the price	dĕ-PREIS	de prijs
the merchandise	dĕ-WAAR	de waar
the quality	dĕ-kwaalieTEIT	de qualiteit
The prices are'nt high there, and they have good stuff.	dĕ-PREIzĕn zein-ĕr-niet-HOOCH, en-dĕ-WAAR is-van-GHOEdĕ kwaalieTEIT.	De prijzen zijn er niet hoog, e. ᴄᴄ waar is van goede qualiteit.

Clerk

What can I do for you, gentlemen?	wat-iz-ĕr-van-uuw-DIENST, HEErĕn?	Wat is er van uw dienst, heeren?

Mr. Bell

I need some shirts.	ik-hep-OOvĕr-hemdĕ-noodich.	Ik heb overhemden noodig

Clerk

Here are some shirts, sir.	hier-zein-HEMdĕn, mĕNEER.	Hier zijn hemden, mijnheer.
These are of the finest quality.	DIE-zein van-dĕ-bestĕ-kwaalieTEIT.	Die zijn van de beste qualiteit.
What's your size, sir?	wat-is-uu-NUMMĕr, mĕNEER?	Wat is uw nummer, mijnheer?

the collar	dĕ-BOORT	de boord
the sleeve	dĕ-MOU	de mouw
the measure	dĕ-MAAT	de maat
The collar is sixteen and one half and the sleeve thirty-five, in American sizes.	BOORT ZEStien en-ĕn-HALF, MOU zez-ĕn-DERtich, in-dĕ--ameerieKAANsĕ MAAT.	Boord zestien en een half, mouw vijf en dertig, in de Ameri- kaansche maat.

Clerk

Very good, sir.	GHOET-mĕneer.	Goed, mijnheer.
We know the American sizes here.	wei-KENNĕ-hier dĕ-ameeriekaansĕ--MAAtĕn.	Wij kennen hier de Amerikaansche maten.

Clerk

to look	KEIkĕn	kijken
Neckties, sir?	DASSĕn, mĕNEER?	Dassen, mijnheer?
Will you please look over here?	wilt-uu-HIER als-t-uu-BLIEFT eevĕn-KEIkĕn?	Wilt u hier alstublieft even kijken?
of them	ĕr	er
the color	dĕ-KLEUR	de kleur
We have them in all colors.	wĕ-HEBBĕn-zĕ-hier in-ALLĕ KLEUrĕn	We hebben ze hier in alle kleuren.

Mr. Bell

really	WERkĕlik	werkelijk
white	WIT	wit
black	ZWART	zwart
gray	GHREIS	grijs
brown	BRUIN	bruin
red	ROOT	rood
blue	BLOU	blauw
yellow	GHEEL	geel

Yes, there really are all colors: white, black, gray, brown, red, blue, green, and yellow.

JAA, ĕr-ZEIN-werkĕlik ALLĕ--kleurĕn: WIT, ZWART, GHREIS, BRUIN, ROOT, BLOU, GHROEN, en-GHEEL.

Ja, er zijn werkelijk alle kleuren: wit, zwart, grijs, bruin, rood, blauw, groen en geel.

I'll take this blue one here, and two of those gray ones.

ik-neem-deezĕ-BLOUwĕ-hier, en-TWEE van-die-GHREIzĕ.

Ik neem deze blauwe hier, en twee van die grijze.

Clerk

to fit	PASSĕn	passen
to try on	AAN-passĕn	aanpassen

Will you just try on this suit, sir?

wilt-uu-dit-PAK eens-eevĕn-AAN--passĕn, mĕNEER?

Wilt u dit pak eens even aanpassen, mijnheer?

How do you like this suit, Mr. Olpers?	hoe-vint-uu-DIT-pak, měneer-OLpěrs?	Hoe vindt u dit pak, Mijnheer Olpers?
the attendant	dě-běDIENdě	de bediende
The salesman says it fits very well.	dě-WINkěl-bědiendě-zecht dat-ět-ghoet-PAST.	De winkelbediende zegt dat het goed past.

Mr. Olpers

It doesn't fit you very well.	ět-past-uu-NIET erch-GHOET.	Het past u niet erg goed.

Mr. Bell

the coat	dě-JAS	de jas
the vest	hět-VEST	het vest
wide	WEIT	wijd
Yes, I think (that) the coat and the vest are too long and too wide.	JAA, ik-DENK dat-dě-JAS en-ět-VEST tě-LANG en-tě-WEIT-zein.	Ja, ik denk dat de jas en het vest te lang en te wijd zijn.

Mr. Olpers

the pair of trousers	dě-BROEK	de broek
tight	NOU	nauw
to stand or to suit	STAAN	staan
And I don't think the trousers fit either.	en-dě-BROEK-past OOK-niet.	En de broek past ook niet.

They're too tight and too short.	zĕ-is-tĕ-NOU en-tĕ-KORT.	Ze is te nauw en te kort.
No, Mr. Bell, that suit isn't right for you.	NEE, mĕneer-BEL, dit-PAK STAAT-uu-niet.	Nee, Mijnheer Bell, dit pak staat u niet.

Mr. Bell

I won't take this suit.	DIT-pak neem-ik-NIET.	Dit pak neem ik niet.

Clerk

something or *anything*	IETS	iets
Anything else I can do for you sir?	noch-iets-van-uu-DIENST, mĕNEER?	Nog iets van uw dienst, mijnheer?
to send	STUUrĕn	sturen
Shall I send the other things to the hotel for you?	zal-ik-dĕ-ANdĕrĕ-kleerĕn-voor-uu--naar-ĕt-hooTEL-stuurĕn?	Zal ik de andere kleeren voor u naar het hotel sturen?

Mr. Bell

rather	LIEvĕr	liever
No, I'd rather take them with me now.	NEE, ik-NEEM-ze-lievĕr MEE.	Neen, ik neem ze liever mee.

Clerk

to pack	PAKKĕn	pakken
to wrap up	IN-pakkĕn	inpakken
Then I'll wrap them up for you right away.	dan-zal-ik-zĕ-DAAdĕlik voor-uu--IN-pakkĕn.	Dan zal ik ze dadelijk voor u inpakken.
the pack or *the bundle*	het-PAK	het pak
Here's the package, sir.	HIER is-ĕt-PAKjĕ, mĕNEER.	Hier is het pakje, mijnheer.

Mr. Olpers

For the suit we'd better go to a store that just sells clothes.
or you can have one made at a tailor's.

(Here with us) in Holland that isn't quite as expensive as in America.

voor-ĕt-PAK kunnĕn-wĕ-BEEtĕr naar-ĕn-KLEERĕn-winkĕl-ghaan.
uu-kunt-ĕr-OOK-een bei-ĕn-KLEER-maakĕr-laatĕ-maakĕn.
hier-bei-ons-in-HOLLant is-dat-NIET-zoo-duur als-in-aMEEriekaa.

Voor het pak kunnen we beter naar een kleerenwinkel gaan.
U kunt er ook een bij een kleermaker laten maken.
Hier bij ons in Holland is dat niet zoo duur als in Amerika.

Mr. Bell

(Yes) and I still have to have a warm overcoat, and a raincoat.

JAA, en-dan-moet-ik-OOK-noch ĕn-warmĕ-OOvĕr-jas-hebbĕn, en-ĕn-REEghĕ-jas.

Ja, en dan moet ik ook nog een warme overjas hebben en een regenjas.

B. Word Study

1. Word Study

Point 1. To Look. To try to see something (as by turning one's head or eyes) is *kijken* (participle *gekeken*):

Kijk eens hier.	(keik-ĕs-HIER.)	'*Just look here.*'
Kijk dat meisje eens.	(keik-dat-MEIsjĕ-ĕs.)	'*Just look at that girl.*'
Zij heeft uit het raam gekeken.	(zĕ-HEEFT uit-ĕt-RAAM-ghĕkeekĕn.)	'*She looked out of the window.*'

To have such and such an appearance is expressed in several different ways; one is *er uitzien* (a literal trans- lation would make no sense in English):

U ziet er goed uit.	(uu-ZIET-ĕr ghoet-UIT.)	*'You are looking well.'*
Hij heeft er gisteren niet goed uitgezien.	(hei-heeft-ĕr-GHIStĕrĕ NIET- -ghoet UIT-ghĕzien.)	*'He didn't look well yesterday.'*

Point 2. Er. The word *er* is always unstressed, pronounced *ĕr* (and sometimes, by some people, *dĕr*), and it means literally 'of them' or 'some of them'. But the Dutch use it in many connections where we do not say '(some) of them' in English:

Heb je nog cigaretten?	(hep-jĕ-noch-sieghĕRETTĕn?)	*'Got any more cigarettes?'*
Ja, ik heb *er* nog een paar.	(JAA, ik-HEB-ĕr-noch ĕn-PAAR.)	*'Yes, I still have a couple.'*
Ja zeker, ik heb *er* nog.	(jaa-ZEEkĕr, ik-HEB-ĕr-noch.)	*'Sure, I've still got some.'*
Neen, ik heb *er* niet meer.	(NEE, ik-HEB-ĕr niet-MEER.)	*'No, I haven't got any more.'*

There are three words *ĕr* (all three sometimes pronounced *dĕr*):

1. unstressed for *daar*

Is er een restaurant in dit hotel?	(is-ĕr-ĕn-rĕstoRANG in-dit- -hooTEL?)	*'Is there a restaurant in this hotel?'*

2. unstressed for *haar*

Ik ken haar niet.	(ik-KEN-ĕr-niet.)	*'I don't know her.'*

3. 'of them, some of them'

Ik zou er graag een dozijn willen hebben.	(ik-ZOU-ĕr-ghraach ĕn-dooZEIN- -willĕn-hebbĕn.)	*'I'd like a dozen of them.'*

Point 3. Het staat u niet. The verb *staan* 'to stand' also means 'to be becoming, to suit', of clothes and the like:

Die hoed staat haar.	(die-HOET STAAT-ĕr.)	*'That hat is becoming to her.'*
Die hoed staat haar goed.	(die-HOET STAAT-ĕr-GHOET.)	(same meaning)
Blauw staat u beter dan rood.	(BLOU staat-uu-BEEtĕr dan--ROOT.)	*'Blue is more becoming to you than red.'*

Point 4. Clothing. The general word for a shirt is *het hemd*, but when nothing more is said this is likely to be taken to mean an undershirt. To specify, one says *het overhemd* (*ĕt-OOvĕrhemt*) for 'the (outer) shirt'. In the case of trousers and drawers it is different; the simple word means trousers only: *de broek* (*dĕ-BROEK*) 'the (pair of) trousers', *de onderbroek* (*dĕ-ONdĕrbroek*) 'the (pair of) drawers'.

Het pak means a pack or big bundle, and also a suit (of clothes). The diminutive *het pakje* means a package or small bundle, of the size you would get in shopping, and also a package of set size, as in *een pakje cigaretten* 'a pack of cigarettes'.

The verb *pakken* means 'to pack'; with the end-word *in* it means 'to pack up, to wrap up':

Zal ik het voor u inpakken?	(zaI-ik-ĕt-voor-uu-IN-pakkĕn?)	*'Shall I wrap it up for you?'*

Point 5. Verb Forms. The following verbs in this Unit have irregular participles:

dragen, P gedragen

helpen, P geholpen
kijken, P gekeken
koopen, P gekocht

Examples:

Ze heeft haar nieuwe hoed nog niet gedragen.	(zĕ-heeft-ĕr-niewĕ-HOET noch--niet-ghĕDRAAghĕn.)	*'She hasn't yet worn her new hat.'*
Ik heb hem geholpen.	(ik-heb-ĕm-ghĕHOLpĕn.)	*'I helped him.'*

Ze heeft uit het raam gekeken.	(ze-heeft-uit-ět-RAAM-ghěkeekěn.)	*'She looked out of the window.'*
Ik heb een paar schoenen gekocht.	(ik-hep-ěn-paar-SCHOEněn- -ghěkocht.)	*'I've bought a pair of shoes.'*

The remaining verbs in this Unit have regular participles:

Hebt u uw koffer al gepakt?	(hept-uu-uu-KOFFěr al-ghěPAKT?)	*'Have you (already) packed your trunk?'*
Hebt u de kleeren al ingepakt?	(hept-uu-dě-KLEErěn al-IN- -ghěpakt?)	*'Have you wrapped up the clothes?'*
De broek heb ik nog niet aangepast.	(dě-BROEK heb-ik-noch-niet- -AAN-ghěpast.)	*'I haven't yet tried on the trousers.'*

Point 6. Prepositions and End-Words. Some words are both *prepositions* ('*in* the room') and *end-words* ('he locked me *in*'). In Dutch, a preposition comes before a noun or a pronoun, but an end-word comes at or near the end of a sentence:

De hemden zijn *in de koffer.*	(dě-HEMděn zein-*in-dě-KOFF*ěr.)	*'The shirts are in the trunk.'*
Hij pakt de hemden *in.*	(hei-PAKT dě-HEMděn-*IN*.)	*'He is wrapping up the shirts.'*
Ik hoor hun *op de trap.*	(ik-HOOR-hun *op-dě-TRAP*.)	*'I hear them on the stairs.'*
Ze loopen de trap *op.*	(zě-LOOpěn dě-TRAP-*op*.)	*'They're running up the stairs.'*

However, some prepositions are not used as end-words; instead, some other word or expression is used. The most important are the three following cases:

1. The preposition *met* 'with' is matched by the end-word *mee* 'along':

Zij eet *met ons.*	(zě-EET *met-ONS*.)	*'She's eating with us.'*
Zij gaat *mee.*	(zě-ghaat-*MEE*.)	*'She's going along.'*
Zij gaat *met ons mee.*	(zě-GHAAT met-ons-MEE.)	*'She's going along with us.'*

2. The preposition *aan* (*AN*) 'on, at, to' is matched by the end-word *aan* (*AAN*) 'on, at':

Geef het geld *aan uw vriend*.	(GHEEV-ĕt-GHELT *an-uu--VRIENT*.)	*'Give the money to your friend.'*
Geef me even de suiker *aan*.	(GHEEF-mĕ-eevĕ dĕ-SUIkĕr-*aan*.)	*'Please pass me the sugar.'*

3. The preposition *naar* 'to' is matched by the (compound) end-word *naar toe* (*naar-TOE*) 'to, toward':

Ik ga *naar het station*.	(ik-GHAA *naar-ĕt-staaSJON*.)	*'I'm going to the station.'*
Waar gaat u *naar toe?*	(waar-GHAAT-uu *naar-TOE?*)	*'Where are you going (to)?'*

In some expressions (but not in all) the preposition *van* 'of, from' is matched by the compound end-word *vandaan* (*van-DAAN*) 'from':

Hij komt *van de bank*.	(hei-KOMT *van-dĕ-BANK*.)	*'He's coming from the bank.'*
Waar komt hij *vandaan?*	(waar-KOMT-ie *van-DAAN?*)	*'Where's he coming from?'*

Uses of End-Words. End-words have three principal uses, but one cannot really draw a line between these uses. They are mentioned here only because this will help you to understand Dutch.

1. The end-word goes with a verb:

Ze *pakt* het waschgoed *in*.   *'She's wrapping up the things for washing.'*

2. The end-word goes rather with a preceding noun:

We gaan *de stad in*.   *'We're going down town.'*

3. The end-word goes rather with *waar* 'where', *daar*, *er* 'there', or *hier* 'heer':

Hier is een pakje, maar wat is *er in?*   *'Here's a package, but what's in it?'*

It would be very hard to assign every instance of an end-word to one of these three uses, but you will find it helpful to go through the following outline.

1. The combinations of a verb with an end-word often have some odd and unexpected meaning. In Dutch dictionaries these combinations are entered as separate items, with end-word and verb (in the infinitive form) written together, as *aannemen* 'to accept'.

Examples:

Fooien *neemt* hij niet *aan.*	'*He doesn't accept tips.*'
Geef me even het zout *aan.*	'*Pass me the salt, please.*'
Wilt u het even voor me *inpakken?*	'*Will you just wrap it up for me?*'
Op het plein *stappen* we *over.*	'*At the main square we change cars.*'
Hier moeten we de straat *oversteken.*	'*Here we must cross the street.*'
Ik mag vandaag niet *uitgaan.*	'*I mayn't go out today.*'
Hij zegt dat ik er niet goed *uitzie.*	'*He says I'm not looking well.*'

In combination with verbs many end-words occur which are not like prepositions. Such end-words are usually plain as to their meaning; for instance, *terug* 'back' and *vooruit* 'ahead, in advance':

Wanneer *komt* u *terug?*	'*When are you coming back?*'
Ga maar *vooruit.*	'*Just go on ahead.*'
We *betalen* de huur *vooruit.*	'*We pay the rent in advance.*'

2. Combinations of end-words with nouns sound much like the combinations with verbs, except that the end-word is oftener unstressed. The noun comes right before the end-word. The end-word matches some preposition. The meanings are fairly plain, and so the combinations are often not listed in dictionaries.

Ik moet *de stad in*gaan.	(ik-moet-*dĕ-STAT-in*-ghaan.)	'*I have to go down town.*'
Ik moet *de stad in.*	(ik-moet-*dĕ-STAT-in.*)	(same meaning)
Hij gaat juist *de deur uit.*	(hei-ghaat-JUIST *dĕ-DEUR-uit.*)	'*He's just now going out the door.*'

3. Combinations of a preposition with *what, this, that, it* are rarely used in Dutch. Instead, they use the words *waar, hier, daar, er* with an end-word that replaces the preposition. The end-word sometimes comes immediately after these words instead of coming at the end of the sentence. In their conventional spelling, the Dutch are very inconsistent about running the two words together.

Ik snijd het vleesch *met dit mes.*		'*I cut the meat with this knife.*'
Waarmee snijdt u het vleesch?	(WAAR-mee . . .)	'*With what do you cut the meat?*'
Waar snijdt u het vleesch *mee?*	(WAAR SNEIT-uu ět-VLEES--mee?)	'*What do you cut the meat with?*'
Dit is het mes *waarmee* ik vleesch snijd.		'*This is the knife with which I cut meat.*'
Dit is het mes *waar* ik het vleesch *mee* snijd.	(DIT-is-ět-MES waar-ik-ět-VLEES mee-sneit.)	'*This is the knife (that) I cut the meat with.*'
Hiermee kan ik het vleesch niet snijden.	(HIER-mee kan-ik-ět-VLEES niet-SNEIděn.)	'*With this I can't cut the meat.*'
Hier kan ik het vleesch niet *mee* snijden.		'*I can't cut the meat with this.*'
Daarmee kan ik geen vleesch snijden.		'*With that I can't cut any meat.*'
Daar kan ik geen vleesch *mee* snijden.		'*I can't cut any meat with that (thing).*'
Dit mes is niet meer scherp; ik kan *er* het vleesch niet *mee* snidjen.		'*This knife isn't sharp any more; I can't cut the meat with it.*'
Ik kan het vleesch *er mee* niet snijden.		'*I can't cut the meat with it.*'

Other examples, with the word *over:*

Ze praten altijd *over de oorlog.*   '*They're always talking about the war.*'

Waarover praten ze?	'*About what are they talking?*'
Waar praten ze *over?*	'*What are they talking about?*'
Ik weet niet *waarover* ze praten.	'*I don't know what they're talking about.*'
Hierover praten ze altijd.	'*They're always talking about this.*'
Hier praten ze altijd *over.*	'*They're always talking about this.*'
Daarover praten ze altijd.	'*They're always talking about that.*'
Daar praten ze altijd *over.*	'*They're always talking about that.*'
Ze praten *er* altijd *over.*	'*They're always talking about it.*'
Ze praten altijd *er over.*	'*They're always talking about it.*'

Compounds. Notice that prepositions or end-words often appear as the first parts of compound words:

het overhemd	(ĕt-OOvĕrhemt)	'*the (outer) shirt*'
de overjas	(dĕ-OOvĕrjas)	'*the overcoat*'
overschoenen	(OOvĕrschoenĕn)	'*overshoes, rubbers*'
het ondergoed	(ĕt-ONdĕrghoet)	'*the underwear*'
de onderbroek	(dĕ-ONdĕrbroek)	'*the pair of drawers*'

2. Review of Basic Sentences with English Covered

C. WHAT WOULD YOU SAY?

1. What Would You Say?

1. *The coat fits, but the trousers don't.*   *You tell the salesman:*

   a. dĕ-BROEK-past, maar-dĕ-JAS is-tĕ-nou.   De broek past, maar de jas is te nauw.

   b. dĕ-JAS-is-tĕ-nou, maar-dĕ-BROEK past-GHOET.   De jas is te nauw, maar de broek past goed.

   c. dĕ-JAS PAST, maar-dĕ-BROEK-past-niet.   De jas past, maar de broek past niet.

2. *Your friend is looking better today than yesterday.   You tell him:*

a. van-DAACH ziet-uu-ĕr-NIET ghoet-UIT.   Vandaag ziet u er niet goed uit.
b. van-DAACH ziet-uu-ĕr-SLECHT UIT.   Vandaag ziet u er slecht uit.
c. van-DAACH ziet-uu-ĕr-BEEtĕr UIT.   Vandaag ziet u er beter uit.

3. *The salesman, by misunderstanding, has shown you undershirts, but you need regular (outer) shirts.   You say:*

a. ik-hep-OOvĕr-hemdĕn-noodich, GHEEN HEMdĕn.   Ik heb overhemden noodig, geen hemden.
b. ik-hep-HEMdĕn-noodich, GHEEN OOvĕr-hemdĕn.   Ik heb hemden noodig, geen overhemden.
c. als-ik-"OOvĕr-hemdĕn"-zech gheeft-ie-mĕ-ONdĕr-   Als ik "overhemden" zeg, geeft hij me ondergoed.
   -ghoet.

4. *You are waiting for your change to come back.   At last you say:*

a. ik-kreich-noch-GHELT-tĕruch.   Ik krijg nog geld terug.
b. ik-hep-KLEIN-ghelt-noodich.   Ik heb kleingeld noodig.
c. GHEEF-mĕ mĕn-GHELT-tĕruch.   Geef me mijn geld terug.

2. What Did You Say?

D. Listening In

Annie Jansen goes with Mr. Carver to buy him a new hat.

Carver:	wil-jĕ-mĕt-mĕ-MEE-ghaan en-mĕ-HELpĕn ĕn-HOET-koopĕn?	Wil je met me meegaan en me helpen een hoed koopen?
Annie:	jaa-ZEEkĕr. WAAR-wil-jĕ-ĕm KOOpĕn?	Ja zeker. Waar wil je hem koopen?
Carver:	hier-LINKS vlak-BEI, in-DIE-straat, is-ĕn-	Hier links vlak bij, in die straat, is een kleine

	-KLEInĕ-WInkĕl waar-ik-eens-SOKKĕn ghĕKOCHT-hep.	winkel waar ik eens sokken gekocht heb.
Annie:	dat-was-SEEkĕr dĕ-KLEErĕn-winkĕl van--HETTĕmaa en-ZOON?	Dat was zeker de kleerenwinkel van Hettema en Zoon?
Carver:	ik-heb-dĕ-NAAM vĕrgheetĕn, maar-die-IS--ĕt-mischien	Ik heb de naam vergeten, maar die is het misschien.
De winkelbediende:	ghoedĕn-DACH, mĕvrou. ghoedĕn-DACH, mĕneer.	Goeden dag, mevrouw. Goeden dag, mijnheer.
	Wat-is-ĕr-van-uu-DIENST?	Wat is er van uw dienst?
Carver:	ik-sou-GHRAACH ĕn-HOET-willĕn-hebbĕn.	Ik zou graag een hoed willen hebben.
De winkelbediende:	WAT-is-uu-NUMMĕr-mĕneer?	Wat is uw nummer, mijnheer?
Carver:	ZEEvĕn-en-ĕn-HALF.	Zeven en een half.
De winkelbediende:	HIER-heb-ik ĕn-HEElĕ-ghoede HOET--voor-UU.	Hier heb ik een heele goede hoed voor u.
	WILT-uu-ĕm EEvĕn OP-passĕn?	Wilt u hem even oppassen?
Carver:	hoe-VINT-jĕ deezĕ-HOET, ANNie?	Hoe vind je deze hoed, Annie?
Annie:	ik-HOUT-niet van-dĕ-BRUInĕ KLEUR.	Ik houd niet van de bruine kleur.
	GHREIS staat-jĕ-BEEtĕr dan-BRUIN.	Grijs staat je beter dan bruin.
De winkelbediende:	HIER-hept-uu ĕn-GHREIzĕ, mĕVROU.	Hier hebt u een grijze, mevrouw.
	WILT-uu DEEzĕ-eens-eevĕn OP-passĕn, mĕNEER?	Wilt u deze eens even opassen, mijnheer?
Carver:	hoe-vint-jĕ-DEEzĕ-hoet, ANNie?	Hoe vind je deze hoed, Annie?
Annie:	JAA, DEEzĕ staat-jĕ-BEEtĕr.	Ja, deze staat je beter.
Carver:	HOE-veel KOST deeze-HOET?	Hoeveel kost deze hoed?
De winkelbediende:	DIE-hoet-is ZEEvĕn-ghuldĕ-TACHtich.	Die hoed is zeven gulden tachtig.

Annie (to Carver):	VINT-jĕ-niet dat-die-PREIS ĕn-beetjĕ-HOOCH-is?	Vind je niet dat die prijs een heetje hoog is?
De winkelbediende:	wel-NEEN, mĕvrou.	Wel neen, mevrouw.
	neem-mĕ-NIET KWAAlik, maar-DIT-is NIET DUUR-voor-ZOO-ĕn-hoet.	Neem me niet kwalijk, maar dit is niet duur voor zoo'n hoed.
	ĕt-is-dĕ-BEStĕ kwaalieTEIT-mĕvrouw.	Het is de beste qualiteit, mevrouw.
Carver:	als-jĕ-VINT dat-ie-mĕ-GHOET STAAT, dan-NEEM-ik-ĕm-maar.	Als je vind, dat hij me goed staat, dan neem ik hem maar.
	HIER zein-TIEN GHULdĕn.	Hier zijn tien gulden.
De winkelbediende:	dank-uu-WEL-mĕneer.	Dank u wel, mijnheer.
	dus-uu-KREICHT-noch TWEE-ghuldĕn--TWINtich tĕRUCH.	Dus u krijgt noch twee gulden twintig terug.
	ZAL-ik-ĕm-voor-uu-laatĕn IN-pakkĕn?	Zal ik hem voor u laten inpakken?
	OF-wilt-uu-lievĕr dat-ik-ĕm-naar-uuw HUIS-stuur?	Of wilt u liever dat ik hem naar uw huis stuur?
Carver:	ik-sal-ĕm-LIEvĕr MEE-neemĕn.	Ik zal hem liever meenemen.
	mĕn-OUdĕ-hoet kunt-uu-voor-mĕ-IN--pakkĕn, als-i-uu-BLIEFT.	Mijn oude hoed kunt u voor me inpakken, alstublieft.
De winkelbediende:	GHRAACH, mĕneer.	Graag, mijnheer.
	hept-uu-NOCH-iets NOOdich, mĕneer?	Hebt u nog iets noodig, mijnheer?
	wĕ-HEBBĕn-hier ERCH-ghoedĕ-DASSĕn.	We hebben hier erg goede dassen.
	ĕt-is-dĕ-BEStĕ kwaalieTEIT, en-dĕ--PREIzĕn zein-WERkĕlik niet-HOOCH.	Het is de beste qualiteit en de prijzen zijn werkelijk niet hoog.
	MACH-ik-zĕ-uu laatĕn-ZIEN?	Mag ik ze u laten zien?
Carver:	NEE. DANK-uu-WEL. van-DAACH lievĕr-NIET. ghoedĕn-DACH.	Neen. Dank u wel. Vandaag liever niet. Goeden dag.

De winkelbediende:	ghoedĕn-DACH, mĕvrou. ghoedĕn-DACH, mĕneer.	Goeden dag, mevrouw. Goeden dag, **mijn**heer.
Carver:	dĕ-WINkĕl-bĕdiendĕ denkt-SEEkĕr dat--jĕ-mein-VROU-bent.	De winkelbediende denkt zeker, dat **je mijn** vrouw bent.
Annie:	NEE, KAARvĕr, DAT-moet-jĕ niet--SEGHĕn.	Nee, Carver, dat moet je niet **zeggen**.
	ik-HOUT-niet van-die-GHRAPjĕs.	Ik houd niet van die grapjes.
Carver:	jaa-ZEEkĕr; dat-HEEFT-dĕ-bĕDIENdĕ ZEEkĕr-ghĕDACHT.	Ja zeker; dat heeft de bediende **zeker** gedacht.
	en-ik-wou-GHRAACH-dat-ĕt-ook--WERkĕlik zoo-WAS.	En ik wou graag dat het ook werkelijk **zoo** was.
Annie:	als-jĕ-ZOO-praat, ghaa-ik-NOOJT-meer--met-jĕ naar-dĕ-KLEErĕn-winkĕl.	Als je zoo praat, ga ik nooit meer met **je** naar de kleerenwinkel.

E. Conversation

1. Review of Basic Sentences with Dutch Covered

2. Vocabulary and Word Study Check-up

3. Carrying on Conversation

FINDER LIST

aanpassen 'to try on'

de bediende (bĕDIENdĕ) 'the attendant'
  best 'best'
  blauw (BLOU) 'blue'
de boord 'the collar'

de broek 'the (pair of) trousers'
bruin 'brown'

de das 'the necktie'
dragen P gedragen 'to carry, to wear'

geel 'yellow'
grijs 'gray'
   een grijze hoed 'a gray hat'

de handschoen 'the glove'
  helpen P geholpen 'to help'
het hemd 'the shirt'
de hoed 'the hat'

   iets 'something, anything'
   inpakken 'to wrap up'

de jas 'the coat'

   kijken P gekeken 'to look'
de kleur 'the color'
   koopen P gekocht 'to buy'

   liever 'rather'

de maat 'the measure'
meer 'more'
   niet meer (NIET MEER, NIE-měr) 'no longer'
   nooit meer 'never again'

de mouw (MOU) 'the sleeve'
  onder 'under'
   de onderbroek 'the (pair of) drawers'
   het ondergoed 'the underwear'

oud 'old'
   mijn oude hoed (měn-OUdě-HOET) 'my old hat'
over 'over'
   het overhemd 'the (outer) shirt'
   de overjas 'the overcoat'
   de overschoen 'the overshoe'

het pak 'the pack, the big bundle; the suit of clothes'
   het pakje 'the package'
   pakken 'to pak'
  passen 'to fit'
de prijs 'the price'
   hooge prijzen 'high prices'

de qualiteit (kwalieTEIT, kwaalieTEIT) 'the quality'

de regenjas 'the raincoat'
  rood 'red'
   een roode das (ěn-ROOdě-DAS) 'a red tie'

de schoen 'the shoe'
de sok 'the sock'
   staan P gestaan 'to stand, to suit'
   sturen 'to send'

het vest 'the vest'

de waar 'the merchandise'
het warenhuis 'the department store'
    werkelijk (WERkĕlik) 'truly, really'
    wijd 'wide'

de winkelbediende 'the store clerk'
    wit 'white'
        het witte hemd 'the white shirt'
    zwart 'black'

PART TWO

REVIEW

To the Leader: This Review Unit is organized like Unit VI, not like Units I–V and VII–XI.   Be careful to look it over in advance and be sure you know what is to be done.

Like Unit 6, this will furnish you with a thorough review of what you have learned in the previous five Units.   Remember to make every occasion you have to speak out loud a practice in pronunciation; your Guide, if you have one, will never stop pointing out mistakes so long as there are mistakes to point out.

A. TRUE-FALSE TEST

Each student is to take a sheet of paper and write down along the side the numbers from 1 through 80. Then the Guide, or the records, will give you a series of eighty statements, repeating each one twice.   You should have no trouble understanding these statements if you have done the work properly up to this point. Each statement is either *obviously* true, or else *usually* false: put down T or F accordingly.

Afterwards the Leader will tell you the answers, give you the English when necessary, and you can mark your own papers.   65 to 70 correct means that you have mastered the material so far well enough to go on; if you make more mistakes than that, then you need more thorough review.

To the Leader: The True-False Statements, together with their English equivalents and the indications of whether they are true or false, are in the Key to exercises and tests at the end of the book.

B. Putting It into Dutch

1. Individual Study

Go through the following English sentences and prepare to say the Dutch equivalents when the group works together. Practice the Dutch out loud to yourself so that you have them all down cold.

I

1. Have you rooms for rent?
2. Come in.
3. Will you come upstairs?
4. Are light and heat included?
5. The rent is always paid in advance.
6. The bathroom and the toilet are at the end of the hall.
7. Bring my baggage upstairs.
8. Our rooms are two flights up.
9. How much are the rooms by the week?
10. My room is number 288.

II

11. I have to get a haircut.
12. I have to get shaved.
13. Just be seated, please.
14. Your turn will come right away.

III

15. Are you ready?
16. I still have to bring my things to the laundry.
17. I have to have my suit cleaned and pressed.
18. I have a good laundress.
19. Haircut, please!
20. Don't make it too short in back.

21. My clothes are old.
22. I guess I'll have to buy new ones.
23. What do you need?
24. Will you help me?
25. The prices are not high there.
26. I'll take this blue necktie here.
27. How do you like this suit?
28. The coat is too tight.
29. The trousers are too wide.
30. Shall I wrap it up for you?

IV

31. Have you already eaten dinner?
32. It's time to eat.
33. Give me some soup (a plate of soup).
34. I'll take steak and potatoes.
35. What sort of vegetables have you today?
36. Give me beans with the pork.
37. I don't like carrots.
38. Children like ice cream.
39. This spoon is not clean; bring me another, please.
40. We need a few more spoons.

V

41. The bank is near the main square.
42. We have to cross the street here.
43. The street car stops at the other side of the street.
44. Which line must I take?
45. At the park you have to transfer.
46. We have to ask a policeman where the bank is.
47. You'd better take a taxi.
48. Where are you going?
49. I find it more pleasant to walk than to ride.
50. This big building here is the city hall.

2. How Do You Say It?

This is the group drill on the above sentences. The Leader will call on the other members of the group for the Dutch equivalents of the above sentences. All but the Leader should keep their books closed. If the Guide is present, he will listen and check on your Dutch.

C. MORE PUTTING IT INTO DUTCH

1. Individual Study

Prepare this, working individually, just as in Section B.

I

1. Just look at that girl!
2. You're looking well.
3. I've bought a pair of shoes.
4. She's going along with us.
5. Please pass me the sugar.

6. I mayn't go out today.
7. When are you coming back?
8. I have to go down town.
9. What are they talking about?
10. This is not expensive.

II

11. I'm going to the barber's.
12. The coffee is getting cold.
13. Give me a cup of coffee.
14. I should like some razor blades.
15. How long will it take?
16. How are you getting along?
17. Can you mend this suit for me?
18. I have only forty guilder.
19. I'm coming at six o'clock sharp.
20. Can you wash these things for me?

III

21. I'll show you the rooms.
22. Let me see the room.
23. I'm having my car repaired.
24. My baggage is still at the station.
25. I should like to take a warm bath.
26. The heating doesn't work.
27. I've been living here two weeks **already.**

28. May I have a match?
29. The furniture is good.
30. I have a room with two beds.

IV

31. I still have some change coming.
32. Today you're looking better.
33. Here's the package.
34. Shall I send the baggage to the hotel?
35. I don't like that color.
36. I need a warm overcoat.
37. We'd best go to a department store.
38. I've forgotten the key.
39. I haven't washed yet.
40. We've had the auto repaired.

V

41. I haven't had time.
42. You haven't understood me **right.**
43. I've shaved.
44. I've cut myself.
45. I've already seen it.
46. Has the movie started yet?
47. We rode to The Hague.
48. They're sitting and talking.
49. They've been sitting and talking all **evening.**
50. She's never been in Holland.

2. How Do You Say It?

Go over the above sentences under the direction of the Leader, as in Section B.

D. CONVERSATION

The members of the group are to carry on short conversations, lasting not more than one or two minutes, which use the entire contents of Units 7 through 11, and as much of the contents of the first five Units as may be necessary. Everyone in the group should have a chance to take part as many times as possible. The situations of the conversations should be varied and combined as much as possible. Each conversation should begin with the usual polite greetings and inquiries about health, and should end with polite leave-taking. Here are a few of the many possibilities:

1. Asking a person whether he has rooms for rent. Discussing location, price, cleanliness, bathroom, number of rooms, heating and baggage.

2. Making inquiries about the place where a friend lives.

3. Going to the barber. A shave or haircut. Giving directions as to how hair should be cut. Explanations of why you don't shave yourself.

4. Taking things to the laundry. When will they be ready?

5. Taking things to the tailor; pressing and cleaning.

6. Ordering lunch or dinner. Variety of dishes. Asking for additional silverware. The bill and change; tip.

7. Going to the museum, theater, or town hall. Asking directions and comparing several means of conveyance. Transfers, bus lines, taxis. Asking for a guide. Voicing preference for walking over going by street car.

8. Calling on friends or relatives. Discussing what you did the day before or what happened.

9. Talking about all different kinds of clothing; quality, color, size. Stores where they can be bought. Discussing whether clothes fit or not. Asking attendant to wrap things up and send them to the hotel or home.

UNIT 1.

UNIT 1. SECTION A. §2. *Hints on Pronunciation.* (Hoofdstuk 1, Afdeeling A, §2, *Wenken voor de Uitspraak.*)

De leider zal aangeven wanneer de groep klaar is voor elk van de volgende groepen woorden. Lees dan elk woord *één maal* voor en wacht daarna lang genoeg zoodat de groep het woord kan herhalen en uw uitspraak kan nabootsen. Het is mogelijk dat men U vraagt de heele groep twee of drie maal te herhalen, voordat de klas aan de volgende groep wil gaan beginnen.

Practice 1.

man
dag
wat
dat
danken

Practice 2.

met
en
zeggen
rechts

Practice 3.

kop
kom
vol
koffie
om

Practice 4.

bus
zuster
kunnen
zullen
juffrouw

Practice 5.

water
gaan

kwalijk
waar

Practice 6.

peer
heer
nemen
spreken

Practice 7.

boot
brood
zoon
komen

Practice 8.

boek
goed
hoe
broer
moeten

Practice 9.

diep
vriend
niets
hier

A

Practice 10.

deur
meubel
kleur
neus
keuken

Practice 11.

duur
lucifer
student
natuurlijk

Practice 12.

trein
mij

vijf
zij
zijn

Practice 13.

nou
vrouw
ik zou
ik wou

Practice 14.

huis
muis
uit
tuin
tuig

5. a.
6. b.
7. a.

UNIT 1. SECTION C. KEY.

1. b
2. b.
3. b.
4. a.

UNIT 2.

UNIT 2. SECTION A. §2. *Hints on Pronunciation.* (Hoofdstuk 2, Afdeeling A, §2. *Wenken voor de Uitspraak.*)

Ga op dezelfde manier te werk als met de *Wenken voor de Uitspraak* in Hoofdstuk I. Wacht totdat de leider aangeeft, dat de groep klaar is voor de woorden van elke groep. Herhaal dan elk woord één maal en wacht zoodat de klas gelegenheid heeft de uitspraak na te bootsen voordat U verder gaat. Herhaal elke groep net zoo veel malen als de leider U dat vraagt te doen.

Practice 1.

zeggen
gaan
geen

gulden
graag
schip
misschien

B

Practice 2.

fier, vier, wier
vond, wond

visch, wisch
vang, wang
vinden, winden

UNIT 2. SECTION C. KEY.

1. b.
2. a.
3. c.
4. b.
5. a.
6. c.
7. c.
8. c.
9. a.

UNIT 3.

UNIT 3. SECTION A. §2. *Hints on Pronunciation.* (Hoofdstuk 3, Afdeeling A, §2. *Wenken voor de Uitspraak.*)

Ga op dezelfde manier te werk als met de *Wenken voor de Uit-spraak* in Hoofdstukken 1 en 2.

Practice 1.

man, maan
stad, staat
ras, raas

mis, Mies
liggen, liegen

Practice 4.

rot, rood
mot, moot
ros, roos

Practice 2.

met, meet
het, heet
hel, heel

Practice 5.

lus, leus
Rus, reus

Practice 3.

visch, vies

UNIT III. SECTION C. KEY.

1. a.
2. a.
3. c.
4. b.
5. c.
6. c.
7. a.
8. b.

UNIT 4.

UNIT 4. SECTION A. §2. *Hints on Pronunciation.* (Hoofdstuk 4, Afdeeling A, §2. *Wenken voor de Uitspraak.*)

Ga als gewoon te werk.

Practice 1.

deur
meubel
kleur
neus
keuken

vijf
zij
zijn

Practice 4.

nou
vrouw
ik zou
ik wou

Practice 2.

duur
lucifer
student
natuurlijk

Practice 5.

huis
muis
uit
tuin
tuig

Practice 3.

trein
mij

UNIT 4. SECTION C. KEY.

1. b.
2. a.
3. b.
4. b.
5. c.
6. a.
7. c.

UNIT 5.

UNIT 5. SECTION A. §2. *Hints on Pronunciation.* (Hoofdstuk 5, Afdeeling A, §2. *Wenken voor de Uitspraak.*)

Ga als gewoon te werk.

Practice 1.

man, maan
stad, staat
ras, raas

Practice 2.

met, meet
het, heet
hel, heel

D

Practice 3.

visch, vies
mis, Mies
liggen, liegen

mot, moot
ros, roos

Practice 5.

Practice 4.

rot, rood

lus, leus
Rus, reus

UNIT 5. SECTION C. KEY.

1. b.
2. a.
3. c.
4. b.
5. c.
6. c.
7. a.
8. b.

UNIT 6.

UNIT 6. REVIEW. SECTION A. TRUE-FALSE TEST.
(Hoofdstuk 6, *Herhaling.* Afdeeling A. *Goed of Fout Test.*)

Zoodra de leider U zegt, dat de groep klaar is, lees dan elk van de volgende zinnen *twee maal* voor en wacht een oogenblik voor U ze herhaalt en aan de volgende zin begint. De leider leest een nummer voor (in het Engelsch), dat bij elke zin hoort. Als U geen Engelsch kent, volg de nummers dan met uw vinger, zoodat U steeds weet aan welke zin men toe is. Zorg dat de klas niet kan zien wat U voorleest, want de T's en F's links, geven de oplossing aan.

I

F 1. Twee en drie is acht.
F 2. Het regent zelden in Holland.
F 3. In de winter hebben wij altijd warm weer.
T 4. In Amerika spreken wij Engelsch.
T 5. Nieuw-York is in de Vereenigde Staten.
F 6. Boeren werken in fabrieken.
F 7. Kleine kinderen eten nooit.
F 8. In hotels zijn geen W.C.'s.
F 9. Matrozen werken niet op schepen.
F 10. Hollanders spreken altijd langzaam.

E

II

F 11. In de zomer hebben wij veel sneeuw.
T 12. In Florida is het dikwijls warm.
T 13. Hollanders spreken Hollandsch.
T 14. In de meubelfabriek maken zij meubels.
F 15. Naar Holland gaan geen schepen.
F 16. Hollanders drinken nooit bier.
F 17. Chicago is een stad in Holland.
T 18. Nieuw-York is een groote stad.
T 19. De zoon van mijn broer is mijn neef.
T 20. De zoon van mijn zuster is mijn neef.

III

F 21. In Amerika zijn weinig autos.
T 22. Er gaan veel treinen naar Nieuw-York.
T 23. Amerikanen en Hollanders drinken veel koffie.
F 24. Er zijn tien dagen in een week.
T 25. Wij verstaan een beetje Hollandsch.
F 26. Het regent altijd.
T 27. Het regent veel in Holland.
T 28. Er zijn veel dagen in een jaar.
T 29. In Engeland spreken zij Engelsch.
F 30. Alle Amerikanen trouwen met Hollandsche meisjes.

IV

F 31. Alle meisjes zijn erg mooi.
F 32. Het weer is altijd mooi in Holland.
T 33. Zeven en drie is tien.
F 34. Een cigaret is zoo groot als een auto.
F 35. In een restaurant repareeren zij autos.
T 36. Een boer woont op een boerderij.
T 37. Studenten moeten veel studeeren.
T 38. Als U leven wilt moet U eten.
T 39. In Amerika zijn veel fabrieken.
F 40. Een man spreekt nooit met zijn zuster.

V

F 41. Kinderen kunnen autos repareeren.
F 42. Wij spreken nooit met vrouwen of meisjes.

F

T 43. Veel mannen heeten Jan.
F 44. Veel mannen heeten Annie.
T 45. In Chicago sneeuwt het dikwijls in de winter.
F 46. In Nieuw-York hebben zij nooit sneeuw.
F 47. Er gaat geen schip naar Nieuw-York.
T 48. De staat Nieuw-York is een van de staten van de Vereenigde Staten.

T 49. De stad Nieuw-York is in de staat Nieuw-York.
T 50. Veel Hollanders spreken een beetje Engelsch.

VI

T 51. Veel Amerikaansche meisjes zijn mooi.
T 52. Veel Amerikaansche vrouwen zijn mooi.
F 53. Amerikanen gaan nooit naar de bioscoop.
F 54. Nieuw-York is een kleine stad.
T 55. Er zijn veel autos in Nieuw-York.
T 56. Er zijn veel Amerikaansche matrozen.
F 57. En Engeland zijn geen groote steden.
T 58. In Californië sneeuwt het niet veel.
T 59. Wij drinken dikwijls koud water.
T 60. Wij drinken dikwijls warme koffie.

VII

F 61. Rotterdam is zoo groot als Nieuw-York.
F 62. In de morgen zeggen wij goeden avond.
F 63. Als ik een vliegmachine zie, weet ik dat het voorjaar is.
T 64. In de zomer heb ik het dikwijls warm.
F 65. Als het sneeuwt weten wij dat het warm weer is.
F 66. In de zomer sneeuwt het veel.
F 67. Boeren eten nooit brood.
T 68. Wij eten dikwijls aardappelen bij het vleesch.
T 69. Amerikanen eten veel vleesch.
T 70. U kent veel Amerikanen.

VIII

T 71. Een goede dokter moet veel weten.
T 72. In een groote stad zijn er veel hotels.
T 73. Als ik vliegen wil, moet ik een vliegmachine hebben.
F 74. Alle Amerikanen kunnen vliegen.

G

F 75. Geen Amerikanen kunnen vliegen.

F 76. Geen Amerikanen kunnen autos repareeren.

T 77. Veel Amerikanen kunnen autos repareeren.

F 78. Er zijn maar twee Amerikanen die vliegen kunnen.

T 79. Veel Amerikanen kunnen vliegen.

T 80. In Amerika maken zij veel autos.

UNIT 6. REVIEW. SECTION B. KEY. (Hoofdstuk 6, *Herhaling.* Afdeeling B. *Sleutel.*)

De klas heeft een lijst Engelsche zinnen, die overeen komen met de Hollandsche, en moet die zinnen in het Hollandsch vertalen. Als ze niet precies dezelfde bewoording kiezen, die U voor zich heeft, maar als ze iets anders zeggen, dat goed Hollandsch is, en dat ongeveer dezelfde beteekenis heeft, maak er dan geen aanmerking op. Maar als ze iets zeggen, dat in het Hollandsch geen zin maakt, of als ze iets zeggen, dat een geheel andere beteekenis heeft, verbeter ze dan en zeg hun de zin voor, die hier staat afgedrukt.

I

1. Goeden avond, mijnheer.
2. Hoe laat is het?
3. Het is vier uur.
4. Het regent weer.
5. Het sneeuwt vandaag.
6. Ik versta niet wat U zegt.
7. Spreek langzaam als 't U blieft.
8. Waar is er een restaurant?
9. Er is een restaurant links.
10. Ga links.

II

11. Ik wou graag wat eten.
12. Ik zou graag een cigaret willen hebben.
13. Ik zou graag vleesch en aardappelen willen hebben.
14. Hoeveel is het?
15. Wilt U lucifers hebben?
16. Dat is drie gulden.
17. Hoe laat begint de bioscoop?
18. De bioscoop begint om acht uur.

H

19. Wanneer gaat de trein?
20. Gaat deze trein naar Amsterdam?

III

21. Hoe is Uw naam? Hoe heet U?
22. Hoe heet uw vriend? Hoe is de naam van uw vriend?
23. Zijn naam is Alfred Dekker. Hij heet Alfred Dekker.
24. Waar woont hij?
25. Waar woont zijn zuster?
26. Zij woont in dit hotel.
27. Leeft zijn vader nog?
28. Zijn zijn broers nog in Amerika?
29. Ja, zij zijn in Amerika.
30. Haar vader werkt in een fabriek.

IV

31. Ik moet naar het station.
32. Mijn trein gaat om vier uur.
33. Het gaat wel sneeuwen. Het zal wel sneeuwen.
34. Bij dit weer kan ik niet werken.
35. Spreekt U Engelsch?
36. Ik kan de auto niet repareeren.
37. Ik weet niet waar onze vriend is.
38. Ik weet niet of hij komt.
39. Hij komt vanavond.
40. Ik moet mijnheer Vos opzoeken.

V

41. Is zij getrouwd?
42. Hoeveel kinderen hebben zij?
43. Zij hebben geen kinderen.
44. Zij hebben alleen maar een kind.
45. Zij hebben vier kinderen, twee zoons en twee dochters.
46. Boeren werken op het land.
47. Ik ga naar de boerderij.
48. Zij is typiste.
49. Haar broer is matroos.
50. Onze zoon studeert voor dokter.

VI

51. Hij is zoo groot als zijn vader.
52. In de winter is het hier erg koud.
53. Ik heb het koud.
54. In Californië sneeuwt het maar zelden.
55. Het regent dikwijls een heele week.
56. Bent U ooit in Amerika geweest?
57. Ik ben nooit in Den Haag geweest.
58. Wat blieft U?
59. Neem me niet kwalijk.
60. Tot vanavond.

UNIT 6. REVIEW. SECTION C. KEY. (Hoofdstuk 6, *Herhaling.* Afdeeling C. *Sleutel.*)

Ga op dezelfde manier te werk als in Afdeeling B.

I

1. Deze koffie is koud.
2. In de winter is het koud.   Het is koud in de winter.
3. Wij moeten nog naar de kleerenwinkel.
4. Het is laat.
5. Het voorjaar is hier heel mooi.
6. Aangenaam kennis te maken, mevrouw.
7. Mijnheer Jansen ken ik al.
8. Veel Hollanders spreken Engelsch.
9. Spreekt U Hollandsch?
10. Ik spreek het maar een beetje.

II

11. Verstaat U wat ik zeg?
12. Ik woon al vijf jaar in Den Haag.
13. Ik heb een nicht die met een Hollander getrouwd is.
14. Zij woont in een kleine stad in Holland.
15. Waar bent U vandaan?
16. Ik kom van de Vereenigde Staaten.
17. Van welke stad komt U?
18. Drinkt U bier of water?
19. Ik drink geen bier.
20. Hij heeft een vrouw en vier kinderen.

III

21. Mijn vrouw en mijn dochter zijn natuurlijk in Amerika.
22. Mijn vrouw en ik zijn al tien jaar getrouwd.
23. Er zijn maar weinig Amerikanen die niet werken.
24. Mijn dochter is nog jong.
25. Zij is studente.
26. Mijn zuster is een goede typiste.
27. Kom vanavond bij ons eten.
28. Wie is die man?
29. Ik ken hem niet.
30. Ik weet niet wie dat is.

IV

31. Ik ben blij dat U komt.
32. Dank U wel, mevrouw.
33. Niets te danken, mijnheer.
34. Wij zijn allemaal Amerikaansche matrozen.
35. Ik kan die melk niet drinken. Die melk kan ik niet drinken.
36. Waar zijn de aardappelen?
37. Hier zijn zij.
38. Dit zijn mijn vrienden.
39. Wilt U met me naar de bioscoop gaan?
40. Neen, mijnheer; met U ga ik niet naar de bioscoop.

V

41. Waarom wilt U niet met me naar de bioscoop gaan?
42. Ik ken U immers niet.
43. Ik kan dat niet eten. Dat kan ik niet eten.
44. Ik kan dat bier niet drinken. Dat bier kan ik niet drinken.
45. Hij werkt in deze fabriek.
46. Komt U vanavond?
47. Wij gaan vanavond naar de bioscoop.
48. Wat zegt hij?
49. Wat zegt zij?
50. Wat zeggen zij?

K

UNIT 7.

UNIT 7. SECTION C. KEY.

1. b.
2. a.
3. a.
4. a.
5. c.
6. b.
7. c.
8. b.

UNIT 8.

UNIT 8. SECTION C. KEY.

1. a.
2. b.
3. b.
4. c.
5. c.
6. c.
7. a.
8. b.
9. a.

UNIT 9.

UNIT 9. SECTION C. KEY.

1. a.
2. a.
3. b.
4. c.
5. a.
6. c.
7. c.
8. c.

UNIT 11.

UNIT 11. SECTION C. KEY.

1. c.
2. c.
3. a.
4. a.

L

UNIT 12.

UNIT 12. REVIEW. SECTION A. TRUE-FALSE TEST.
(Hoofdstuk 12, *Herhaling.* Afdeeling A. *Goed of Fout Test.*)

Als de leider U zegt, dat de groep klaar is, lees dan elk van de volgende zinnen *twee maal* voor, en wacht een oogenblik tusschen twee zinnen, zoodat de klas tijd heeft te begrijpen wat er is gezegd. De leider geeft (in het Engelsch) elke zin een nummer terwijl U ze voorleest.

I

T 1. Ik neem een bad in de badkamer.
T 2. Mannen dragen sokken.
F 3. Er zijn geen groote gebouwen in Washington.
F 4. Er zijn vijf en twintig uren in een dag.
T 5. De waschvrouw wascht het goed.
T 6. Kellners werken in restaurants.
T 7. Een kapper knipt haar.
T 8. We eten in een eetkamer.
F 9. Er zijn geen trams in Chicago.
F 10. Rundvleesch wordt nooit gegeten

II

T 11. We drinken water uit glazen.
F 12. Niemand eet aardappelen.
F 13. Alle huizen hebben drie verdiepingen.
T 14. Kleermakers persen pakken op.
T 15. Veel steden hebben een stadhuis.
F 16. Ik wasch me met warme soep.
F 17. Dassen zijn altijd geel.
T 18. Zes en zes is twaalf.
T 19. Een bus stopt nooit.
F 20. We drinken alleen maar bier als we in een taxi rijden.

III

F 21. Als mijn waschgoed schoon is, stuur ik het naar de wascherij.
T 22. We koopen kleeren in een kleerenwinkel of in een warenhuis.
F 23. Wanneer het regent mag ik nooit uitgaan.
T 24. We dragen schoenen.

M

T 25. Veel steden hebben mooie parken.
T 26. In veel steden zijn de winkels en warenhuizen vlak bij het plein.
F 27. Tachtig cent is meer dan een gulden.
T 28. Bagage gaat in treinen.
T 29. Een schoenmaker kan schoenen repareeren.
F 30. Het scheren duurt uren lang.

IV

F 31. Als ik een gast heb, betaalt hij de rekening.
T 32. Een overjas dragen we in de winter.
F 33. Wanneer ik honger heb, zoek ik een waschvrouw.
F 34. Lucifers kosten meer dan schoenen.
F 35. Kinderen houden niet van dessert.
T 36. Als dessert eten we dikwijls ijs.
F 37. Alle agenten dragen witte dassen.
F 38. In een restaurant zit ik altijd op de tafel.
T 39. Boorden zijn dikwijls wit.
T 40. Wanneer ik de rekening betaal, geef ik de kellner een fooi.

V

T 41. We beginnen het middageten dikwijls met een bord soep.
F 42. Jonge meisjes gaan nooit naar de bioscoop.
T 43. U kunt in een bus rijden.
T 44. In een restaurant kunt U dikwijls een biefstuk krijgen.
T 45. Pakken van de beste qualiteit zijn duur.
T 46. Er zijn matrozen op een schip.
F 47. In de zomer kan niemand een bad nemen.
F 48. Een kleermaker maakt autos schoon.
T 49. Om aan de andere kant te komen, moeten we de straat oversteken.
F 50. Amerikanen maken nooit grappen.

VI

T 51. Een park is groen in de zomer.
F 52. Dassen kun je niet in een winkel koopen.
F 53. Een kaart van de stad zal ons niet helpen de weg te vinden.
F 54. Lepels en vorken vindt U in mijn bed.
T 55. Veel mannen dragen een vest onder hun jas.
F 56. Winkelbedienden mogen geen water drinken.

N

T 57. Bij het vleesch eten we aardappelen en groente.
F 58. Een sleutel en nog een sleutel, dat zijn twee sleutels.
F 60. Mijn bed staat voor het hotel.

VII

T 61. Eerst eet ik sla en dan het dessert.
T 62. In een hotel zijn kamers te huur.
F 63. Het ontbijt kunt U het beste in een garage krijgen.
F 64. Autos zijn goedkooper dan cigaretten.
T 65. Ik ga niet uit voor ik klaar ben.
F 66. Amerikanen trouwen altijd in een theater.
T 67. Er zijn mooie steden in Holland.
F 68. Als ik een overhemd aanheb, kan ik geen biefstuk eten.
F 69. Nieuw York is dicht bij Rotterdam.
T 70. Sokken kunt U in een winkel koopen.

VIII

T 71. Ik eet brood met boter.
T 72. Als ik ziek ben ga ik naar de dokter.
F 73. Morgen ga ik het stadhuis koopen.
T 74. Wanneer ik genoeg gegeten heb, heb ik geen honger meer.
T 75. Boeren werken de heele dag lang.
F 76. Ik draag boorden in alle nummers.
T 77. Als U een taxi neemt en ik loop, dan kunnen we niet samen gaan.
T 78. De zoons van mijn broers, van mijn zusters, van mijn ooms en van mijn tantes zijn allemaal mijn neven.
F 79. Varkens rijden altijd in treinen.
F 80. Ik houd niet van mooie vrouwen en meisjes.

UNIT 12. REVIEW. SECTION B. KEY. (Hoofdstuk 12, *Herhaling.* Afdeeling B. *Sleutel.*)

De klas heeft een lijst Engelsche zinnen, die overeenkomen met de Hollandsche en moet die zinnen in het Hollandsch vertalen. Als ze iets zeggen, dat grootendeels neerkomt op wat er in het Hollandsch staat, maak er dan geen aanmerking op. Maar als het slecht Hollandsch is, of wanneer het een andere beteekenis heeft, verbeter ze dan en zeg hun de zin voor, die hier staat afgedrukt.

O

I

1. Hebt U kamers te huur?
2. Kom binnen.
3. Wilt U even naar boven komen?
4. Is licht en verwarming inbegrepen?
5. De huur wordt altijd vooruitbetaald.
6. De badkamer en de W.C. zijn aan het eind van de gang.
7. Breng mijn bagage naar boven.
8. Onze kamers zijn twee trappen hoog.
9. Hoeveel kosten de kamers per week?
10. Mijn kamer is nummer tweehonderd acht en tachtig.

II

11. Ik moet mijn haar laten knippen.
12. Ik moet me laten scheren.
13. Ga even zitten, als 't U blieft.
14. U komt dadelijk aan de beurt.
15. Bent U al klaar?
16. Ik moet nog mijn goed naar de wasscherij brengen.
17. Ik moet mijn pak laten schoon maken en persen.
18. Ik heb een goede waschvrouw.
19. Haar knippen, als 't U blieft!
20. Maak het niet te kort van achteren.

III

21. Mijn kleeren zijn al oud.
22. Ik zal wel nieuwe moeten koopen.
23. Wat hebt U noodig?
24. Wilt U me helpen?
25. De prijzen zijn er niet hoog.
26. Ik neem deze blauwe das hier.
27. Hoe vindt U dit pak?
28. De jas is te nauw.
29. De broek is te wijd.
30. Zal ik het voor U inpakken?

IV

31. Hebt U al middag gegeten?
32. Het is tijd om te eten.
33. Geef me een bord soep.

P

34. Ik neem een biefstuk en aardappelen.
35. Wat voor groente hebt U vandaag?
36. Geef me boonen bij het varkensvleesch.
37. Ik houd niet van worteltjes.
38. Kinderen houden van ijs.
39. Deze lepel is niet schoon; breng me een andere, als 't U blieft.
40. We hebben nog een paar lepels noodig.

V

41. De bank is vlak bij het plein.
42. We moeten hier de straat oversteken.
43. De tram stopt aan de andere kant van de straat.
44. Welke lijn moet ik nemen?
45. Bij het park moet U overstappen.
46. We moeten een agent vragen waar de bank is.
47. U neemt beter een taxi.
48. Waar gaat U naar toe?
49. Ik vind het prettiger te loopen dan te rijden.
50. Dit groote gebouw hier is het stadhuis.

UNIT 12. REVIEW. SECTION C. KEY. (Hoofdstuk 12, *Herhaling.* Afdeeling C. *Sleutel.*)

Ga te werk als in Afdeeling B.

I

1. Kijk dat meisje eens!
2. U ziet er goed uit.
3. Ik heb een paar schoenen gekocht.
4. Zij gaat met ons mee.
5. Geef me even de suiker aan.
6. Ik mag vandaag niet uitgaan.
7. Wanneer komt U terug?
8. Ik moet de stad in.
9. Waar praten ze over?
10. Dit is niet duur.

II

11. Ik ga naar de kapper.
12. De koffie wordt koud.
13. Geef me een kop koffie.
14. Ik zou graag scheermesjes willen hebben.

Q

15. Hoe lang zal het duren?
16. Hoe maakt U het?
17. Kunt U dit pak voor me repareeren?
18. Ik heb alleen maar veertig gulden.
19. Ik kom om zes uur precies.
20. Kunt U dit goed voor me wasschen?

III

21. Ik zal U de kamers laten zien.
22. Laat me de kamer zien.
23. Ik laat mijn auto repareeren.
24. Mijn bagage is nog aan het station.
25. Ik zou graag een warm bad willen nemen.
26. De verwarming werkt niet.
27. Ik woon hier al twee weken.
28. Mag ik een lucifer?
29. De meubels zijn goed.
30. Ik heb een kamer met twee bedden.

IV

31. Ik krijg nog geld terug.
32. Vandaag ziet U er beter uit.
33. Hier is het pakje.
34. Zal ik de bagage naar het hotel sturen?
35. Ik houd niet van die kleur.
36. Ik heb een warme overjas noodig.
37. We gaan het beste naar een warenhuis.
38. Ik heb de sleutel vergeten.
39. Ik heb me nog niet gewasschen.
40. Wij hebben de auto laten repareeren.

V

41. Ik heb geen tijd gehad.
42. U hebt me niet goed verstaan.
43. Ik heb me geschoren.
44. Ik heb me gesneden.
45. Ik heb het al gezien.
46. Is de bioscoop al begonnen?
47. We zijn naar Den Haag gereden.
48. Ze zitten te praten.

49. Ze hebben de heele avond zitten praten.
50. Ze is nooit in Holland geweest.

T